Walzer and Justice: Spheres of Justice in the 2020s

"Michael Walzer's *Spheres of Justice* was a bombshell of a book in the field of political theory when it was published in 1983. Four decades later, Walzer's theory has become even more influential, not just because of its philosophical insights, but also because it helps us to think in practical ways about how to promote social justice in the modern world. Read this book by leading political theorists to find out more!"

—Daniel A. Bell *(University of Hong Kong), Chair Professor of Political Theory, Faculty of Law, University of Hong Kong, Distinguished Chair Professor of Fudan Institute for Advanced Study in Social Sciences*

"The idea of justice means different things in different spheres of life. In the age of capitalist globalization, one must consider how such an idea is exchanged, commodified, and performed. The contributors to this volume are committed to this task. By rereading *Spheres of Justice* forty years after its publication, they demonstrate that social liberalism makes it possible to tackle epistemic conflicts over the idea of justice, a prerequisite for peace and the pursuit of a decent life. A timely and indispensable work."

—Bruno Perreau *(Cynthia L. Reed Professor of French Studies, Massachusetts Institute of Technology)*

J. Toby Reiner
Editor

Walzer and Justice: Spheres of Justice in the 2020s

palgrave
macmillan

Editor
J. Toby Reiner
Political Science
Dickinson College
Carlisle, PA, USA

ISBN 978-3-031-87808-4 ISBN 978-3-031-87809-1 (eBook)
https://doi.org/10.1007/978-3-031-87809-1

This Palgrave Macmillan imprint is published by the registered company Springer Nature Switzerland AG
The registered company address is: Gewerbestrasse 11, 6330 Cham, Switzerland

Preface and Acknowledgements

This book emerged out of a seminar held in October 2023 at the **Institute for Advanced Study, Princeton**, to mark the fortieth anniversary of the publication of *Spheres of Justice*, **Michael Walzer**'s seminal account of **distributive justice**. We wrote it to demonstrate the enduring contribution and ongoing relevance of Walzer's account of **social democracy** at a time when it is in retreat across much of the world. Many of Walzer's arguments seem to us to contain the resources to revitalize leftist and **egalitarian politics** and to provide alternatives to right-wing **populism** that can win the allegiance of democratic citizens by virtue of their appeal to indigenous norms that they share.

We are grateful to the Institute for hosting and supporting the seminar, and especially to Wendy Brown, Laura McCune, and Miriam Harris for their help with the arrangements. Thanks also to *Dissent*—the intellectual magazine that Walzer edited for 40 years—for participating in the seminar, and especially to Michael Kazin, Mark Levinson, Mitchell Cohen, Jo Ann Mort, Nick Serpe, Natasha Lewis, and David Marcus for their interest in and encouragement of our endeavors. Bruno Perreau presented a paper at the conference on the importance of Walzer's work for **left-wing politics** today. The editor also wishes to thank Daniel Bell, Avner de-Shalit, Sarah Song, Nicola Lacey, Elizabeth Fraser, Joseph Blasi, Graham Parsons, and Marcus Agnafors for helpful discussion of this project.

At Palgrave, Anca Pusca and Esther Sundar have been extremely helpful and supportive editors, and we are grateful for their promotion of this work. I am grateful to Dickinson College for the sabbatical support that enabled me to complete this project, and to my wife, Margaret Winchester, for encouraging me to pursue it.

Carlisle, USA J. Toby Reiner

Contents

Notes on Contributors

Geoffrey Kurtz is Associate Professor of Political Science at Borough of Manhattan Community College (City University of New York). He is the author of *Jean Jaurès: The Inner Life of Social Democracy* (2014). His recent essays have appeared in publications such as *Current*, *Front Porch Republic*, and *Public Seminar*.

Steven Lukes, retired Professor of Sociology, New York University, previously taught at Balliol College, Oxford, the London School of Economics, and the European University Institute. He is the author of *Emile Durkheim: His Life and Work, Individualism, Power: A Radical View, Marxism and Morality, Moral Relativism,* and *The Diversity of Morals* (forthcoming).

David Miller is Professor of Political Theory and Senior Research Fellow at Nuffield College, University of Oxford. He has written or edited over twenty books, including *Market, State, and Community* (Clarendon Press, 1989), *On Nationality* (Clarendon Press, 1995), *Principles of Social Justice* (Harvard University Press, 1999), *National Responsibility and Global Justice* (Oxford University Press, 2007), and *Strangers in Our Midst: the political philosophy of immigration* (Harvard University Press, 2016). He was elected as a Fellow of the British Academy in 2002, and in 2020 the European Consortium for Political Research gave him its biennial Lifetime Achievement Award.

J. Toby Reiner is Associate Professor and Chair of Political Science at Dickinson College. He has a Ph.D. in Political Science from the University of California, Berkeley and an MPhil in International Relations from the University of Cambridge. He wrote a book on Michael Walzer as part of Polity Press's series on Key Contemporary Thinkers (Polity, 2020). His book on Community for Polity's series on Key Concepts will be published in 2025. He has published in various journals, including *Political Research Quarterly, Polity, American Political Thought,* and the *Critical Review of International Social and Political Philosophy*. He is currently working on a book manuscript on migration and global justice.

Michael Rustin is a Professor of Sociology at the University of East London and Visiting Professor at the Tavistock and Portman NHS Trust. He is author of *The Good Society and the Inner World* (1991), *Reason and Unreason (*2001*)*, and *The Inner World of Doctor Who* (2014) (with Iain MacRury), and co-author with Margaret Rustin of *Narratives of Love and Loss: Studies in Modern Children's Fiction* (1989/2001), *Mirror to Nature: Drama Psychoanalysis and Society* (2002) and *Reading Klein* (2017). He edited, with David Armstrong, *Social Defences against Anxiety: Explorations in a Paradigm* (2014).

Margo Trappenburg studied political science and obtained her doctorate at Leiden University in the Netherlands. In 1993 she co-organized a conference on Citizenship and Local Justice in Amsterdam where Michael Walzer was a keynote speaker. She co-edited a volume based on the conference papers including Walzer's contribution in Dutch. She published various Walzer-inspired articles on the distribution of health care and the admission of migrants. She currently works at Utrecht University and at the University of Humanistic Studies. Her research is about health care policy, professionalism and the welfare state. Publications can be found at https://www.margotrappenburg.nlwww.margotrappenburg.nl

Astrid von Busekist is Professor of Political Theory at Sciences Po, Paris, where she directs the political theory program at the graduate school. She has been visiting professor at the Goethe Universität Frankfurt (2020–2021), at New York University (2017, 2018, 2019, 2020), Tel Aviv University (2009–2011), and the Université Libre de Bruxelles (2001). She is the author, with Michael Walzer, of *Justice is Steady Work* (Polity, 2020).

Michael Walzer is Professor Emeritus of Social Science at the Institute for Advanced Study, in Princeton, New Jersey. As a professor, author, editor, and lecturer, he has addressed a wide variety of topics in political theory and moral philosophy: distributive justice, just and unjust wars, nationalism and membership, social criticism, and many others. His books (among them *Just and Unjust Wars, Spheres of Justice, The Company of Critics, Thick and Thin: Moral Argument at Home and Abroad, On Toleration,* and *Politics and Passion*) and essays have played a part in the revival of situated, issue-focused political thought and in the development of a pluralist approach to political and moral life. Walzer edited *Dissent* from 1975 to 2013 and is a former contributing editor for the *New Republic.* His articles and interviews appear frequently in the world's foremost newspapers and journals. His most recent book is *The Struggle for a Decent Politics* (Yale, 2023).

Georgia Warnke is professor emerita in Political Science at the University of California, Riverside. She writes on issues in political and critical social theory, **Gadamer's** philosophical **hermeneutics** and contemporary **feminism**. She is the author of five books and an edited volume.

CHAPTER 1

Introduction

J. Toby Reiner

Michael Walzer's *Spheres of Justice*[1] (1983) is a landmark work in post-war political theory that changed the way in which scholars think about equality and about distributive justice. Walzer advances a "rich and compelling"[2] social-democratic conception of distributive justice that he calls "complex equality" (Walzer 1983: 3–30), which seeks to reconcile egalitarianism with the pluralism of contemporary life, both across and within diverse cultures and societies. As a social-democratic account of distributive justice, *Spheres* is the most important counterpoint to both John Rawls's *A Theory of Justice* (1971)[3] and Robert Nozick's *Anarchy, State, and Utopia* (1974),[4] the classic statements of left-liberalism and libertarianism in recent Anglophone theory.

This book is dedicated to demonstrating the on-going relevance of *Spheres* both to theorizing about distributive justice and to social-democratic politics in the twenty-first century. It emerges out of a seminar on *Spheres* held at the Institute for Advanced Study in Princeton, New Jersey—where Walzer worked while he wrote the book—in October

J. T. Reiner (✉)
Political Science, Dickinson College, Carlisle, PA, US
e-mail: reinerj@dickinson.edu

J. T. Reiner (ed.), *Walzer and Justice: Spheres of Justice in the 2020s*,
https://doi.org/10.1007/978-3-031-87809-1_1

2023. The seminar marked the fortieth anniversary of the publication of *Spheres*. There are contributors from the United States, United Kingdom, France, and the Netherlands, who tackle a broad array of Walzer's arguments, relating to equality, immigration, shared understandings, philosophical interpretation, workplace rights, pluralism, and polarization. Social democracy—and even left-liberalism—has been in retreat across the region in recent years, thanks to the electoral success of the populist right. Yet *Spheres* was written in 1983, in the middle of Reagan's first term, which was hardly the heyday of social democracy. It is our contention that Walzer's approach offers fruitful avenues for a revitalized left politics and political theory in an era of polarization, one that can uncover areas of deep consensus that underlie our surface disagreements and ground a revitalization of egalitarian politics for today.

Similarly, Walzer's theory continues to make major contributions to political theory. Then, as now, liberal theories such as those of Rawls and Nozick represented the mainstream, agenda-setting positions in political theory and philosophy, at least on matters of socio-economic justice. Some of Walzer's most significant overarching contributions offer alternatives to positions that are shared by both egalitarian liberalism and libertarianism. Walzer's attention to pluralism leads him to argue that goods have distinctive meanings that vary across different "spheres" of social life and that goods should be distributed in accordance with those sphere-specific meanings (Walzer 1983: 6–10). He thus sets out to analyze the social meanings of a wide range of prominent goods, including money and commodities (95–128), political power (281–311), office (129–640, education (197–226), security and welfare (64–94), and membership (31–63), as well as goods less frequently studied by political theorists, such as kinship and love (227–42) and divine grace (243–48). As a result, Walzer's book makes contributions to most of the major debates in political philosophy. Indeed, Walzer's attention to social meanings led him to focus attention on topics such as immigration, citizenship, multiculturalism, employee relations, and hard work long before they became the major research areas in political thought that they are today. Moreover, Walzer's engagements with disciplines such as anthropology, history, and sociology make *Spheres* resonate powerfully beyond political theory and philosophy.

Notably, complex equality conceives of equality as a political relationship that breaks with patterns of oppression and domination (Walzer 1983: 10–13), or as a "complex relation of persons" rather than "an identity of possessions" (18). Related to this, in conceiving of goods as social products, Walzer makes community central to an understanding of distributive justice.[5] In addition, Walzer's method of analyzing the meaning of social goods breaks with the universalism of much traditional political philosophy, suggesting in its place an interpretive method of social criticism, in which theorists start from the social meanings of their fellow citizens but argue that current practices fail to do justice to those deeper understandings.[6]

Both Walzer's interest in social and political context and his understandings of equality and of social criticism reflect *Spheres*' debt to public-intellectual debate: Walzer wrote the book while editing *Dissent*, the social-democratic magazine of the New York Intellectual community.[7] Walzer continued to edit *Dissent* until 2013 and still writes for it. He has also written frequently for outlets such as the *New Republic* and the *New York Review of Books*. In these forums, he extended and developed many of the arguments of *Spheres* in response to subsequent developments. Summing up the relationship between his political theory and his public-intellectual work, Walzer argues that there is a "political theory license" that allows scholars to stake out politically engaged positions in ways denied to almost all other academics.[8] Pursuing this license makes Walzer's work of continuing interest and concern to both scholars and intellectuals and has led to a series of books and articles dedicated to *Spheres* and to Walzer's work more broadly in recent years.[9] Furthermore, Walzer's engaging and elegant prose often makes political theory come alive to readers new to the subject. *Spheres* is of enduring relevance and contains the resources to help us think afresh about the predicaments of social democracy and left politics and theory in challenging times.

The Argument and Contribution of Spheres

The most distinctive feature of the conception of distributive justice that Walzer develops in *Spheres* is that, rather than proposing a series of principles that are to apply to the distribution of all goods, he proposes that different goods be "distributed to different people for different reasons."[10] This makes for a great variety of distributive principles that vary with the meaning of goods and across both time and space (Walzer 1983: 6–10).[11] Walzer grounds this pluralism in the argument that justice is a "human construction" (Walzer 1983: 5) that begins with the conception and creation of goods, and can only then develop principles of distribution (6–8). Goods, on Walzer's account, are not "idiosyncratically valued," because their conception and creation are "social processes" that produce shared meanings within a society even as goods mean different things in different societies (7–8). The conception and creation of goods are among the central phenomena in any society, because it is through our relationship to goods that we develop our "concrete identities" and become "recognizable" as individuals (8). As a result, a theory of distributive justice cannot proceed in abstraction from the political, philosophical, and economic debates within societies. These debates are what give meaning to the goods that are the objects of the theory, as well as giving the subjects who are to distribute the goods among themselves the materials out of which to fashion their identities. Social meanings provide the criteria by which goods should be distributed, for Walzer contends that distributive principles follow from the meanings of goods (8–9).[12] For this reason, the bulk of the argument of *Spheres* consists of an examination of the meanings of the most important contemporary social goods. Walzer holds that, "If we understand what [a good] is, what it means to those for whom it is a good, we understand how, by whom, and for what reasons it ought to be distributed" (9–10). Thus, Walzer concludes, theories of distributive justice should focus on goods and their relationship to the people who hold them, not on comparative assessment of distributive principles, conceived generally and abstractly.

Walzer argues that distributing goods for reasons relevant to their social meaning will produce complex equality because, although there may and in fact must be inequality of possession within each sphere, citizens will not be "unequal generally" (Walzer 1983: 19) so long as those inequalities are confined to the appropriate sphere.[13] Equalizing possessions within any one sphere will produce only "simple" equality by preventing people from monopolizing certain goods (13–17), whereas the true egalitarian task is to prevent particular goods—above all, money and political power—from becoming socially dominant (10–13). When goods achieve dominant status, their possessors can achieve a social status inimical to the development of a society of equals, dominating society by using those goods that they rightfully possess to gain access to all sorts of other goods with which they stand in a more distant relationship. This creates the sort of subordination that egalitarians seek to prevent, chasing instead a world with "no more bowing and scraping; fawning and toadying; no more fearful trembling; no more high-and-mightiness" (xiii). To prevent domination, and establish egalitarian relationships, we must prevent goods from accruing to people because of those people's relationship to other goods, for domination "is always mediated by some set of social goods" (xiii). Walzer thus reformulates the doctrine of right reasons, whereby goods are distributed for reasons relevant to their meaning, in negative terms, arguing that equality depends on ensuring that "*No social good x [be] distributed to men and women who possess some other good y merely because they possess y and without regard to the meaning of x*" (20). If this occurs, we will live in a complexly egalitarian society.

Simple equality—in which possession of important goods such as money is equalized—will not, on Walzer's account, last, because people's decisions will soon render possession unequal again (Walzer 1983: 14).[14] This would be a problem for egalitarians, Walzer contends, only if the same people won out in every sphere (Walzer 1983: 20; see also Walzer 2007: 81–95). Walzer acknowledges that the "subtle and indirect" convertibility of social goods (Walzer 2007: 83) across lines of class, ethnicity, and race may make such hierarchy appear likely in a capitalist society (87). Yet he argues that the range of human talents and goods makes it in fact unlikely. Consider, first, the different skills: "intelligence, physical strength, agility and grace, artistic creativity, mechanical skill, leadership, endurance, memory, psychological insight, the capacity for hard work—even, moral strength, sensitivity, the ability to express compassion" (Walzer 1980: 239–40). Each of these talents might well be distributed unequally along a bell curve, but if they are all distributed along the *same* bell curve, then equality is a chimera, and it is worth making a "democratic wager" that they are not (Walzer 2007: 92). Consider, next, the various goods we might wish to acquire: "Political power, celebrity, admiration, leisure, works of art, baseball teams, legal advice, sexual pleasure, travel, education, medical care, rare books, sailboats" (Walzer 1980: 239–40). We have different entitlements to each of these because different reasons are relevant to the distribution of each. For example, while in contemporary society, the appropriate reason for forming a romantic relationship is love and affection, such a reason amounts to nepotism or cronyism when it infiltrates the sphere of public office (Walzer 1983: 234–39; 147–48). Even if talents are unequally distributed overall, we can discern this only by investigating each talent as it relates to each good, and so there is no getting away from an approach to distributive justice that proceeds with reference to distinct social goods. This is especially because some of the relevant reasons for possessing a good are nothing to do with any sort of talent but depend entirely on relational standing. For example, one of Walzer's most famous arguments is that medical care should go to the sick (Walzer 1983: 86–91).[15] Distribution on the basis of health is a form of distribution for right reasons, but not one to which notions of merit are relevant at all. It is, rather, a form of distribution in accordance with need, but need, too, will not work for the distribution of all goods (Walzer 1983: 25–26).

In short, the argument for complex equality is an argument for pluralism of both skills and meanings, and for a relational approach to both equality and distributive principles. Walzer's other major contribution—the insistence that social meanings, and hence principles of justice, vary across cultures (see especially Walzer 1983: 312–16)—is in part a consequence of his theory of goods. If goods are produced by groups of humans in specific settings, it follows that goods will have different meanings in different societies. For example, Walzer notes, bread can be "the staff of life, the body of Christ, the symbol of the Sabbath, the means of hospitality" (8), etc. Non-natural products will not only have different meanings but be different goods. If the relevant principles of distribution follow from a good's meaning, then distributive principles will vary as goods and their meanings do. Offices and positions of responsibility can be treated as something to which the principle of equality of opportunity should apply only once those offices have been created. Moreover, they rely on the notions of the career and of life being lived according to a plan—both of which are modern ideas that are products of liberalism and of capitalism (Walzer 1994: 22–24).[16]

Walzer's argument for a more contextual approach to distributive justice, paying attention to specific goods in the settings in which they are created and used, offered a corrective to the abstract universalism of dominant accounts from the liberal tradition, in both its egalitarian and its libertarian guises. Walzer's theory of goods counters Rawls's notion of "primary goods," those things that all people need if they are to pursue their goals, whatever those goals happen to be (Rawls 1971: 54–55; c.f. Walzer 1983: 8–9). On Walzer's account, there are no such goods, because the range in social meanings is so great that almost anything might be necessary for the pursuit of our life plan, and almost nothing will be essential to all such plans. Even foodstuffs only meet this requirement in situations of extreme necessity, and "even there, we can't be sure. If the religious uses of bread were to conflict with its nutritional uses—if the gods demanded that bread be baked and burned rather than eaten—it is by no means clear which use would be primary" (Walzer 1983: 8; see also

1994: 21–40).[17] Universal principles based on appeal to universal goods must give way to particular principles based on contextual investigation of specific goods in specific contexts.

Walzer's critique of philosophical universalism departs from liberalism not only in the particularism of his conclusions but also in rejecting the abstraction of its methods. In developing his contractual theory of justice, Rawls starts by positing that parties to the contract reason from behind a "veil of ignorance" that denies them knowledge of any of the particularities of their situation and personality. Rawls argues that permitting such knowledge would introduce illegitimate bargaining advantages into negotiations on the contract and would produce outcomes based on morally arbitrary reasons (Rawls 1971: 17–22; 118–92). Rawls's theory seeks to produce principles that are fair to everyone, but the abstract way in which he cashes this out sets up, in Walzer's view, a clash between political theory and democratic prerogative.[18] Nozick's theory starts by presupposing the context of Locke's depiction of the state of nature (Nozick 1974: 9–12) and seeking to consider whether residents of such a state of nature might avoid establishing a state as quickly as Locke has his do (12–15). Nozick concludes that a minimal state would inevitably emerge from a clash between private protection agencies (22–25). Bruce Ackerman and Ronald Dworkin also base their theories on hypothetical scenarios that abstract from political contexts—Ackerman sets his on a spaceship that is on route to an uninhabited planet, Dworkin sets his on a desert island.[19]

Walzer's more contextual method has provided a valuable corrective to philosophical abstraction, such that contextualism is now much more common in political theory than it was in the 1980s, inspiring scholars generally at odds with some aspects of Walzer's work.[20] Walzer's contextualism proceeds via interpretation of the meaning of goods. Philosophical interpretivism was a prominent feature of Anglophone political theory in 1983,[21] but using interpretive method to construct a theory of distributive justice was less so. Moreover, Walzer's argument that interpretivism can be allied to an egalitarian account via social criticism of established practices that are at odds with deeper meanings (Walzer 1983: 318–21; 1987: 33–65) adds a way of reconciling equality with particularism that strikes us as fruitful for rethinking social democracy in an age of political polarization and a surge of populism on the right. For Walzer's appeal to social meanings, couched as it is in the language of shared understandings,[22] has frequently been criticized on the grounds that it is implicitly conservative or less critical of quotidian norms than a theory of justice should be.[23] Critics have taken Walzer to exaggerate the degree of social consensus, holding that any shared understandings that do exist likely result from domination and so lack moral force.[24]

If it were the case that interpretation is inevitably insufficiently critical of established practices, then an egalitarian theory would have no recourse but to abandon Walzer's particularism and return to the universalism of much left-liberalism. Yet if goods really are created by groups and societies, then a universal theory lacks purchase on the objects of distribution. It is its attention to goods-in-their-context that gives Walzer's theory its richness and flavor. I have argued elsewhere that critics overstate the degree of consensus to which Walzer appeals (Reiner 2017; 2020: 69–75), for his argument is not that citizens of a society always have an identical moral worldview but that whatever understandings of goods do exist are culturally specific. Interpretation does not "commit us to a positivist reading of the actually existing morality" (Walzer 1987: 29), nor does it assume that meanings are "just *there*, agreed on once and for all" (Walzer 2007: 42). Rather, "they are always subject to dispute" (42). Walzerian interpretivism is a plea for political theory to use as its materials the messy, semi-articulated, seemingly incoherent arguments of daily life, not the tidy, formal rigorous thought experiments of analytic philosophers (Walzer 2007: 1–37). Walzerian egalitarianism is in part the claim that equality can emerge from engagement with the political traditions of particular societies, as social critics find fertile ground in pointing out the gap between social practices and underlying principles (Walzer 1987: 33–65). The argument is that distributive justice always has its roots in a political tradition, because the goods available for distribution are the products of that tradition's society, but that traditions are always contested and can always be read in democratic, egalitarian ways that undercut hierarchy.

The rich flavor of Walzer's situated arguments related to migration, cultural diversity, workplace rights, and so on, thus stem from his insistence that goods are social products with social meanings embedded in political traditions that are sites of social contestation. Consider his oft-stated position on healthcare (Walzer 1983: 86–91; 1994: 26–31).[25] Walzer argues that healthcare in the United States ought to be distributed on the basis of need; that is, provided free at the point of delivery to those already sick and to prevent future illness. The implication is that the private medical insurance system ought to be replaced by at least a "Medicare for All" scheme and probably a national health service that provides universal coverage for all citizens. Walzer repeatedly made this argument during the 1980s, in a period when the Reagan Government won repeated heavy victories in Presidential elections on a platform dedicated to cutting public spending on welfare (Walzer 1986). How could Walzer plausibly claim that there was a shared understanding in the United States that healthcare was a need? The answer is that Walzer's claim that healthcare should be distributed on the basis of need is an implication of his account of its social meanings, not the account itself. For Walzer, what makes socialized distribution morally necessary is our shared commitments to health (the avoidance and minimization of pain and suffering) and longevity, commitments that are particular to the modern age (see especially Walzer 1994: 26–28). Walzer argues that past cultures did not value long life as we do, both because they were less likely to achieve it and because of more widespread belief in the afterlife, which encouraged stoicism about death that few contemporaries share. Which of us today would choose, with Achilles, to live a short but glorious life, rather than a longer, obscure one? It is Walzer's contention that few contemporaries would do so. Rebutting Walzer's position cannot proceed simply by arguing that most Americans think that healthcare should be treated as a commodity, bought and sold on the marketplace. Rather, it requires either showing that he is mistaken about our commitment to longevity or making a case for the compatibility of such a commitment with the commodification of medical care.[26]

I detail Walzer's healthcare argument for two reasons. First, one of Walzer's central contributions in *Spheres* (and follow-up work) is to demonstrate the case for theories of justice emerging out of enquiry into social meaning and using said meanings to argue for distributive principles. Walzer's interest in social meanings is thus one of the reasons why *Spheres* covers myriad topics that were not then widely discussed in political theory but are important today Political theory today looks far more Walzerian than it did in 1983, because there is far greater focus on applied work on topics of importance in political life, and perhaps less on intellectual and moral foundations. Walzer is a direct influence on the content of some important works in some of these growth areas.[27] In some cases, his influence is apparent in the choice of topic and is briefly acknowledged, but his claims are less important to the author's arguments (for discussion, Moore 2016).[28] Yet even where the overlap is coincidental, *Spheres* is important for bringing to attention significant political issues such as migration, free time, and hard work, and for demonstrating that one of the tasks of a theory of distributive justice is to grapple and engage with them rather than proceeding in abstraction from them.

A corollary of Walzer's insistence in *Spheres* that distributive justice engages with political issues is his claim that it should pay attention to our specific attributes.[29] Walzer devotes a chapter of *Spheres* to recognition, arguing that complex equality in this area would break with a system of recognition based on rank but insisting that "individual men and women would still be differentially honored" (Walzer 1983: 258) beyond a minimal respect, because admiration loses its meaning if all are equally admired. In this argument, Walzer breaks with the rejection of moral desert in the theories of Rawls and Dworkin (Rawls 1971: 310–15),[30] insisting that abstracting from both goods and personal qualities cannot "possibly do justice to persons as they are, in search of goods as they conceive them. We don't encounter other people as moral and psychological blanks…[Justice] begins with persons-in-the-social world, with goods in their minds" (Walzer 1983: 261). A complexly egalitarian society must ensure equality of democratic citizenship (277), but alongside this, special honors for noteworthy achievements—including dishonors and criminal punishments—must continue if justice is to be meaningful for us. Recognition freely given, and not linked to inherited status, is integral to the development of democratic self-respect (279–80). Complex equality should allow for inequality of certain types of recognition.[31] So long as honors and punishments do not determine people's overall life chances, they are compatible with complex equality. As Walzer later put it, "John Rawls deserved the honors he won by writing *A Theory of Justice*—even if his intelligence was an accidental effect of the natural lottery" (Walzer 2007: 304). The crucial point is that, just as theories of justice must engage with specific social goods, so they must consider people as they are, for who "we are necessarily has consequences in the social world" (304). An egalitarian theory can be truly egalitarian only if it speaks to its purported beneficiaries, and too great a use of philosophical abstraction jeopardizes its attempts to speak to ordinary citizens.

Second, Walzer's claims about healthcare illustrate the plausibility of his argument that enquiry into social meaning can uncover areas of surprising overlap and agreement between political opponents that is obscured by dispute over principles of distribution and other normative dissensus. This is one of the things that makes *Spheres* a lasting work, for it offers an approach to distributive justice grounded in the claim that members of a society share more in common than our political disputes suggest.

What we share is a tradition of arguing about how to live together (Walzer 1987: 32). Theories of justice can help to narrow disagreement by showing that it is often rooted in different understandings of a shared way of life and by focusing on justice "*right here*" (Walzer 1980: 49), rather than sub specie aeternitatis (on this, see especially Walzer 2007: 68–80; c.f. Rawls 1971: 587). This does not mean that Walzer's theory of society is one of consensus. Indeed, in *Spheres* he offers an account of a society wracked by disagreement, arguing that "when understandings are controversial, justice requires that the society be faithful to the disagreements, providing institutional channels for their expression, adjudicative mechanisms, and alternative distributions" (Walzer 1983: 313). Thus, Walzer's approach can be a fruitful way to think through political conflict in eras of polarization such as the 2020s, by drawing our attention to the fact that citizens share a common life,[32] participate together in the creation of goods, and that their disagreements are often nested within a political tradition that is meaningful to them all.

That is, Walzer makes the case for a more overtly *political* theory of distributive justice that engages with debates in institutional politics. In this sense, his work anticipates "new realist" thought[33]—one of the major growth areas in Anglophone philosophy in recent decades—in suggesting that political theory avoid abstract moralizing. Walzer argues that such criticism "doesn't touch the conscience of the people to whom it is addressed" (Walzer 1988: 151). Unlike new realists, however, Walzer does not advance a sharp distinction between "political" and "moralist" approaches to philosophy (for examples of realists who do so, see especially Larmore 2013 and Williams 2005, the latter of whom bakes such a distinction into his title), but offers a moral argument rooted in political discourse. Walzer suggests that criticism that works within a discourse is more effective because it shows us what we aspire to be (Walzer 1988: 151), and that this is necessary to inspire popular mobilization by appealing to our "historically formed" and "culturally specific" values and ideals (126).

With that said, recent waves of migration and the resulting increase in cultural diversity around the world provide a stark test case of the theory that Walzer advances in *Spheres*. Disparate cultural and ethnic groups may *not* share the goods, meanings, or values to which Walzer appeals. If not, the same arguments that I adduced above in critique of a universal theory of justice would apply internally, within a nation-state, to the different groups. If social goods are the key bedrock of the theory—the things that we first conceive and create, and only then can distribute among ourselves (Walzer 1983: 6–7)—then it is an open question to what extent radically different groups within the same polity can be subjects of the same theory of distributive justice. It is one thing to arrange for alternative distributions of *similar sets of social goods* and another to have different distributive schemes of entirely different goods set up alongside each other. Put differently, the extent to which citizens today share a social world is one of the major themes of this book, for it strikes at the heart of the plausibility of the theory that Walzer advances in *Spheres*.

Spheres entered a field of political theory that was somewhat saturated after the burst of work on distributive justice over the previous decade, following the release of Rawls's *A Theory of Justice*. In this respect it was in a significantly different position than was Walzer's other great work, *Just and Unjust Wars* (1977).[34] Although theorizing about military ethics has a history as long as that of distributive justice, when Walzer wrote *Just and Unjust Wars*, it was, in the United States, mostly studied by theologians who assumed Christian values.[35] Hence Walzer opened *Wars* by stating that his ambition was to "rediscover the just war for political and moral theory" (Walzer 2015: xxvi). In 1983, theories of distributive justice were a cottage industry. It is a hallmark of Walzer's achievement that *Spheres* was able to make a distinctive contribution in a field so well-trodden. Complex equality, social goods, the spheres of justice, shared understandings, and more are concepts that have changed the way in which political theorists approach questions of distribution, and they remain as relevant today as they were in 1983.

Structure of the Book

This volume has eight contributions, by Walzer scholars from the United States, the United Kingdom, France, and the Netherlands. We combine consideration of some of the deep theory of *Spheres* with focus on its application to political debate in the 2020s and what it has to offer going forward into subsequent decades. Because of Walzer's appeal to the social meanings of specific societies, our focus in the more political chapters is on North America and Western Europe. Michael Walzer concludes the volume with a response that also reconsiders the project of *Spheres* from today's perspective.

The first chapter, by Astrid von Busekist, sets Walzer's work in its intellectual and political context. Von Busekist traces the influence on

Walzer of various elements of thought in which he was immersed while writing *Spheres*, including the analytic political philosophy of the Rawlsian tradition, the social democracy of the *Dissent* circle, and the interpretive social sciences, in particular the anthropology of Clifford Geertz, Walzer's colleague at the Institute for Advanced Study. In her chapter, von Busekist draws on a series of interviews that she conducted with Walzer.[36]

The next two chapters consider the intellectual foundations of Walzer's project. Georgia Warnke subjects Walzer's interpretive method and appeal to social meanings to critical scrutiny. She argues that critics of Walzer's interpretivism have failed to note that what is shared is not an understanding of distributive principles but of the meaning of goods and that critics overstate the degree to which Walzer's position relies upon consensus. Comparing Walzer's account to traditions of literary interpretation, however, she suggests that understandings of social meaning may be less widely shared within communities than Walzer suggests. Considering his healthcare example, she reconstructs a market-based account that appeals to social meanings. She suggests that the hermeneutic tradition can help provide criteria with which to adjudicate debates about meaning. She concludes that appeal to interpretive methods can promote greater civility in public and political debate.

Geoffrey Kurtz asks whether we can uncover moral foundations to Walzer's socialism despite Walzer's disinclination to explore those foundations (Walzer 1983: xii; 1987: 14–18). Kurtz's goal is to suggest possible sources of commitment to equality, rather than the entailments of such commitment. Kurtz focuses on Walzer's note that equality may stem from our recognition of each other as human beings with "bodies and minds and feelings and hopes and maybe even souls" (Walzer 1983: xii). In exploring this appeal to souls, Kurtz considers the debt that Walzer owes to R. H. Tawney, an oft-neglected aspect of the literature, as well as to *Dissent*niks such as Irving Howe. Kurtz argues that moral foundations can serve as sources of orientation or bases for commitment. Kurtz concludes that viewing the soul as an orienting foundation for egalitarianism might help both to revive egalitarian politics today and to reverse the erosion of civic life.

J. Toby Reiner takes up Kurtz's question about the nature of Walzerian egalitarianism, while focusing on its conception of equality as complex equality rather than its source. Much of the secondary literature on *Spheres* has taken Walzer's word that egalitarianism is an abolitionist project, concerned to deconstruct hierarchies (Walzer 1983: xii–xiii).[37]

While accepting this aspect of Walzer's egalitarianism, Reiner argues that there exists alongside it an activist conception of equality, which sees equal citizenship as founded on rights to participation in a self-governing community. That is, equality requires not merely abolition of hierarchy, but its replacement with an institutional framework founded on shared commitment to, and involvement in, political projects of community governance. Reiner considers Walzer's defense of industrial and workplace democracy as an aspect of this vision. Walzer's arguments for extending democracy from the polity to the workplace and on to industrial organization are a crucial site of Walzer's social-democratic critique of liberalism and showcase the distinctiveness of his conception of equality as a positive vision.

David Miller's contribution focuses on the first substantive chapter of *Spheres*, on membership (Walzer 1983: 31–63), and particularly on Walzer's arguments about immigration. Miller notes the innovativeness of Walzer's position, because Walzer combines the claim that states have a right to restrict entry with insistence on robust membership rights for those admitted, including paths to citizenship. Miller scrutinizes this position, defending much of it but suggesting that some temporary migration programs that do not grant paths to citizenship should be permissible, so long as they do not exploit the migrant workers. Miller also connects Walzer's position to his own contributions to the migration debate (see especially Miller 2016), which focuses on the extent to which the welfare state, and socio-economic redistribution, depend on public cohesion that mass immigration may undermine.

Steven Lukes asks whether shared understandings survive in the contemporary world. Lukes notes that we live in an era of political polarization that was only beginning to emerge when Walzer wrote *Spheres*. Lukes suggests that polarization produces understandings that depend increasingly on party affiliation and result in what has been called "tribal epistemology." However, Lukes suggests, this polarization is asymmetrical, at least in the United States, where many Republicans oppose society's central information-gathering institutions (such as universities and mass media), while Democrats remain reliant on them. Lukes argues that polarization need not mean that few shared understandings survive. Polarization is largely driven by the mobilization of power to comfort the comfortable, while inflaming the grievances of the disadvantaged. Ethnography can reveal, and experiments in deliberative democracy can help enable people to discover, what interests they have in common—despite that mobilization—and what values they share.

Michael Rustin analyzes the political importance of *Spheres* as a work of social democracy in an era of retrenchment from the post-war period of enhanced equality in North America and Western Europe. He explores how Walzer's argument aimed to rescue equality from its association with conformity following the state socialism of Eastern Europe, from which Western social democrats struggled to differentiate themselves. The contribution of *Spheres*, Rustin argues, was to connect equality with pluralism. However, he holds, *Spheres* might have offered greater focus on the good life, rather than on justice per se. Rustin suggests that such focus would lead to examination of the relationship between complex equality and hierarchy within particular spheres, and that some forms of hierarchy are compatible with leftist goals (see also Bell and Wang 2020).

Finally, Margo Trappenburg provides a thoroughgoing defense of Walzer's pluralism. She notes that, in the 1980s and 1990s, pluralism helped Walzerians such as herself to rebut the marketization of society and the prevailing neoliberalism. She suggests that we currently face new challenges to Walzer's claim that talents are (more or less) randomly distributed and spheres of justice should be kept separate. One rising contemporary challenge is the idea that all types of injustice are connected and should be fought in coherence, an idea advanced by scholars and activists under the rubrics of intersectionality and identity politics. Another challenge is that current policymakers tend to feel that they have to solve societal problems and help needy citizens as well as possible, disregarding the boundaries between governmental organizations and their respective societal spheres. Trappenburg argues that Walzer's theory might help us be more critical about these new types of boundary crossings.

Competing Interests The author has no conflicts of interest to declare that are relevant to the content of this chapter.

Notes

1. Michael Walzer, *Spheres of Justice: A Defense of Pluralism and Equality* (New York: Basic Books, 1983).
2. Margaret Moore, "Michael Walzer, *Spheres of Justice*," in *The Oxford Handbook of Classics in Contemporary Political Theory*, ed. Jacob Levy (Oxford Handbooks Online, 2016): https://doi.org/10.1093/oxfordhb/9780198717133.013.45. Last accessed 31 October 2024.
3. Cambridge, MA: Harvard University Press, 1971.
4. New York: Basic Books, 1974.
5. Indeed, much of the early reception of *Spheres* called it a "communitarian" work. See, for example, Stephen Mulhall and Adam Swift, *Liberals and Communitarians* (Oxford: Blackwell, 1992); Shlomo Avineri and Avner de-Shalit, ed. *Communitarianism and Individualism* (New York: Oxford University Press, 1992).
6. Michael Walzer, *Interpretation and Social Criticism*, (Cambridge, MA: Harvard University Press, 1987); *The Company of Critics: Social Criticism and Political Commitment in the Twentieth Century* (New York: Basic Books, 1988).
7. On the New York Intellectuals, see Neil Jumonville, ed. *The New York Intellectuals Reader* (New York: Routledge, 2007); for discussion of *Dissent* and Walzer, J. Toby Reiner, "Michael Walzer in Historical Context: Complex Equality and the American Social-Democratic Tradition," *American Political Thought* 6 (2017): 455–75.
8. Michael Walzer, "The Political Theory License," *Annual Review of Political Science* 16 (2013): 1–9.
9. Astrid Von Busekist, *Justice is Steady Work: A Conversation on Political Theory* (Cambridge: Polity, 2020); J. Toby Reiner, *Michael Walzer* (Cambridge: Polity, 2020); Graham Parsons and Mark Wilson, ed. *Walzer and War: Reading Just and Unjust Wars Today* (London: Palgrave Macmillan, 2020); Yitzhak Benbaji and Naomi Sussmann, ed., *Reading Walzer* (New York: Routledge, 2014).
10. Michael Walzer, *Radical Principles: Reflections of an Unreconstructed Democrat* (New York: Basic Books, 1980): 242. In *Spheres*, this is the last of Walzer's six propositions that makes up his theory of goods. See Walzer 1983: 10.

11. For discussion of the relationship between these two axes of pluralism, see Jacob Levy, "What it Means to be a Pluralist," in Benbaji and Sussmann 2014: 111–28.
12. This, as well as the conclusion that theories of justice should be culturally relative, has been among the most controversial parts of Walzer's theory. See Ronald Dworkin, "To Each His Own," *New York Review of Books* 30 (1983): 4–6; Govert Den Hartogh, "The Architectonic of Michael Walzer's Theory of Justice," *Political Theory* 27 (1999): 491–522; Brian Barry, "Intimations of Justice" *Columbia Law Review* 84 (1984): 806–15 and "Spherical Justice and Global Injustice," in *Pluralism, Justice, and Equality*, ed. David Miller and Michael Walzer (Oxford: Oxford University Press, 1995): 67–80; Norman Daniels, "Book Review: *Spheres of Justice*," *Philosophical Review* 94 (1985): 142–48; Joshua Cohen, "Book Review: *Spheres of Justice*," *Journal of Philosophy* 83 (1986): 457–66; Robert Van der Veen, "The Adjudicating Citizen: On Equal Membership in Walzer's Theory of Justice," *British Journal of Political Science* 29 (1999): 343–62; George Kateb, "Walzer's Radicalism," in Benbaji and Sussmann 2014: 196–221. For defense of Walzer's positions, see J. Toby Reiner, "Social Meanings and the Cultural Theory of Goods in Michael Walzer's Ethical Anthropology," *Polity* 48 (2016): 359–86; Margo Trappenburg, "In Defence of Pure Pluralism: Two Readings of Walzer's *Spheres of Justice*," *Journal of Political Philosophy* 8 (2000): 343–62.
13. Walzer defends this proposition in "Justice Here and Now" [1986] and "Exclusion, Injustice, and the Democratic State," [1993], each of which is reprinted in Michael Walzer, *Thinking Politically: Essays in Political Theory* (New Haven: Yale University Press, 2007): 68–80 and 81–95, respectively.
14. On this point, Walzer agrees with Nozick's critique of "patterned" theories of justice (see Nozick 1974: 149–64). However, Walzer disagrees that all egalitarian theories are "patterned.".
15. See also Michael Walzer, *Thick and Thin: Moral Argument at Home and Abroad* (Notre Dame: Notre Dame University Press, 1994): 26–31.
16. See also Michael Walzer, "Liberalism and the Art of Separation" [1984] in Walzer 2007: 53–67 at 54–55.
17. For Walzer's theoretical defense of this proposition, see "Objectivity and Social Meaning" [1993] in Walzer 2007: 38–52.

18. See especially Michael Walzer, "Philosophy and Democracy" [1981] and "A Critique of Philosophical Conversation" [1989/90] in Walzer 2007: 1–21 and 22–37, respectively.
19. Bruce Ackerman, *Social Justice in the Liberal State* (New Haven: Yale University Press, 1980); Ronald Dworkin, "What is Equality? Part 2: Equality of Resources." *Philosophy and Public Affairs* 10 (1981): 283–345.
20. See, for example, Joseph Carens, "A Contextual Approach to Political Theory," *Ethical Theory and Moral Practice* 7 (2004): 117–32. See Carens, "Complex Justice, Cultural Difference, and Political Community," in Miller and Walzer 1995: 45–66 for critique of *Spheres* and Carens, "Aliens and Citizens: The Case for Open Borders," *Review of Politics* 49 (1987): 251–73 for an account of immigration ethics in which the position Walzer develops in *Spheres* (Walzer 1983: 31–63) is a foil.
21. See especially Alasdair MacIntyre, *After Virtue: A Study in Moral Theory*, (London: Duckworth, 1981); Charles Taylor, "Interpretation and the Sciences of Man," [1971] in his *Philosophical Papers: Volume 2, Philosophy and the Human Sciences* (New York: Cambridge University Press, 2012): 15–57. For discussion, Jason Blakely, *Alasdair MacIntyre, Charles Taylor, and the Demise of Naturalism* (Notre Dame: Notre Dame University Press, 2016).
22. See especially *Spheres*: 313, where Walzer argues that "A given society is just if its substantive life is lived…in a way faithful to the shared understandings of the members."
23. Critics of Walzer on this point include those listed in note 12. See also William Galston, "Community, Democracy, Philosophy: The Political Thought of Michael Walzer," *Political Theory* 17 (1989): 119–30; Joseph Raz, "Morality as Interpretation," *Ethics* 101 (1991): 392–405; Elisabeth Bounds, "Conflicting Harmonies: Michael Walzer's Vision of Community," *Journal of Religious Ethics* 22 (1994): 355–74; Tyler Roberts, "Michael Walzer and the Critical Connection," *Journal of Religious Ethics* 22 (1994): 333–53; Veit Bader, "Citizenship and Exclusion," *Political Theory* 23 (1995): 211–45; Melissa Orlie, "Beyond Identity and Difference," *Political Theory* 27 (1999): 140–49; Toni Erskine, "Qualifying Cosmopolitanism? Solidarity, Criticism, and Michael Walzer's 'View from the Cave'," *International Politics* 24 (2007): 125–49. I provide a fuller list in Reiner 2020: 186–97.

24. For discussion, Brian Orend, *Michael Walzer on War and Justice* (Cardiff: University of Wales Press, 2000): 17–25.
25. See also "The Long-Term Perspective," *Bulletin of the New York Academy of Medicine* 62 (1986): 8–14.
26. In her contribution to this volume, Georgia Warnke considers this case in more detail. See also Reiner 2016.
27. For example, Walzer's work on both the nation and migration influences David Miller, *National Responsibility and Global Justice* (New York: Oxford University Press, 2007) and *Strangers in Our Midst: The Political Philosophy of Immigration* (Cambridge, MA: Harvard University Press, 2016), and his accounts of commodification and workplace rights are an inspiration for the groundbreaking work on these subjects by Elizabeth Anderson, *Private Government: How Employers Rule Our Lives (and Why We Don't Talk About It)* (Princeton: Princeton University Press, 2017). See also Sarah Jaffe, *Work Won't Love You Back* (Bold Type Books, 2021).
28. See, for example, Julie Rose, *Free Time* (Princeton: Princeton University Press, 2016) and Michael Sandel, *What Money Can't Buy: The Moral Limits of Markets* (London: Penguin, 2012). See also much of the philosophical literature on multiculturalism. Will Kymlicka discusses Walzer's influence on that literature in "Categorizing Groups, Categorizing States: Theorizing Minority Rights in a World of Deep Diversity" in Benbaji and Sussmann 2014: 129–45.
29. This follows from his argument that it is through involvement in the conception and creation of goods that we acquire our concrete identities (Walzer 1983: 7–8).
30. Ronald Dworkin, "Why Bakke Has No Case," *New York Review of Books* 24 (1977): 11–15; for discussion, Michael Sandel, *Liberalism and the Limits of Justice* (Cambridge: Cambridge University Press, 1982): 137–43.
31. On this point, see also Daniel Bell and Wang Pei, *Just Hierarchy: Why Social Hierarchies Matter in China and the Rest of the World* (Princeton: Princeton University Press, 2020).
32. On the common life, see especially Michael Walzer, "The Moral Standing of States: A Response to Four Critics" [1980] in Walzer 2007: 219–36.

33. On new realism, see William Galston, "Realism in Political Theory," *European Journal of Political Theory* 9 (2010): 385–411; Bernard Williams, *In the Beginning Was the Deed: Realism and Moralism in Political Argument* (Princeton: Princeton University Press, 2005); Charles Larmore, "What is Political Philosophy?" *Journal of Moral Philosophy* 10 (2013): 276–306; Matt Sleat, "Legitimacy in Realist Thought: Between Moralism and *Realpolitik*," *Political Theory* 42 (2014): 314–37; Enzo Rossi and Matt Sleat, "Realism in Normative Political Theory," *Philosophy Compass* 9/10 (2014): 689–701; Lorna Finlayson, "With radicals like these, who needs conservatives? Doom, gloom, and realism in political theory," *European Journal of Political Theory* 16 (2017): 264–82.
34. Michael Walzer, *Just and Unjust Wars: A Moral Argument with Historical Illustrations* (New York: Basic Books, 2015 [1977]).
35. See especially R. Paul Ramsey, *War and the Christian Conscience: How Shall Modern Warfare be Conducted Justly?* (Durham, NC: Duke University Press, 1961); *The Just War: Force and Political Responsibility* (Rowman & Littlefield, 2002 [1968]).
36. These interviews are the basis of Von Busekist 2020.
37. On this point, see especially Robert Mayer, "A Walzerian Theory of Exploitation," *Polity* 34 (2002): 337–56.

CHAPTER 2

The Factory of *Spheres:* Michael Walzer and Practical Equality

Astrid von Busekist

Michael Walzer is a warm and generous intellectual, a passionate albeit patient activist. He calls himself a social democrat and has been called a socialist. He calls himself a liberal and has been called a communitarian. In the writings of his friends and critics, he is alternately internationalist, statist, or nationalist. In life, he is a militant and professor, an intellectual and a political writer. He has been inspired by *Dissentniks* and Talmudists.

His thinking and writing bring together different but overlapping strings: a constant awareness of the right distance in politics; an anthropological or phenomenological approach to justice; a firm commitment, theoretical and practical, to egalitarian pluralism. What connects these strings—and connects Michael Walzer to the real world as an ever-contemporary thinker—is what I call a "politics of comradeship."[1]

My contribution is an attempt to tie the threads of a long involvement in academic and political debate and to offer a cartography that will, I hope, shed some new light on *Spheres of Justice*.[2] I will begin with a brief

A. von Busekist (✉)
Political Theory, Sciences Po, Paris, France
e-mail: astrid.vonbusekist@sciencespo.fr

J. T. Reiner (ed.), *Walzer and Justice: Spheres of Justice in the 2020s*,
https://doi.org/10.1007/978-3-031-87809-1_2

biographical detour on the context in which *Spheres of Justice* [SJ] was written; I will then look at the genealogy of Michael Walzer's practical theory; I will finally propose a reading of SJ rooted in social-democratic egalitarian theory and practice against domination, rather than in the classical liberal kind of distributive justice.

Justice, equality, and politics before Spheres

In the early 1970s, Michael Walzer became a professor at Harvard. The *social studies* department he chaired included Barrington Moore and Albert Hirschman; Theda Skocpol arrived in 1974, the same year Raymond Boudon became a visiting professor. *Philosophers* included John Rawls, Stanley Cavell, Hilary Putnam (who was a Maoist at the time), W.V.O. Quine and Robert Nozick. *Sociology* is represented by Talcott Parsons, Seymour Lipset, Daniel Bell and Shmuel Eisenstadt; the *Government* department employs Stanley Hoffman, Karl Deutsch, Samuel Huntington, Joseph Nye, Carl Friedrich, Zbigniew Brzeziński, Louis Hartz and Samuel Beer (Walzer's thesis advisor). This impressive list of scholars debated across disciplinary divides, campaigned together or against each other depending on the year and the topic. Chapters of Rawls' *Theory of Justice were* circulated before the book was released in 1971; the same year that *Obligations*[3] was published, along with the first issue of a journal with a promising future, *Philosophy and Public Affairs*, co-founded by Michael Walzer.[4] *Anarchy, State and Utopia* [ASU] was published in 1974.[5] *Just and Unjust Wars*[6] appeared a few years later, but one had to wait until 1983 to read Walzer's contribution to the discussion on justice set in motion by Rawls. When *Spheres of Justice* [*SJ*] was finally published, its author had already joined Princeton.

What explains this late publication? At the time, Michael Walzer was more of an intellectual historian than a theorist; as a *Dissentnik*—the nickname given to members of the *Dissent* editorial team—he was a civil rights activist and opposed the Vietnam War, the real emergencies of the day. He also felt that the formal debates of analytic philosophy were too far removed from real life[7]—and I believe he never ceased to think so.[8] It was in 1971 that he nevertheless decided, with his comrade Bob Nozick[9], to give a class simply entitled "Capitalism and Socialism[10]"—and this is the first lesson in comradeship, beyond the political preferences of each.[11] The course,[12] which the *Crimson* quotes only once,[13] had a crucial influence on the writing of *Spheres*, even though Nozick is barely mentioned.[14]

Students and assistants alike remember two qualities from Walzer's lectures in that class that still describe him quite well today. Firstly, what might be called "honest adversarial presentations", i.e. a line of reasoning that incorporates the opposing point of view.[15] Secondly, what Michael Walzer later called the "the political theory license[16]", i.e. the conviction that it is legitimate to defend one's own ideas and political preferences, as long as the opposing arguments are presented as fairly as possible. A fine lesson in probity. Finally, about comradeship: No doubt Nozick was quicker and wittier. Walzer knew this, and later confided: "I think Bob probably won the argument (if anyone was keeping score), but it was 1970, so the majority of the students were with me—though Bob was as radical as I was in his own way". But Walzer was the one who made a longer lasting impression according to the students who took the class. After class, the two men played handball together.

In Defense of Equality

"In Defense of Equality" [IDE], published by *Dissent* in 1973, takes up Walzer's contribution to the class with Nozick and announces *Spheres.* The main ideas and the terminology are there.[17] IDE may be less elaborate, more realistic perhaps, this being 1973—"the welfare state cannot provide social love[18]"—and undoubtedly also more steeped in socialism:

> What socialists want is a society in which wealth is no longer convertible into social goods with which it has no intrinsic connection. [...] In capitalist society, the actual exchange value of the work they do is largely a function of market conditions over which they exercise no control. It has little to do with the intrinsic value of the work or with the individual qualities of the worker. [...] I want to argue that in our society the only way to do that, or to begin to do it, is to worry about the tyranny of money.[19]

IDE is very explicit about an idea that Michael Walzer cherishes and defends throughout his entire work (whether all socialists have defended the equal standing of liberty and equality—and in that order—may be wishful…): "the case is exactly as socialists have always claimed it to be: liberty and equality are the two chief virtues of social institutions, and they stand best when they *stand together*[20]". IDE also tests the main theses developed in SJ: the question of the nature of goods (their concreteness: goods do not magically appear in the hands of those who create and produce them)—this is why they express a certain relationship between individuals and goods; the problem of the unequal distribution of talents[21]; the pre-eminent role of money as converter *par excellence*; the important role played by tyranny (inspired by quotations from Pascal and Marx[22]); the leading example of health and healthcare[23]; and lastly of course the main argument: there is no single criterion for the fair distribution of goods.[24]

On this last point, Walzer and Nozick agree. The best evidence is the funny paragraph in *Anarchy State and Utopia* about the incommensurable desires of Wittgenstein and Elizabeth Taylor, Ghandi and a Lubavitcher rebbe.[25] Both professors also opposed single models, Walzer because he fears for equality, Nozick because he fears infringements on freedom.[26]

In essence, IDE argues that an equal distribution of goods according to a single parameter (cardinality) will not lead to a society of equals; that equality cannot be equated with the equal distribution of a particular good, that it is above all a political principle that is negotiated concretely, collectively, politically. If there is no substantial equality, if equality is contextual, it is also relative—Walzer would later say "complex". Relativism however does not have a good reputation in this field: some critics will associate relativism with conservatism as we shall see.

Another idea crucial to understanding SJ finds its first formulation in this pioneering article: the "capacity" (my term) namely of a good to be distributed. It clarifies Michael Walzer's conception of goods (they are both material and immaterial) and puts some limits on an interpretation of SJ focused exclusively on distributive justice[27] Not all goods can be distributed in the same way. Intuitively, this seems obvious: divine grace or free time are not distributed in the same way as housing or access to healthcare. If certain goods have a low capacity for distribution, we need to find other ways of accessing them without going through monetary conversion.

On the other hand, some important themes that will hold the attention of the readers of *Spheres* are still missing in IDE: Walzer's interest in "shared understandings"; concerns about monopoly and dominance, and the importance of belonging (the future chapter 2 of SJ) which has been often criticized in the light of the literature on the "boundary problem" and "justice in immigration" as David Miller would put it.[28]

Here, then, is a glimpse of how Michael Walzer thought about a more diverse framework for social justice before writing SJ. The author's pendulum always swings from politics to theory and back again: convictions in one world feed commitments in the other. Clearly, the class he taught with Nozick enabled him to refine his thinking and his political commitment to putting equality at the heart of his work. We don't campaign alone, and we don't think alone: comradeship must be cultivated, in theory and in the field.

A Genealogy of Practical Theory, or the Politics of Comradeship: Thinking and Acting Together

The relationship between politics and political theory is strong, as is the important role played by friends and allies. I believe Michael Walzer has an *ethical triangle* in mind whose three vertices are equality, comradeship, and political action.

Commitment and friendship translate into action: "Action is the crucial language of moral commitment[29]" says Walzer. Theory comes a little later, just out of step. But Michael Walzer does have high hopes and expectations for left-wing intellectuals[30]: "What do I want from my young friends and comrades, what would I like them to do, say or write?[31]" he asks. He also advises on the way we should act: with gentle manners, an inquisitive and open mind[32]. This politics of comradeship—which is also a politics of equality, as his early texts show[33]—is the thread that links his *œuvre* to his political commitments.

References to comradeship are numerous in his books and his *Dissent* articles, one example being the Algerian war, when the magazine supported Messali Hadj: it is always about fighting together, across borders, for a democratic, egalitarian socialism. Thus in 1981: "[People] come to pluralism only through an act of empathy and identification[34]"; or in 2019: Leftists must pursue a politics of kindness right now, for our contemporaries and for ourselves: arguing softly (even when injustice makes us angry), raising consciousness, forming coalitions, building a majority, making lives better, one step at a time[35]"; and again in 2023, in his latest book: "So, what does liberal morality have to do with politics? I don't have an answer for everyone. I want to write about myself and my political friends and comrades and tell stories about our life together".[36]

Indeed, Michael Walzer is constantly reminding us of the program Lewis Coser announced in the first issue of *Dissent*: anti-sectarianism[37], with *fellow travelers*, and *comrades*: "No revolution, no transformation, no left-wing politics *without you and me*[38]". This idea of comradeship also shows in the respect we owe any of our fellow citizens.[39] The lesson is the following: you have to take reality seriously in order to transform it, and you have to take society as it is, and you shouldn't denigrate people's daily lives or think in their place. To achieve a "feasible socialism"[40], you need to give collective decision-making a chance.

Such a program will disappoint the revolutionaries among us and does indeed express a solid distrust of "too much politics" among the radical left of the 1960s and 1970s. Michael Walzer is convinced that one cannot be a full-time citizen, that one cannot ask individuals to be mobilized day and night[41]; he believes in the value of representation and insists on shared understandings.

Political time in his view is long and slow. Walzerian politics—a patient commitment, incremental results, coalitions and compromises—is indeed the opposite of the radical, revolutionary impatient left and its *Avant-garde*: "I still hope for a transformative politics, but I am certain that transformation will be, should be, slow and steady work. There won't be a messianic moment or a final revolution[42]"; "two steps forward, one step back is better than three steps forward over the bodies of our enemies".[43]

A practical wisdom that perhaps bears the hallmark of Talmudic thought: "a dissenting opinion may turn out to be true".[44]

Partisans and Prophets: Against Domination

The subject of political theory, as Walzer often reminds us, must be politics, not theory.[45] A political theory must speak to everyone, not just the happy few in academia—he shared this idea with his colleagues Judith Shklar and Stanley Hoffman, and the *Dissentniks* of course. You need to know "from where" people are talking and to whom. Being a citizen, a partisan and a scholar is a style and an ethos. As Michael Walzer has often said, the clear language of a political argument is also a proof of political politeness, George Orwell being a good example. The theorist does an *inside job*, his theory has to be "connected". The language, the style of the hundreds of papers published by Michael Walzer in the columns of *Dissent*, incisive *and* accessible to all, is also a political commitment: any democratic argument must be supported by intelligible writing.[46] The philosopher does not have any special status to assert. He is a "pedestrian" whose role, if it is to be effective, is to speak to all, from the inside. To talk from the same sidewalk.[47]

This requirement, a way of conveying the idea of anti-domination, finds its source in part in Walzer's reading of the Hebrew Bible, particularly the Prophets who called upon the powerful and confronted them with their contradictions. Prophets may have no "philosophical imagination", but they live among their own people, and, therefore, can channel an unrivaled power of social transformation, they have a "pluralistic wisdom".[48] He is particularly fond of Amos, the Socratic prophet, and believes, with Max Weber, that prophecy is the earliest form of a political pamphlet.[49] But he is also inspired by the Yiddish tradition and the character of the grumbler, who interferes and makes uninvited comments, the *Kibbitzer*[50]

He puts it forcefully in a text from 1987:

> "Amos' prophecy is social criticism because it challenges the leaders, the conventions, the ritual practices of a particular society and because it does so in the name of values recognized and shared in that same society [...] What makes the difference is Amos' membership. [...] he knows the fundamental values of the men and women he criticizes (or because he tells them a plausible story about which of their values ought to be fundamental). And since he in turn is recognized as one of them, he can call them back to their 'true' path. He suggests reforms that they can undertake while still remaining fellow members of the same society.[51]

Walzer's true conviction is that ideas can only be effective in real life if they are backed by shared and sharable practices, an insight he shares with his colleague and friend, anthropologist Clifford Geertz.

The Practice of Political Theory: A Narrative Coherence

Walzerian political theory is "narrative" in essence.[52] He indeed writes stories and often surprises his readers—who hasn't been startled to see divine grace or kinship and love included among the spheres of justice? To be embarked on a trip to a space Hilton to show that morality can't be reinvented with every generation?

Walzer always respects a basic literary rule: you need to start with a real-life problem—some form of injustice or inequality—and think about the best way to fix it and to be useful, beyond the circle of scholars. Stories, as theories, to be effective, must be on the side of hope, Jane Mansbridge calls this "aspirational ideals".[53]

A narrative theory? "It's undoubtedly useful to have a theory ... but it's better to tell stories [...] even if there is no definitive story"[54], says Michael Walzer, who often shows that stories outperform theory, and that (analytic) political philosophy, as practiced by his colleagues, is in some sense anti-political or rather anti-democratic: philosophical founding is an "authoritarian business", the claim of the philosopher is that he knows "the pattern set up in the heavens", he knows what ought to be done; participants to the conversation are idealized, hypothetical actors specifically designed to reach a consensus, but democratic talk is always messier than that.[55] In short, democracy trumps philosophy. In this sense, Walzer is a pragmatist:

> When theory crashes, we can always rely, as [Ignazio] Silone says, on our moral sense to 'guide us towards knowledge' [...]. When I first read that sentence, I assumed that Silone meant to say, a guide to moral knowledge. I now think that he was more ambitious: the moral sense is also a guide to social and political knowledge and perhaps a better guide than, the crashed theory ever was – if only because more widely shared. [...] Who can doubt that this language [liberty, justice, democracy] are better employed by a person of moral sensitivity without a theory, than by a morally obtuse with the grandest possible theory? [...] Moral sensitivity is the armor of critical survival.[56]

Walzer also defends an "indirect normativity" that fits the structure of *Spheres* quite well: what we do and what we ought to do normatively depends on context. To have an opinion on how things should be, we need to know how things *are*; and deciding on how they *should* be requires us to have an idea of how they *could* be. This makes it possible to think about the contingency and the dynamics of history: there are no transhistorical spheres of justice, justice is tied to its time because the value of goods depends on the pertinent timeframe and spatial location. They are particular, as are our shared understandings: they are "relevant to the social world in which [they] were developed; [they are] not relevant, or not necessarily, to all social worlds".[57] A theory must be attentive to changes in the real world.[58]

The emphasis on stories is not fortuitous: "The liberal sensibility that goes hand in hand with morality is undoubtedly better represented in literature than in politics[59]", writes Walzer.

Rereading Spheres of Justice: Against Domination

Rereading our book, I realized that we hadn't talked that much about *Spheres*, although one chapter is devoted to "The experience of minority and *Spheres of Justice*". Michael Walzer didn't object to the title of that chapter, so I may not have been wrong in making the connection: it is through the experience of minority—and thus, one might say, through a certain experience of "domination"—that one can understand *Spheres*. Michael Walzer grew up in a minority and has had a clear sense of social spheres from very early on.

It seems appropriate to read *Sphères* as a composition, or coordination, of minority spaces, as an attempt to thwart the imposition of the rules of majorities on minorities.

As we all know, there are two spheres that are, to varying degrees, objectively in the majority: money and politics.[60] The former because it enables everything to be converted, the latter because it regulates all other (public) spheres.

The very important quotation that follows usually escapes readers (it is a footnote). It will guide me and enable me to reconsider two questions posed above: firstly, the gap in time between *A Theory of Justice*; secondly Walzer's anthropological theory of justice, and the meaning of "shared understandings".

> I should note here what will become more clear as I go along, that political power is a special sort of good. It has a twofold character. First, it is like the other things that men and women make, value, exchange, and share: sometimes dominant, sometimes not, sometimes widely held, sometimes the possession of a very few. And, second, it is unlike all the other things because, however it is had and whoever has it, *political power is the regulative agency for social goods generally*. It is used to defend the boundaries of al the distributive spheres, including its own, and to enforce the common understandings of what goods are and what they are for. (But it can also be used, obviously, to invade the different spheres and to override those understandings.) In this second sense, we might say, indeed, that *political power is always dominant at the boundaries, but not within them.* The central problem of political life is to maintain that crucial distinction

between "at" and "in". But this is a problem that cannot be solved given the imperatives of simple equality.[61] (Emphasis added).

Anti-Domination or the Other Principle of Difference

Michael Walzer believes that *A Theory of Justice* is implausible.[62] He himself advocates an "art of *differentiation*[63]" rather than a "principle of *difference*". His approach of Justice, neither hypothetical nor procedural, is "phenomenological".[64]

Spheres and *A Theory of Justice* belong to two different theoretical planets—it is not by accident that the rather artificial quarrel of the 1990s between "liberals" and "communitarians" has placed Rawls in the former category and Walzer in the latter, but the real reason for the divide lies elsewhere.

It seems to me that, apart from the major difference in style between *A Theory* of Justice and *Spheres of* Justice, a few fundamental distinctions can be made.

If there is a Walzerian difference principle, it lies in the *relevant* distribution as opposed to *fair* distribution. There is no "if"—"then" sequence in *Spheres* (if inequalities persist, then they must benefit the less well endowed). Nor are there any objectifiable "have-nots" in Walzer's view; there are only, if I may say so, "local" have-nots. Relevant distribution is based on need and the relative importance of the good to be distributed. Rice in a poor Indian village is not distributed in the same way as access to healthcare in Paris, but the former distribution is no more important than the latter, and vice versa.

For Walzer, the dominance of a good is more harmful than its monopoly. Monopolies are undoubtedly often unjust, but a fairer distribution of monopolistic goods will not solve the equality issue. The dominance of a good is also unjust. Money, for example, is a dominant good because it allows the conversion of all other goods.[65] It is therefore potentially tyrannical since it allows access to the desired goods in another sphere and by other means than those prevailing in the pertinent sphere. The aim of Walzer's anti-domination strategy is therefore to prevent the emergence of dominant goods of this type (high convertible goods), since the *dominance* of a good is the counterpart to *domination* over individuals.[66] It is literally an abuse in the Marxian sense.

Here then is the connection with boundaries, or the need to maintain the crucial distinction between political power "at the boundaries" and political power "within boundaries": a monopoly can ideally be contained within its sphere[67], whereas dominant goods illegally cross the boundaries between spheres.[68]

This view of domination is different in an important sense from Philipp Pettit's republican view.[69] Although Pettit argues forcefully in favor of non-domination, and against arbitrary interference, his main goal is the protection of freedom. The justification of accountability, transparency, and equal influence is meant mainly to prevent unchecked power over individual agents. These criteria would in principle meet Walzer's idea of a common good rather than sectorial interests, of structural conditions of domination that must be countered in every sphere (political and social) and among spheres, but for Pettit (as for Rawls), it is *freedom* that needs to be protected from domination. For Walzer, it is *equality*. Pettit and Walzer both offer an alternative to liberal theories of freedom: Pettit by extending non-denomination beyond mere absence of interference, as in classical liberal theory ("The Greatest Liberty of Subjects, depends on the silence of the Law"),[70] Walzer by articulating dominance of goods, domination over individuals, and the relative importance of goods in the relevant sphere.

Rawls's *A Theory of Justice* is about a fairer distribution of socially monopolistic goods. "Primary social goods" (rights, liberties, opportunities, powers, income and wealth) must be distributed more fairly. The just distribution of these goods must compensate for the "naturally" unequal distribution of primary goods, such as inherited wealth or natural talents. The distribution of "natural" endowments is morally arbitrary and political liberalism corrects this arbitrariness.

In this sense, *A Theory of Justice* is a response to the imperfection of our societies and the inequality of individual endowments. Rawls aspires to rectify social inequalities; but he recognizes that he cannot erase them (a realist utopia). His premise is individualistic.

For Rawls, the monopoly of politics is not "local", his political liberalism is the umpire of all other spheres, or rather: the sphere of politics may be bounded by the frontiers of other spheres (comprehensive morality, religious conscience, the "good"), but its own borders must be watertight. Rawls carefully excludes everything that does not meet the standard of public reason from the political realm.[71]

Walzer, on the contrary, devotes autonomous spheres to non-political spaces. The former aims for a watertight political sphere, the latter for a complex composition in which equality can be concretely experienced in places other than the political. In the dialectic between non-political and fully political spheres, Walzer defends a "phenomenological", local approach, Rawls a liberal-procedural, more integrative approach.

The Anthropological Theory of Justice and Social Meanings

This anthropological theory of justice raises some questions: the privilege Walzer grants the local, and the meaning of what he calls reiterative universalism[72]; the question of its "communitarianism", maybe of his relativism; and finally, to a certain extent, that of statism and the importance of the notion of belonging.

Communitarian? Michael Walzer doesn't define himself as such, but he has learned the most profound lesson of communitarianism: not all allegiances are voluntary. Loyalty sometimes trumps consent. In principle, this would connect communitarianism, nationality, and religious affiliation.[73] As for justice, "[it] cannot be conceived without reference to the values which pre-exist it and which are carried by a community". This is the statement that has so troubled critical commentators, notably Dworkin, who gave SJ a particularly hostile reception.[74] As we all know, however, Walzer's "universalist relativism", the dialectic kind, is clearly not a *moral* relativism.

To respond adequately to Dworkin, we need to explain what Walzer means by common values or meanings. Individuals are caught in a web of social meanings that they themselves have contributed to create over time. These meanings have normative consequences on our behavior (this is what Walzer calls "moral legislation").

What he has in mind is simple and profound: we assign norms and values to things and goods that govern our relationship with them and with other individuals. Things, or (material and immaterial) goods, are therefore intermediaries of social relations, and must be understood as something more than goods *simpliciter*. They become, through their circulation and through the complex process of determining their meaning, liaison officers between individuals. They literally create the social world.[75]

A just distribution of goods must obey the following principle:

> No social good x should be distributed to men and women who possess some other good y merely because they possess y and without regard to the meaning of x.[76]

It is through social meanings that the theory of goods and the justice of spheres meet.

We are, in fact, both designers and creators: of goods and of meaning: "We are (all of us) culture-producing creatures; we make and inhabit a meaningful world[77]". Goods, writes Walzer, "with their meanings—because of their meanings—are the crucial medium of social relations. Things are our anchors in the world. But while we all need to be anchored, we don't all need the same anchor".[78]

It seems to me, however, that it is the level of generality of *shared understandings* that is mistaken by many readers, and Dworkin is no exception. Let's take an example that Michael Walzer often uses: health-care.[79] At the most general level, the measure of good health is longevity. Good health is a core value in our culture. The debate is not about the importance of health in general, but about how we should politically distribute the means to protect us against health hazards. That is the right scale. Not an agreement on the reasons why each of us individually values access to healthcare, but an agreement on the indispensability of a defining good like health. Consensus on a general value does not prevent profound political dissensus on how to achieve it. This is another lesson in pragmatic morality.

As a native French speaker, I would like to add that many people are, in my opinion, confused by the translation of the term. The notion of *shared understandings* has undoubtedly misled the French reader; it may have led English language natives astray also (Dworkin), but for different reasons.[80] Pascal Engel, the French translator, notes that he sometimes translates the term "compréhension partagée" (shared understanding), sometimes "conception partagée" (shared conception). The meaning Walzer has in mind is, I would suggest, "equal access to a same system of meanings", which is not very elegant and too long, but maybe more accurate.

This slight modification sheds light on the approximation that Walzer often uses to morally justify this or that action, the "right reasons".[81] It also helps to understand two elements that temper the accusation of conservatism: a revised definition of his particular understanding of equality on the one hand, and his interpretative anthropology of justice on the other.

For Michael Walzer, equality is about treating people *as equals*, not *equally*.[82] Let's start with the latter: treating people *equally* means treating them similarly. The same crime will always call for the same sentence. Treating individuals *as equals* means treating them with the same consideration and respect, i.e. not imposing anything on them that goes against their own sense of equality.[83] Certainly, Walzer, like Dworkin, prefers to treat people "as equals", despite the inherently relativistic nature of the argument.

That social meanings do not necessarily have to be coordinated or well matched is further evidence of Walzer's connection with interpretive or symbolic anthropology[84], but also with social psychology as practiced by Alfred Schütz, for example: the most contradictory thoughts can coexist while forming part of the same mental universe; all we need is a same sense of acquaintance. The common culture of shared meanings—the cultural semiotics and the common establishment of meaning by social actors—is a "cultural code" according to Clifford Geertz: without mastering this common cultural code, it is impossible to act together.[85] This brings us full circle: equality, politics, joint action.

Against the literal reading that has been given to shared understandings and has distorted their meaning, Jeremy Waldron proposes to describe them as some form of "public goods[86]", dynamic, regularly revised, never the same over time and in space. But, through alluviations and the passage of time, they do create a "moral legislation", and—importantly—the dialectic between the individual and the collective is maintained: shared or understood meanings do not exclude "individual meanings", the ones that particular individuals attach to specific social goods (the yacht example).

> The *reiterated* social construction is thus the best way to account for the uses and values of goods in different societies. All societies construct their social meanings – therein lies their share of the universal – but all do so according to different imperatives. Individuals, as co-constructors, are also their principal critics and interpreters. What is objective is that all social meanings are constructed. Shared meanings are not "objectively" right or wrong, true or false; our behavior, on the other hand, is objectively right or wrong in terms of the shared meaning of good.[87]

These observations lead me to conclude with a comment on the coherence of Walzer's career and theory. He may not be a "systematic thinker", as he himself says, but his work is ordered around some stable lines: the pre-eminence of practical political experience; the place given to comradeship in action and thought; the firm opposition to domination expressed in complex equality, the subtitle of *Spheres of Justice*.

Since the late 1950s, Walzer's participation in the most important political and social debates—the fight for civil rights and against the Vietnam War, his defiance vis à vis every kind of sectarianism, his firm objection to the war in Iraq, his commitment to feminism to name but a few—exemplifies a constant battle against *abuse*.

Complex equality is first and foremost a response to oppression and the unjust spillover of power from one sphere to another. The division of political and social life into relatively autonomous sections, into "spheres", is meant to prevent or to contain the most *scandalous* inequalities. The aim is not to do away with all forms of inequality, at the risk of generating new ones; rather, we must rebel against inequalities that result from *abuse* (another form of tyranny).

Abuse in my view is precisely the conversion of property into domination. It is not because you have the control over—or the ownership of—this or that good that you may abuse it. Think of the dead wood story in Marx's early writings. You may have the power to exclude poor peasants from collecting dead wood on your property, but this is both unjust and immoral. Using that kind of control-power, is abusive and tyrannical.

Michael Walzer has remained true to his political idea(l)s and faithful to his friends and comrades, the liberal socialists who still believe in "decent politics".[88]

But what about his Talmudist comrades? Is the path as smooth here as it is with his political comrades? Yes and no. Although Walzer's interest in the stories of the Hebrew Bible goes back a long way[89], with the Exodus story occupying a place of honor, the three large volumes on the *Jewish political tradition*[90] as well as *In the Shadow of God*[91] point toward a kind of gradual and friendly rapprochement between political theory, the Bible and its readers.[92]

The share of comradeship and the pre-eminent role of equality may well have its origins in one of the biblical covenants, the very one that so inspired the inventors of the Commonwealth in the seventeenth and eighteenth centuries. Of the two covenants, Abrahamic and Mosaic, only one is an alliance of choice, consent, and respect for the law. Walzer is part of the Abrahamic tradition, but prefers, I believe, the political, Mosaic, covenant because it is passed on "by words and not by weapons".

Competing Interests A previous, slightly different, version of this chapter was published in a special issue of *Raisons Politiques* (94, 2: 2024), as "Relire *Sphères de Justice.*"

Notes

1. A previous, slightly different, version of this chapter was published in a special issue of *Raisons Politiques* (94, 2: 2024), as "Relire *Sphères de Justice.*".
2. Michael Walzer himself likes the idea of the map. The plan of SJ is to "map out a particular social world. For the analysis that I propose is imminent and phenomenological in character. It will yield not an ideal map or a master plan but, rather, a map and a plan appropriate to the people for whom it is drawn, whose common life it reflects.", SJ, p. 26.
3. Michael Walzer, *Obligations. Essays on Disobedience, War and Citizenship*, Cambridge University Press, 1971.
4. Michael Walzer contributes to this first issue with an article "Why was this war different", *Philosophy and Public Affairs,* 1971, 1/1, pp. 3–21. In the same issue, Judith Jarvis Thomson publishes her famous article "A Defense of Abortion", pp. 47–66.
5. Nozick's preparatory work for *State, Anarchy and Utopia* ("A framework for Utopia") is quoted in the *Reading list* Walzer gave me. The article was which is to become the final section of the book.
6. Michael Walzer, *Just and Unjust wars*, New York, Basic Books, 1977.
7. In the early 1960s, Michael Walzer was *Dissent*'s youngest contributor. Still a student, he published two articles on the Civil Rights struggle in several Southern states. "The Young: a Cup of Coffee and a Seat", *Dissent*, Spring 1960, "Politics of nonviolent resistance", *Dissent*, Fall 1960.
8. See Michael Walzer, Astrid von Busekist, *Justice is steady work, A conversation on Political Theory*, Cambridge, Polity, 2020.

9. The course was listed as "Philosophy 174: A moral examination of capitalism and socialism", according to Harvard and Radcliffe's Official Register. Walzer won the prize for best teacher that year (1971).
10. The class was offered in both Philosophy and Social Studies, a relatively new multidisciplinary department at Harvard headed by Michael Walzer. Under the impetus of Bob Amdur, Marty Peretz and Michael Walzer, the curriculum was first and foremost a reading program (one semester on Weber, another on Durkheim, a semester on Dewey, etc.).
11. "Bob would give two lectures, then I would respond with a critical lecture, and he would respond to the criticism. I would then give two lectures, and so on. Each unit consisted of four lectures, […] each of us giving six lectures stating our positions and arguing in six others". Personal communication from M. Walzer.

    "I worked harder than for any other course in my life. Bob was very, very, quick in a way that the best philosophers are quick. He also had a great wit.", Justice is steady work, p. 122.
12. I was able to interview a few witnesses, including course assistants enrolled in philosophy or social studies. One of them was working on his thesis with Rawls, and is now a lawyer in New York (David Korzenick). Another one, Mickey Morgan (godfather to Nozick's children), now a professor in California, is the one who prompted Michael Walzer and Jon Wiener to republish the "guide to movement politics" (originally published in 1971): *Political Action. A practical guide to movement politics.* Finally, Robert Amdur, former dean of Social Studies and now professor emeritus at Columbia. Most of the students were of course *leftists of some sort*, highly politicized and partly affiliated with SDS or PLP, so it was hardly surprising that some of them gave the course their own name: "Capitalism vs Capitalism", Mickey Morgan told me. No doubt the work of SDS or Progressive Labor, for whom the social democratic left was not radical enoug). Nonetheless, "the Walzer v. Nozick class", was an event; all those who sat in on the class reported that the experience was "dizzying", a kind of "sparkling, provocative joust". Walzer himself told me: "I worked harder in this course than in any of the others. Bob was very smart and incredibly fast as some philosophers are; I'm slower and had to prepare carefully.".

13. "We encourage teachers to experiment with different forms of teaching. Joint seminars should be offered to students, with the participation of professors from outside the Arts and Sciences. The 'debate' between Professors Walzer and Nozick in Philosophy 174 is a method that should be tried more often," *Harvard Crimson*, January 5, 1971, available here: https://www.thecrimson.com/article/1971/1/5/curriculum-flexibility-and-experimentation-restructuring-the/
14. A few anecdotes: the "capitalism" championed by Nozick had little to do with actual capitalism. As Walzer puts it, "the capitalism he [Nozick] defended bore no resemblance to American capitalism, hence his best remark: 'A revolution would be necessary and justified to establish capitalism in the United States'". Nozick was totally indifferent to money; what mattered above all to him was *freedom*. Freedom was a kind of "default" position (as Mickey Morgan puts it), and Nozick worked by axioms ("packages and principles"). According to Morgan, Nozick was *weirdly* charismatic, very precise and sharp, and was often compared to Sydney Morgenbesser (his mentor at Columbia). He himself admired Stanley Cavell, whom he thought was "wise". He was a "*loose canon, dazzling,* had *wild thoughts on everything*. To teach a class, says Morgan, "he got up *and delivered potshots"*.
15. "One of my last courses in Harvard was called simply 'Socialism', and it was a defense of my version of socialist theory and practice. And the only commitment I felt I had to live up to in the classroom was to tell the students about the strongest arguments against socialism". Justice is steady work, p. 117.

    Walzer reproduces this pattern, notably in IDE when he writes against Irving Kristol's "conservative naturalism", asserting that the meaning of goods, of all goods, is cultural, not natural. See Irving Kristol, ("About Equality" *Commentary*, November 1972) who claims, as do all conservatives, that the distribution of wealth and power is natural; that any attempt to change this is futile; that equality is a fad of frustrated intellectuals ashamed of their bourgeois past; and that the distribution of political power (legitimately) follows the same bell curve as that of wealth. In his critique, Michael Walzer ironically reverses Kristol's argument on naturalness: "Nature is re-established as a critical norm, and we are invited to question the strangeness of the existing order".

16. In a short intellectual autobiography written for the *Annual Review of Political Science* (vol. 16, 2013, pp. 1–9), entitled "The Political Theory License". See also *Justice is steady work*: "[...] My political work did shape the way I write political theory; it shaped my commitment to avoid abstraction, to write as concretely as possible, to use historical examples instead of weird hypotheticals the way analytic philosophers do. And it led me to take maximal advantage of the political theorist's 'license'. Political theorists have a license to take and to defend political positions explicitly, which political scientists are not supposed to do.".
17. "Different goods must be distributed to different people for different reasons. Equality is not a simple notion, and it cannot be satisfied by a single system of distribution", IDE, p. 401.
18. See "Politics in the Welfare State", *Dissent*, 15, 1968, p. 26–40; On this topic see J. Toby, "Michael Walzer in Historical Context: Complex Equality and the American Social-Democratic Tradition", *American Political Thought*, vol. 6, 2017, p. 462.
19. IDE, p. 403, 404, 405.
20. Michael Walzer, "Freedom and Equality. Can they stand together?" was the title of the lecture given at Sciences Po, Paris, on March 15, 2018, available here: https://www.youtube.com/watch?v=xZc2YOQG_0A
21. "[...] In fact, there is no single talent or combination of talents which plausibly entitles a man to every available social good—and there is no single talent or combination of talents that necessarily must win the available goods of a free society", IDE, p. 401.
22. "Tyranny is the wish to obtain by one means what can only be had by another. We owe different duties to different qualities: love is the proper response to charm, fear to strength, and belief to learning.", Pascal, *Les Pensées*, trans. L. Brunschvicg, Paris, Hachette, 1921, p. 251. "If you love without evoking love in return, i.e., if you are not able, by the manifestation of yourself as a loving person, to make yourself a beloved person, then your love is impotent and a misfortune.", Marx, "The Power of Money in Bourgeois Society", *Early Writings* (1844), London, Watts, 1963, pp. 193–194.
23. Good health is a core value; the good to be distributed is longevity. The curve should follow the "susceptibility to fall ill", but it follows "the financial capacity to afford treatment", IDE, p. 403.

24. "This suggests that a society in which a single principle of distribution is dominant cannot be an egalitarian society. Equality requires a diversity of principles, reflecting the diversity of humanity and social goods", IDE, p. 407.
25. "Wittgenstein, Elizabeth Taylor, Bertrand Russell, Thomas Merton, Yogi Berra, Allen Ginsburg, Harry Wolfson, Thoreau, Casey Stengel, The Lubavitcher Rebbe, Picasso, Moses, Einstein, Hugh Heffner, Socrates, Henry Ford, Lenny Bruce, Baba Ram Dass, Gandhi, Sir Edmund Hillary, Raymond Lubitz, Buddha, Frank Sinatra, Columbus, Freud, Norman Mailer, Ayn Rand, Baron Rothschild, Ted Williams, Thomas Edison, H..L Mencken, Thomas Jefferson, Ralph Ellison, Bobby Fischer, Emma Goldman, Peter Kropotkin, you, and your parents. Is there really one kind of life which is best for each of these people? Imagine all of them living in any utopia you've ever seen described in detail. Try to describe the society which would be best for all of these persons to live in… ", *Anarchy, State and Utopia*, p. 310.
26. Compare SJ, p. 323, n. 2: the "social share in the production of goods".
27. J. Toby Reiner, art. cit. defends the thesis of a misreading of *Spheres*: against the traditional reading turning Walzer into an advocate of a new model of fair distribution, Reiner asserts that the political understanding of equality prevails over all other dimensions. The centrality of political decision making takes precedence over the fair distribution of goods.
28. This debate has taken place mostly within the context of a discussion on immigration and border control. See A. Abizadeh,"On the Demos and it's Kin", *American Political Science Review*, Vol. 106, No. 4 (November 2012), p. 867–882; Miller, D., « Why immigration controls are not coercive: a reply to Arash Abizadeh», *Political Theory* 38 (1), 2010, p. 111–120; D. Miller, "Immigrants, Nations and Citizenship", *The Journal of Political Philosophy*, vol. 6, n°4, 2008, p. 371–390.
29. See *Obligations*, *op. cit.* p. 98, quoted by J. Toby Reiner, art. cit. p. 462.
30. A "left-wing intellectual, according to Lewis Coser, is someone who reads books outside his field of specialization", writes Michael Walzer in *The Struggle for a Decent Politics: On "Liberal" as an Adjective*, New Haven, Yale University Press, 2023, p. 111.

31. See *Justice is steady work*, *op. cit.* p. 272.
32. See Michael Walzer, *The Struggle for a Decent Politics*, *op. cit.* p. 3.
33. See the conclusion of his article "The Young. A cup of coffee and a seat", art. cit.: "[...] What about the man you're standing next to on a picket line? For it is there, I believe, on the picket line, that real equality is finally won.".
34. M. Walzer, "Philosophy and Democracy", p. 394.
35. See *Justice is steady work*, p. 170.
36. Introduction to *The Struggle for a Decent Politics*, *op. cit.*
37. "Sects are "the ur-model of illiberal political organizations", *The Struggle for a Decent Politics*, *op. cit.* p. 39.
38. See *Justice is steady work*, p. 280, emphasis added.
39. "Respect", writes Hannah Arendt, "comparable to Aristotle's *philia politikè*, is a kind of friendship without intimacy, without proximity".
40. See *The Struggle for a Decent Politics*, *op. cit.* p. 51. J. Toby Reiner, art. cit. would say "realist".
41. See "A Day in the Life of a Socialist Citizen. Two Cheers for Participatory Democracy", *Dissent*, June 1968, p. 245.
42. See *Justice is steady work*, p. 169, and 168: "I have never believed that these engagements require the guidance of an overarching, world-historical, totalizing theory such as Marxism was. Theories like that tend to produce a vanguard of knowers, whose views are always correct, dominating over the mass of men and women who are the victims of false consciousness. This makes for a bad politics, and, as it turns out, the big theories aren't so good either. Again and again, the knowers get the world wrong; vanguard militants also suffer from false consciousness. Still, our critical work requires a better understanding of the social order and its internal contradictions—theories, of course, but modest ones".
43. See *The Struggle for a Decent Politics*, p. 5; see also: "Two steps forward is, for example, a detail of the march, a good moment. Right now, we have to minimize backsliding and make up for lost ground", "Leftism right now, first of all, has to be a defensive politics.", p. 167.
44. See *Justice is steady work*, p. 8. And "The critical enterprise is founded on hope [...] critique is future oriented," *The Company of Critics*, p. 17.

45. Michael Walzer believes for example that there is a "just war industry" among academics that has completely lost sight of the reality of war.
46. "Good prose was never an absolute value in itself but writing clearly and directly about even the most complex of topics, spoke to a shared value of openness and respect for the reader. There was a vision of politics in such prose", says Nicholas Howe (Irving Howe's son) about *Dissent* in an interview with Maurice Isserman, "Steady Work: Sixty Years of *Dissent*", January 23, 2014.
47. See *Justice is steady work*, p. 2.
48. See *Justice is steady work*, p. 12.
49. *Interpretation and Social Criticism*, henceforth ISC, Cambridge MA, Harvard University Press, 1987, p. 59.
50. In Yiddish, «Kibbitzer» refers to a person who literally looks over the shoulder of card players; more generally, someone who interferes in matters that are none of his business, and/or makes uninvited comments. ISC, p. 24.
51. ISC, p. 75–76.
52. See also J. Toby Reiner, art. cit. p. 467.
53. Jane Mansbridge, "A Citizen-Centered Theory", *Journal of Deliberative Democracy* 16/2, 2020, pp. 15–24.
54. See ISC, p. 57.
55. "Philosophy and Democracy", *Political Theory*, 9/3, 1981, p. 279–399, p. 381, 383 and 389. See also: "The distinction that I am trying to draw here, between having a right to decide and knowing the right decision, might be described in terms of procedural and substantive justice. Democrats, it might be said, are committed to procedural justice, and can only hope that the outcomes of just procedures will also be substantively just. But I am reluctant to accept that formulation because the line between procedure and substance seems to me less clear than it suggests. What is at stake in discussions about procedural justice is the distribution of power, and that is surely a substantive matter. No procedural arrangement can be defended except by some substantive argument, and every substantive argument (in political philosophy) issues also in some procedural arrangement. Democracy rests, as I have already suggested, on an argument about freedom and political obligation. Hence it is not only the case that the people have a procedural

right to make the laws. On the democratic view, it is right that they make the laws-even if they make them wrongly.", p. 386.
56. See ISC, p. 229.
57. SJ, p. xiv.
58. Walzer defends the same kind of contextual knowledge in his book *On Toleration*, New Haven, Yale University Press, 1997.
59. See *The Struggle for a Decent Politics*, p. 10.
60. Political power resembles other goods: it is exchanged, manufactured, shared; it is sometimes in the hands of a few, sometimes widely shared. But it is also different from other goods in that it is the regulating agent of other spheres of distribution. This is why it is dominant "at" the boundaries of these spheres and not "within". But if it invades these other spheres, its power is abusive. See below on abuse.
61. SJ, p. 15, note.
62. SJ, p. 26.
63. See "Liberalism and the Art of Separation", *Political Theory*, vol. 12, no. 3, 1984, pp. 315–330.
64. SJ, p. 26.
65. "[...] Money seeps across all boundaries—this is the primary form of illegal immigration; and just where one ought to try to stop it is a question of expediency as well as of principle", SJ, p. 22.
66. Walzer puts it this way: "Tyranny is always specific in character: a particular boundary crossing, a particular violation of social meaning. Complex equality requires the defense of boundaries; it works by differentiating goods just as hierarchy works by differentiating people.", SJ, 56.
67. "Political power is a local monopoly", SJ, p. 29.
68. "Money enables pre-emptive strikes against the political system"; "Complex equality requires borders to be defended", SJ, p. 56.
69. See, for example, Chapter 1 of *On the people's terms: A Republican Theory and Model of Democracy (< < Freedom as non-domination > >), Cambridge University Press, 2012.*
70. Thomas Hobbes, *Leviathan* (1651), 21, 18.
71. John Rawls, "The Idea of Public Reason Revisited", *The University of Chicago Law Review*, 64/3, 1997, p. 765–807.
72. See, for example, *Thick and Thin: Moral Argument at Home and Abroad*, Notre Dame Press, 1994.

See also: "What makes [reiterative universalism] different from covering-law universalism is its particularist focus and its pluralizing tendency". Nation and Universe, p. 513.

73. See *The Struggle for a Decent Politics*, chapter 5 ("Liberal Communitarians") on the quality and intensity of community life and Rousseau's civic republicanism, of which Michael Walzer says that his "Social Contract is an illiberal nation-state", p. 91.
74. "The idea that the world is divided into distinct moral cultures, and that it should be the goal of politics to foster the value of "community" by respecting these differences, has for a long time been associated with political conservatism and moral relativism", writes Dworkin, Ronald Dworkin, "To Each His Own" (the review of *Spheres of Justice*), *New York Review of Books*, April 14, 1983.

    Michael Walzer's (abbreviated) response boils down to a few arguments: "[...] Most relativists would think me just as tiresomely judgmental as he is. Indeed, we share a desire to reach moral conclusions. We only disagree about the force or, better, the scope of our conclusions. I don't hope to make arguments that are conclusive for all human beings in all societies that exist or will exist or have ever existed. I don't subscribe to the idea—it seems to me distinctly odd—that the principles of justice appropriate to Americans must be appropriate as well to ancient Babylonians. Not that such an idea makes it impossibly hard to arrive at principles of justice; it makes it too easy, for the principles need not apply to anyone in particular. The hard task is to find principles latent in the lives of the people Dworkin and I live with, principles that they can recognize and adopt.", "Spheres of Justice: An Exchange", reply by M. Walzer followed by a reply by R. Dworkin, *New York Review of Books*, July 21, 1983.
75. *Justice is steady work*, p. 14–15.
76. SJ, p. 20.
77. See *SJ*, p. 314.
78. SJ, p. 104.
79. Michael Walzer revisits this idea in a beautiful interview with Nancy Rosenblum, available here: https://www.youtube.com/watch?v=TvpnmmLoO38
80. Perhaps because they only apply to societies that are not "profoundly inegalitarian"; But traditional societies may not be "profoundly" inegalitarian, hence Dworkin's criticism.

81. "The doctrine of right reasons suggests that we pay equal attention to the'different qualities', and to the 'individuality' of every man and woman, that we find ways of sharing our resources that match the variety of their needs, interests, and capacities.", IDE, p. 403.
82. This distinction has first been made by Dworkin in *Freedom's Law: The Moral Reading of the American Constitution*, Cambridge, Harvard University Press, 1996.
83. Comp. Richard Rorty: "Anti-eanti-thnocentrism should be seen as a protest against the persistence of Enlightenment rhetoric in an era in which our connoisseurship of diversity has made this rhetoric seem self-deceptive and sterile. It is not a reaction against love, or against justice, or against liberal institutions. It is just a bit of AD HOC philosophical therapy, an attempt to cure the cramps caused in liberals by what Bernard Williams called 'the rationalist theory of rationality'—the idea that you are being irrational, and probably viciously ethnocentric, whenever you cannot appeal to neutral criteria. It urges liberals to take with full seriousness the fact that the ideals of procedural justice and human equality are parochial, recent, eccentric cultural developments, and then to recognize that this does not mean they are any the less worth fighting for. It urges that ideals may be local and culture-bound, and nevertheless be the best hope of the species.", On ethnocentrism: A reply to Clifford Geertz, in *Objectivity, Relativism and Truth*, Cambridge University Press, 1991, p. 85.
84. See also Clifford Geertz, especially "Common sense as a cultural system", *The Antioch Review*, 33/1 1975, pp. 5–26.
85. Properly understood, culture is a mode of common production of meaning. Walzer may have been inspired by "thin" and "thick" descriptions in Geertz when he wrote *Thick and Thin: Moral Argument at Home and Abroad*, Notre Dame University Press, 1994.
86. "Social meanings are in a sense 'public goods'—diffuse in general social and political culture", writes Jeremy Waldron in his review of Michael Sandel (*What Money Can't Buy)* in the *New York Review of Books*, August 16, 2012.
87. "Majority rule does not govern debates about social meanings; it only governs behavior. Rules of behavior are objectively right in relation to shared social meanings, but shared social meanings are not objectively right (or wrong)", Michael Walzer, "Objectivity and

Social Meaning", in M. Nussbaum and A. Sen (eds.), *The Quality of Life*, *op. cit.* p. 44; and Justice is steady work *op. cit.* p. 30–31.

88. See the *Washington Post OpEd* on February 2, 2023, co-written with his some of his old friends: Paul Berman, Marty Peretz, and Leon Wieseltier, available here: https://www.washingtonpost.com/opinions/2023/02/02/wieseltier-peretz-berman-walzer-israel-netanyahu/
89. Ki Tisa in particular (Ex. 30.11)... Exodus is present from the very start of his career. See *The Revolution of the Saints: A Study in the Origins of Radical* Politics, Harvard University Press, 1965; *Exodus and Revolution*, New York, Basic Books, 1985; *The Paradox of Liberation: Secular Revolutions and Religious Counterrevolutions*, Yale University Press, 2015.
90. *The Jewish Political Tradition*, vol. 1 *Authority*, New Haven, Yale University Press; Michael Walzer, Menachem Lorberbaum, Noam J. Zohar, Ari Ackerman, *The Jewish Political tradition*, vol. 2 *Membership*, 2003; Michael Walzer, Menachem Lorberbaum, Noam J. Zohar, Madeline Kochen, *The Jewish Political tradition*, vol. 3 *Community*, New Haven, Yale University Press, 2018.
91. In God's Shadow: Politics in the Hebrew Bible, New Haven, Yale University Press, 2012.
92. Many fellow philosophers and political scientists feature in the table of contents of *The Jewish Political Tradition*.

CHAPTER 3

Interpretation and Social Meanings

Georgia Warnke

The account of distributive justice that Walzer offers in *Spheres of Justice*[1] is an interpretive one that connects the just distribution of social goods to the meanings each has within and for a particular society. "Distributions," he maintains, "are patterned in accordance with shared conceptions of what the goods are and what they are for" (7). Unjust distributions are distributions that violate these shared conceptions, which Walzer also calls shared understandings and social meanings. Criticizing such distributions is internal; it does not import external standards but rather appeals to the shared understandings of the goods themselves. Although some theorists have raised objections to this interpretive account, I want to defend it in this paper.[2] Yet I also want to argue that the recourse to shared understandings may be more complicated than Walzer sometimes lets on. I begin with a summary of his argument and some of the objections to it.

G. Warnke (✉)
University of California, Riverside, USA
e-mail: warnke@ucr.edu

J. T. Reiner (ed.), *Walzer and Justice: Spheres of Justice in the 2020s*,
https://doi.org/10.1007/978-3-031-87809-1_3

Walzer and His Critics

Walzer starts by noting that before a society can distribute its goods it must first create them. A group of people wants to honor certain achievements and it conceives of prizes as a way of doing so; a community develops a democratic form of governing itself and establishes political positions as a way to represent the views and interests of various constituencies in enacting and revising laws and policies. Honors and political positions in a democratic government are not goods that simply exist but are rather goods that communities conceive of, create and develop. As the result and embodiment of such collective conceptions and creations they are social meanings; moreover, as social meanings they determine their own just distribution. If a prize is a way of honoring one or more people for their achievements, it is to be distributed to the person or people that the selection committee decides best meet the criteria of achievement that the prize honors. If a political position in a democracy is a way of representing the views and interests of a particular constituency, it is to be distributed to those who have persuaded the majority of that constituency that they can best fulfill this mandate. "Once we understand what a good is," Walzer writes, "and what it means to those for whom it is a good, we understand how, by whom, and for what reasons it ought to be distributed" (9). The negative corollary to this position is that distributing goods in violation of this understanding—distributing prizes or political positions to those who have the means to pay for them, for example—is unjust. As Walzer puts this point, "No social good x should be distributed to men and women who possess some other good y merely because they possess y and without regard to the meaning of x" (20).

Richard Arneson is skeptical of this formulation: "This 'distribute according to social meanings' norm is an empty vessel, the content of which could be anything."[3] It says only: "(a) that institutions should conform to the moral beliefs of those people affected by them and (b) ... that institutional rules should conform to the preferences of those who live under the institutions, as to what the rules should be."[4] Ronald Dworkin is also doubtful: Walzer "tells us to look to social conventions to discover the appropriate principles of distribution for particular goods, but the very fact that we debate about what justice requires, in particular cases, shows that we have no conventions of the necessary sort."[5] Brian Barry's objection is a hostile one: "Justice has certain formal characteristics and ... the universal validity of this proposition cannot be challenged by showing that a lot of people in some benighted society think otherwise."[6] Finally, Joshua Cohen claims that Walzer's argument relies on an agreement on the values that a specific distributive scheme embodies.[7] Here Cohen imagines a system that relies extensively on the market and thus might be said to exhibit individualistic values. Yet clearly, he continues, not everyone who complies with that system necessarily agrees with it or holds those values. They may comply because they are afraid, self-interested, disinterested, or thinking long-term or strategically.[8] He also thinks that where consensus does exist it can be the result of coercion rather than voluntary assent. Barry agrees: Consensus need not exist and where it may exist it "is invalidated by unequal access to the means of persuasion, or by lack of education, lack of opportunity... for speculation about alternatives, and ignorance about one's own and other societies."[9]

Walzer's critics are clear, then, that questions of justice cannot be answered by discovering what people in "some benighted society" prefer or think about their goods or their distribution, and they also question whether we can assume that they agree in their preferences or thoughts in the first place. Yet these criticisms misconstrue Walzer's argument and do so in at least four ways. First, the social meanings or shared conceptions to which the argument appeals are not thoughts or preferences about goods. Rather social meanings and shared conceptions *are* the goods. A person may have certain thoughts, beliefs and preferences with regard to such goods as honors and political positions and others may share these thoughts, beliefs and preferences but social meanings are not views that people happen either to possess or to share about their goods; instead, as conceived and created by those people, they are the goods themselves. This insight is not as idiosyncratic as Walzer's critics seem to assume. In 1971, Charles Taylor wrote, "We have to admit that intersubjective social reality has to be partly defined in terms of meanings; that meanings as subjective are not just in casual interaction with a social reality made up of brute data, but that as intersubjective they are constitutive of this reality."[10]

Walzer's critics also fail to recognize that the same distinction between meanings and opinions or preferences holds for distributions. Just as one can disagree with others in one's opinions about certain social goods, one can disagree with the way a particular prize committee, say, distributes its prize or disagree with the majority's choice for their political representative. Neither of these disagreements, however, touches on the meanings of prizes or political representatives or on the criteria of distribution embedded in those meanings. If a prize is an honor, it remains one even if certain people disapprove of the selection of a particular honoree; likewise, if a political representative represents a majority choice, it retains this meaning even if a minority disapproves of the choice.

A third way in which Walzer's critics misconstrue his position is to argue, as Cohen does, that he presumes a consensus on the values members of a given society attach to systems for distributing their goods. Walzer's argument, however, is almost precisely the opposite: namely, that people value different goods in different ways. Complex equality is the result of securing the autonomy of different spheres of distribution so that those who value luxury goods, for example, can pursue the wealth needed to purchase them without affecting the distribution arrangements proper to other goods and other values in other spheres—by, say, using their wealth to purchase political influence. The fourth mistake follows. Because Walzer does not presume that members of a society necessarily agree on specific distributions or on the values they attach to different spheres of distribution, he need not deny that members can be coerced into complying with them. Indeed, effective audits of the taxes of the super-wealthy would surely force them into compliance with a progressive tax schema even though their actions clearly indicate they do not agree with it.

Yet, if members of a community can differ in their individual opinions about both a good and its distribution without affecting Walzer's argument about social meanings, what about differences in what they take the good to be or, in other words, differences in their understanding of its social meaning? Take approaches to textual meaning. Intentionalists in literary theory deny the validity of different understandings of a text and insist that it means only what its creator intended it to mean. But, as the hermeneutic philosopher Hans-Georg Gadamer points out, to assume that a text precisely mirrors its author's intention is to overlook its entanglements with the intentions and activities of others. I intend to make a left turn but clash with the intention of another driver to go straight. The meaning of my action is surely not the left turn I intended. While I intended to make a left turn what I actually did was to crash into another car. The meaning of a text is likewise not under the exclusive control of its author but interacts with the circumstances and expectations of its different readers in different times and different circumstances. In this way textual meanings are what Gadamer calls "fusions of horizons."[11]

If so, readers can disagree with one another in two ways: in their opinions about a text and in what they understand the text to be. Literary critics have certainly had different opinions about Herman Melville's, *Moby Dick*. While the contemporary author Nathan Philbrick calls it the "greatest American novel ever written,"[12] in a 1922 comment, the English critic Michael Seidler claimed that it "labours under a sad weight of intolerable prolixity."[13] Literary critics have also had different understandings of its meaning. Some have understood it as a "sea and whaling story,"[14] others as a tragedy of revenge,[15] others as the depiction of "an existential voyage to see if life has any meaning"[16] and still others as a portrayal of the sublime.[17] These interpretive differences reflect the novel's different fusions with different horizons; they are differences in how different interpreters understand it because of their different situations, historical circumstances, interests and expectations. Differences in opinions about a text and differences in understandings of what it is are thus not the same. Indeed, they can fall apart and combine in different ways. Individual readers may differ in their understanding of *Moby Dick* but agree in their opinion of it—as the greatest American novel, say, on any of its interpretations. Conversely, readers can share an understanding of the meaning of the text, as a sea and whaling story, for instance, but disagree on its merits *as* a sea and whaling story. Early English critics found it "poorly constructed."[18]

Understandings of and opinions about social meanings also break apart. We may disagree in how we value a free-market economic system, for instance, but agree that a free-market system is what we have, or we may agree in valuing our economic system but disagree on whether it is or is not a free market. Indeed, we can differ in both: in how we value a free-market system and in whether our system is one at all. Walzer's critics tend to obscure this distinction, failing to separate differences in opinions about a good from differences in understandings of what the good is, about which one can have opinions. At the same time, in *Spheres of Justice* Walzer arguably downplays the latter differences. Only in a parenthesis does he note that members of a community can disagree about the meaning of one or more of their social goods. He continues, "When understandings are controversial, then justice requires that the society be faithful to the disagreements, providing institutional channels for their expression, adjudicative mechanisms, and alternative distributions" (313). Although Dworkin finds this remark "simply mysterious," in what follows

I want to consider it further and do so by looking at the issue of American medical care.

Medical Care in the United States

Walzer argues that as medical knowledge developed in the West, a public commitment to curing bodies gradually took over from a public commitment to curing souls. Concern for the health of the soul once required neighborhood churches and regular church services open to all, while concern for the health and life of the body was largely limited to the wealthy who could afford treatments that were, in any case, mostly useless. Yet as medical care became more effective in preventing and combatting disease, the demand for its more general provision grew. Developing from the recognition, first, that many diseases could be cured or prevented and, second, that if they could be cured or prevented, they must be, physical health and longevity became socially recognized needs. A third recognition followed: cures and preventions promoting health and longevity required common effort. The late nineteenth century thus saw the establishment of licensing boards, medical schools, hospitals and urban clinics, all of which represented, Walzer says, "an important public commitment" (87–8). "Medical research is expensive," he continues, "and the treatment of many particular diseases lies far beyond the resources of ordinary citizens. So the community must step in, and any democratic community will in fact step in, more or less vigorously, more or less effectively, depending on the outcome of particular political battles" (88). The medical care necessary to protect health and longevity becomes part of the sphere of public welfare and a democratic community is "more or less vigorously, more or less effectively" responsible for it.

The American democratic community currently steps in somewhat vigorously with tax-payer funds to help train and license doctors and nurses; support medical research as well as hospitals and institutions such as the National Institutes of Health and the Centers for Disease Control and Prevention; ensure the safety of food and drinking water and assist in the development of virus testing and vaccines. Such measures recognize health and longevity as needs and thus as goods for which the democratic community is responsible. Chances for health and longevity must be available to all members of that democratic community and they must be available "in ways that respect their membership" (88) or, in other words, in ways that respect their status as equal democratic citizens.

Yet despite this use of common funds to support some public health efforts, in the United States, the distribution of health and longevity through direct medical care to individuals remains largely a private and profit-driven affair. The elderly and those with low incomes may qualify for a government sponsored health care program such as Medicare, the Children's Health Insurance Program or Medicaid, both of which are always under threat and under-funded. As a last resort, poorer Americans can also turn to safety net providers such as emergency rooms or free clinics staffed by volunteers. Still, for the most part, if Americans receive medical care at all, they do so through one of three market-based mechanisms. Many can purchase health insurance through employer-sponsored plans where employers subsidize the costs of the insurance in return for government tax breaks. Alternatively, if one can afford to do so, one can pay for one's health care directly. Finally, through the Affordable Care Act, one can buy private health insurance on health care markets where for-profit companies advertise options along a tiered scale of bronze, silver, gold and platinum options, depending on the amount one can or is willing to pay. Less expensive bronze plans offer less coverage for fewer conditions and higher deductibles whereas the most expensive platinum plans offer more coverage for more conditions and lower deductibles.

The Affordable Care Act post-dates the publication of *Spheres of Justice*, but for Walzer, any distributive system in which one's health and life can depend on the resources one has to purchase medical care and/or medical insurance violates the social meanings of health and longevity as needs. If a good is socially recognized as a need, access to it must be available to everyone who needs it in proportion to their need and without consequences for their status as equal citizens. Yet the free clinic and emergency room options available to poor Americans who do not qualify for governmental programs or aid in purchasing health care are clearly far worse than the options available to wealthy citizens. Those who can afford only bronze insurance plans with high deductibles also face a heightened possibility of death and disease or, at the very least, catastrophic debt from medical crises that their insurance plans do not cover. In 2022, the Commonwealth Fund found that 43% of Americans were inadequately insured.[19] Meanwhile, in 2021, UnitedHealth, the largest medical insurance company in the United States, made $17.7 billion in net earnings. This sort of situation clearly represents what Walzer calls "the dominance of wealth in the sphere of need" (91).

Yet as long as the distribution of health and longevity in the United States includes both publicly funded processes and private, profit-driven processes, why criticize this situation as the dominance of wealth in the sphere of need as opposed to, say, the intrusion of need into the sphere where wealth holds sway, namely: the sphere of money and commodities? Barry claims that Walzer's arguments are "a long way from deducing the supersession of the market from the social recognition of health care as a need."[20] Likewise, Cohen writes, "The facts that health care is largely privately, and very unequally, provided are also data for an interpretation of "our" conception of health care. It is not at all clear how Walzer's interpretation fits these data, and, if it does not, why it is legitimate to disregard them."[21]

To be sure, here again Cohen and Barry misread Walzer's point. *Pace* Cohen, *Spheres of Justice* does not try to offer an interpretation of "our" conception of health care nor, *pace* Barry, does it define health care as a need. Rather, Walzer offers an interpretation of health and longevity that understands them, not health care, as socially recognized needs and he claims that if they are socially recognized needs then the medical care required to protect them should be available to all those who need it in a way that preserves their equality as democratic citizens. At the same time, Cohen's reference to the facts about the largely private and very unequal distribution of individual health care in the United States raises the possibility that what Walzer understands as a distributive violation of the social meanings of health and longevity might, on a different interpretation, instead reflect them. On this different interpretation they are not needs but rather commodities and the same holds for the health care required to protect them.

Admittedly, it is unclear how a modern democracy could simply declare itself uninterested in the health and longevity of its sick citizens. Medical researchers already track American life expectancy and, indeed, sounded the alarm as it declined due to COVID-19, the opioid epidemic and lack of access to health care. Moreover, sick Americans often protest when they think their government is doing too little to help them. Take protests against the government during the AIDS epidemic by the ACT-UP organization which insisted that federal agencies were not sufficiently active in accelerating drug testing and lowering the costs of existing drugs. As chronicled by the *New Yorker*, activists "wrapped the home of the North Carolina senator Jesse Helms in a giant yellow condom… laid siege to the Food and Drug Administration… and dumped the ashes of friends who had died of AIDS on the White House lawn."[22] Criticism of the Trump administration for what many saw as its slow response to the COVID pandemic is another example. The administration did, however, ultimately partner with drug manufacturers to develop vaccines in "Operation Warp Speed," thereby indicating its recognition of the government's responsibility for protecting its population from severe illness and death. When the Biden administration claimed that Trump administration "failed to order enough vaccines, failed to mobilize the effort to administer shots [and] failed to set up vaccine centers,"[23] it also announced its own responsibility to do so.

Yet conservatives and libertarians try to limit the role of government in the provision of individual health care. Organizations such as the Cato Institute and the Heritage Foundation do not deny that Americans who want health care should have access to it. But the proposals they advance advocate free market health care delivery systems, ones that they claim will be less expensive and more efficient than those the government can provide. The Cato Institute acknowledges that health care is too expensive for many Americans and admits that the quality of care they often receive "is so low as to be dangerous to patients' health." But the Institute also insists that "The cause of these problems is a dense thicket of state and federal laws that deny workers the right to make their own decisions about their health care, including the right to control whether, to what extent, and where to spend their earnings on health care."[24] Likewise, the Heritage Foundation calls for improving the existing system of public and private coverage to enhance Americans' "personal choice and control."[25]

For many conservative and libertarian groups "personal choice and control" are principles that undercut any social meaning of health and longevity as needs to be communally protected. These groups agree with the Cato Institute and Heritage Foundation that an expanded free market would provide better access to health care than a government-run system. But they also focus on what they call liberty rights, rights not to be interfered with by other people or the state. In the libertarian view my right to property, for instance, does not mean my government must give me land; rather, it prohibits the theft of the land I have already bought on my own. Likewise, my right to life does not mean my democratic government must offer me health care; rather, according to both the Republican Liberty Caucus and David Kelley, head of the Atlas Society, it means "a right to act freely for one's self-preservation. It is not a right to be immune from death by natural causes, even an untimely death."[26] On this view, health and longevity are not needs but are rather simply goods one can choose to protect and nurture if one has the desire and means to do so. Writing in the *National Review* Ben Shapiro draws the consequences for access to care. "Morally, you have no right to demand medical care of me. I may recognize your necessity and offer charity; my friends and I may choose to band together and fund your medical care. But your necessity does not change the basic math: Medical care is a service and a good provided by a third party." Or as he also puts it, "Medical care is a commodity, and treating it otherwise is foolhardy."[27]

Of course, there are very few goods that conservatives and libertarians think are not commodities. Milton Friedman would abolish most government agencies, leaving questions of health and safety to the market, although he does allow for some public health activities to prevent contagion.[28] His descendants do not go even this far: witness the attacks on the perceived authoritarianism of the NIH and CDC during the COVID-19 pandemic and disputes over mask and vaccine mandates. For many Americans even if it could be shown that wearing a mask or being vaccinated would help control the spread of the virus, the individual freedom to decide not to wear a mask trumped questions of community welfare and concern for the lives of others. Indeed, twenty-seven states sued the Biden administration when it sought to impose a vaccine mandate on government workers and private businesses with more than a hundred employees. In January, 2023, members of the U.S. House of Representative introduced a bill prohibiting the government from requiring those working in medical facilities that participated in certain federal programs to be vaccinated. The bill is called the Freedom for Health Care Workers Act.

If we follow Walzer, we will argue that the social meaning of health and longevity as needs requires replacing the current system for their protection, expunging private enterprise from its distribution and instituting a government-run single-payer system. Indeed, he claims that the very first use of tax money for hospitals and the like signals a public commitment that "ultimately can be filled only by turning physicians, or some substantial number of them, into public physicians" (88). Alternatively, if we follow conservatives and libertarians, we will argue that health and longevity, like almost all goods, are consumer items that Americans must be free to choose to buy or not. In this case, syncing patterns of distribution to their social meanings would lead the United States to defund the NIH and the CDC, eliminate programs such as Medicare and Medicaid and establish a completely market-based system. Indeed, syncing might require the elimination of health insurance and establishing direct payment for medical services.

Of course, we might argue that health and longevity possess a mixed social meaning. Their conception and creation as needs is incomplete and co-exists with their older conception and creation as luxury goods. At a certain baseline patterned in free clinics and emergency rooms as well as in such government programs as Medicaid they are needs. At higher levels they are commodities and protecting them through medical care depends on the buyer's wealth and willingness to pay. Neither Walzer nor conservative and libertarian organizations accept this interpretation, however. Walzer insists that the American understanding of health and longevity as reflected in government sponsored institutions and activities such as medical research already goes beyond this analysis and does not admit of different levels of care for different Americans. Conservatives and libertarians insist that the free enterprise system means we need to abolish government sponsorship for all scientific research including medical research and they accuse government programs such as Medicaid and the Children's Insurance Program of crowding out private health delivery and insurance options.[29]

For Rahel Jaeggi, such competing interpretations are reason enough to avoid an interpretive approach from the start. Focusing on Walzer's account of social criticism in *Interpretation and Social Criticism* and on tensions between norms and practices, she claims: "Even if one would like to assume counterfactually the unity of a community, it is apparent that the contradiction between the norms and practices of a community demonstrated by the critics persist as rival interpretations even where these interpretations share a common reference point."[30] Her example is quotas to achieve gender parity for women: both those in favor of using and those against them can appeal to the principle of equal treatment because they interpret it differently. Whereas one side takes equal treatment to mean equality of result, the other takes it to mean equality of opportunity.

Jaeggi thinks matters are even worse for interpretation when different sides in a debate appeal to different principles. In the controversy over asylum and national borders, for example, one side appeals to a "general human solidarity" while the other appeals to the right of communities to protect their way of life.[31] If we follow her line of argument, the same holds for the debate over medical care where one side appeals to principles of personal liberty and the other to principles of equal citizenship. Jaeggi concedes that an internal form of social criticism that contrasts practices to norms has an advantage over an external form in that it need not try to impose standards or principles from outside of the society at issue. Nevertheless, if one side must ultimately impose its interpretation on the other, the difference between internal and external criticism disappears. Each interpretation is external to the other and "the problem of demonstrating and deriving standards of criticism now returns in the guise of the problem of the 'correct' interpretation of norms and practices and...the basis of their authority."[32]

Walzer offers two different ways of resolving this problem. In a footnote in *Spheres of Justice* he notes that Marx would see social meanings as simply "the ideas of the ruling class," but he counters that "A people's culture is always a joint, even if it isn't an entirely cooperative, production and it is always a complex production. The common understanding of particular goods incorporates principles, procedures, conceptions of agency that the rulers would not choose if they were choosing *right now*—and so provides the terms of social criticism" (9). Interpretive social criticism remains internal in that it looks to principles, procedures and conceptions of agency that are lodged in social meanings even if they are not those a ruling class currently acknowledges. An example is his description of a hypothetical village in which the distribution of grain follows an integrated and hierarchical system of social meanings so that members of lower castes receive less grain than those of higher ones. Walzer insists that justice "cannot require a radical redesign of the village against the shared understandings of the members" (313). At the same time, he suggests that because the production of social meanings is complex, it can include alternative principles, procedures and conceptions of agency that may foster anger and indignation at the current distribution and lead to demands for change.

Anger and indignation certainly suffuse both sides in the health care debate in the United States. Both demand change and both appeal to principles, procedures and conceptions of agency to support their demands. Those who share Walzer's account of health and longevity look to principles of equality that tell in favor of providing the same quality of care to all Americans; to procedures for well-being that would undergird a government-run single payer system; and to conceptions of agency that would demand the conditions that can support equal capacities for social and political participation. For this position, the grip of the market on health care is yet another instance of the way corporate power invades too many spheres of American life. In contrast, those who see health and longevity as commodities look to principles of individual freedom that allow individuals to decide for themselves how to spend their money, to procedures for well-being that would allow the market to determine all costs and benefits and to conceptions of agency that valorize the responsible, self-sufficient individual. For this position, any government intervention into health care sets Americans on a slippery slope that would eventually abolish all their civil liberties. Demands for change thus characterize both sides of the American health care debate.

In a reply to critics in 1995 Walzer offers a second answer to concerns about these rival interpretations.[33] He concedes that in *Spheres of Justice* he focused on what he calls the "agents of first resort, the makers, distributors and recipients of the goods in question." As he continues, "My idea was that these people should work out among themselves the meaning of the goods and the appropriate mechanisms of distribution—and that they should defend the integrity of the sphere" (286–7). Thus, it is the priests themselves in the medieval church who opposed nepotism and simony and it is contemporary professors themselves who could object to the automatic admission to the university of the children of wealthy donors. Yet Walzer later suggests that where these agents of first resort fail to resolve an interpretive disagreement on, say, what religion or the university is, they can legitimately appeal to the state and their fellow citizens "to intervene and adjudicate or help one of the sides." This sort of intervention "attends to the goods in questions, honestly attempts to resolve the disagreements about their meaning and then, having reached a temporary resolution, leaves the sphere to its 'inhabitants.'"[34]

This solution provides a possible answer to Dworkin's mystification about what Walzer means by "adjudicative mechanisms" for interpretive disagreements, and it may have been plausible in 1995. It is not clear that it remains so, however, given Americans' increasingly distrust their own fellow citizens and institutions, including Congress, the Supreme Court and the media. Polling data from April 2024 puts approval of Congress at 13%[35] while trust in the Supreme Court dropped more 20-percentage-points between 2020 and 2022, reaching a historic low after the *Dobbs* decision.[36] In May 2024, according to a Marquette Law School poll, approval was at 39%.[37] As for the media, Americans notoriously read different newspapers and watch or listen to different news programs, which not only provide different ideological perspectives on the news but also deliver different news that caters to different audiences. While the liberal press covered Clarence Thomas's trouble with financial deals and disclosures in the spring of 2023, for example, the conservative press covered Hunter Biden. Even so, in September 2023, a Gallup poll found that only 32% of Americans had either a "great deal" or "fair amount" of confidence in the fairness and accuracy of mass media; more—39%—had no trust at all.[38]

Americans' trust in one another fares no better. According to a June 2024 Pew Research Center report, the percentage of Americans who doubt the country can solve many of its important problems rose from 41% in 2022 to 52%; the percentage of doubtful young American adults ages 18 to 29 is 62%.[39] Perhaps worse, the percentage of Americans who say they have little or no confidence in the wisdom of the American people in making political decisions rose from 62% in 2021 to 76%.[40] Political polarization tied to the two major American political parties has not been limited to differences on issues for some time, but it has now transformed into the wholesale contempt each party has for the other. 72% of Republicans think Democrats are more immoral and dishonest than other Americans while around 63% of Democrats think the same of Republicans. Republicans and Democrats segregate themselves in blue states and red states and even blue and red neighborhoods; they shop at different stores, eat at different restaurants and drive different kinds of cars. Indeed, according to one commentator, "The divide between the blue and the red, urban and rural, coastal and heartland, Whole Foods and Cracker Barrel is now so wide and so bitter that maybe, as in a spent marriage, it is time to just hang it up."[41]

Given this data, it is likely that the interventions by the state or fellow citizens to which Walzer gestures would be viewed as simply partisan intrusions. At the same time, as long as Americans do not want to "just hang it up," it is unclear what alternative they have other than one another. Where else can they look to resolve their interpretive disagreements? One of the most compelling images from Walzer's *Interpretation and Social Criticism* describes a debate between Rabbi Joshua agreeing with the majority of the sages present and Rabbi Eliezer, a minority of one. According to Walzer, the latter called for divine help:

> "If the law is as I say, let this carob tree prove it.: Whereupon the carob tree was lifted a hundred cubits in the air...Rabbi Joshua spoke for the majority: "No proof can be brought from a carob tree." Then Rabbi Eliezer said,

> "If the law is as I say, let this stream of water prove it." And the stream immediately began to flow backward. But Rabbi Joshua said, "No proof can be brought from a stream of water."

When Rabbi Eliezer called on the walls of the schoolhouse to prove his point, they began to crumble but they stopped when Rabbi Joshua said the dispute was not their concern.

> And then Rabbi Eliezer called on God himself: If the law is as I say, let it be proved from heaven." Whereupon a voice cried out, "Why do you dispute with Rabbi Eliezer. In all matters the law is as he says." But Rabbi Joshua stood up and explained, "It is not in heaven."

Walzer concludes, "There is a tradition, a body of moral knowledge and there is this group of sages arguing. There isn't anything else."[42] Because there isn't anything else, in the rest of this paper I want to suggest that we acknowledge the conditions of interpretation.

The Conditions of Interpretation

In arguing that with Walzer's approach, "the problem of demonstrating and deriving standards of criticism …returns in the guise of the problem of the "correct" interpretation of norms and practices," Jaeggi inserts scare quotes around "correct." In doing so she may want to suggest that opposing sides will each regard their own interpretation as correct and, as in external social criticism, try to impose it on their adversaries. But the scare quotes also suggest that to call interpretations correct or incorrect misstates the criteria appropriate to them. In relation to textual interpretation, we recognize that different readers with different interests and orientations can understand the same text differently—*Moby Dick*, for example, as a tale of revenge, a sea and whaling story, the account of "an existential voyage" and so on. This difference does not mean that interpretations are solely matters of subjective judgment or that there is no standard by which to discriminate among them. Rather, although no one interpretation is uniquely correct, some may be more sound or plausible than others. At least since Schleiermacher, the German hermeneutic tradition has maintained that the latter are those that are able to show the way a text hangs together—those that show how its parts integrate with one another to compose a unified whole and how the meaning of the whole contributes to the meaning of each of the parts. An interpretation of "The Whiteness of the Whale" chapter in *Moby Dick* that focuses on Ishmael's dread of the color white uses the way that, for him, it reflects "the heartless voids and immensities of the universe"[43] is one of the parts that add up to the account of the novel as "an existential voyage to see if life has any meaning." Conversely, this interpretation of the whole provides the context for understanding the chapter.

If we turn to social meanings, the same hermeneutic conditions apply: our interpretations of them are sound or plausible when they can be integrated with other social meanings as parts in a larger social whole that, in turn, sheds light on them. Walzer's interpretation of the meanings of health and longevity as needs conforms to these conditions. The parts of the interpretation include the historical trajectory that moves from an emphasis on spiritual health and eternity to an emphasis on physical health and longevity, the responsibility of the American government to protect health and longevity as reflected in American institutions and procedures, protests against the government when it is understood to have failed in this responsibility, democratic principles of equality that stress uniform access to health and longevity and ideas about agency that stress community support. The whole into which this interpretation of health and longevity fits as a part is that of an egalitarian, broadly social democratic society. Yet the conservative and libertarian interpretation of the meanings of health and longevity as commodities also conforms to the Schleiermacherian criterion. The parts of this interpretation include American principles of personal liberty, ideas of individual agency that stress self-reliance and personal responsibility and an American commitment to limited government and free-enterprise. The whole into which this understanding of health and longevity fits as a part is that of a free, market-based society.

The field of literary interpretation can accommodate multiple interpretations of a text that each successfully integrates the meaning of its parts and the meaning of the whole. Even after we have rejected textual interpretations that cannot show how a given text holds together, we still recognize the existence of sound, plausible and often enlightening interpretations other than our own. We are able to argue for our own interpretation, provide textual evidence for it and show its merits, all while also recognizing and discussing the merits of the interpretations of others and even trying to learn from them. In the literary domain we not only presume a multiplicity of interpretations of a given text but even encourage it in the hope of new and different insights into both the text and our own understanding of it. Indeed, we often measure the richness of a text by the multiple insightful interpretations it fosters, its ability through time to generate new interpretations geared to new interests and circumstances and the relations of its interpretations to one another in an interpretive tradition.

This interpretive pluralism is more difficult to sustain with regard to political decisions and matters of public policy where we have to act and legislate in one way or another and where not acting or legislating is already a form of action and legislation. Yet we might still look to the way we treat differences in textual interpretation as a model for our political and policy debates. We might acknowledge that, like our interpretations of textual meanings, our interpretations of social meanings are just that: interpretations or ways of understanding our social meanings, ways that are not opinions *about* those meanings but are also not exclusively correct. As in the literary domain, we might both argue for our interpretation and acknowledge that the way we integrate our society's goods, principles and distributions into a coherent whole may be only one of different sound ways of doing so and we might recognize that those who disagree with our integration may be able to provide a coherent integration of their own. They may not, of course, and it is the task of internal criticism to illuminate an interpretation's gaps and inconsistencies. Yet, at least as an initial step, we might presume the plausibility of interpretations other than our own and treat them with respect, if not acquiescence.

Models of discourse and debate geared to overcoming America's current partisan divide are currently a dime a dozen of course. Organizations on college campuses and in the public encourage us to treat those with whom we disagree with consideration and empathy and to appreciate the paths that have led them to their beliefs. As Evan Mandery puts it in *Politico Magazine* we are to listen to "the sincerity of people's convictions, the authenticity of their experiences, and the nuance of their narratives."[44] Unfortunately, these models suggest that the positions others espouse are unintelligible or wrong on their face and that for this reason we must be sensitive to the sincerity, authenticity and nuance with which they are espoused. The condescension evident here is unlikely to close our divide. More promising is the recognition that, like our texts, our social goods and principles must be interpreted and that, like our texts, they can be interpreted in some different equally plausible ways. In the case of health and longevity, leftists and liberals might concede that the conservative and libertarian case against universal health care is part of a coherent understanding of American principles and traditions, one that emphasizes individual rights, the free market and personal responsibility. For their part, conservatives and libertarians might acknowledge that the left-liberal case for universal health care is also part of a coherent understanding of American principles and traditions, one that emphasizes equal rights, social solidarity and the obligations of democratic government. To the extent that neither understanding is unsound, according to Schleiermacherian standards, neither is worthy of the belligerent scorn the opposition currently bestows upon it. The same goes for our debates over immigration, education and so on. Engaging in these debates with hermeneutic charity means listening to the substance of one another's interpretations instead of their sincerity or authenticity. We may still be unable to persuade our adversaries or come to a consensus, but the upshot will at least be less shrillness and more civil public debates. Indeed, we may possibly ease the hostility of factions that currently mirrors a "spent marriage" and threatens a national divorce.

Competing Interests The author has no conflicts of interest to declare that are relevant to the content of this chapter.

Notes

1. Michael Walzer (1983) *Spheres of Justice: A Defense of Pluralism and Equality*. Basic Books. Subsequent citations to this book are in the text.
2. J. Toby Reiner (2020) *Michael Walzer*. Cambridge: Polity Press, 71.
3. Richard J. Arneson (1995) "Against Complex Equality" in *Pluralism, Justice, and Equality* David Miller and Michael Walzer (eds.) Oxford: Oxford University Press. 240.
4. Ibid, 239–240.
5. Ronald Dworkin (1983) "To Each His Own," *New York Review of Books* (April 14) https://www.nybooks.com/articles/1983/04/14/to-each-his-own/?lp_txn_id=1457397.
6. Brian Barry (1995) "Spherical Justice and Global Injustice" in *Pluralism, Justice, and Equality*. 74–75.
7. Joshua Cohen (1986) "Review of Spheres of Justice: A Defense of Pluralism and Equality" in *The Journal of Philosophy* 457–468.

8. Ibid, 462.
9. Barry, "Spherical Justice and Global Injustice," 77–78.
10. Charles Taylor (1971) "Interpretation and the Sciences of Man" in *The Review of Metaphysics*, Vol. 25, No. 1 (September) 29–30.
11. Hans-Georg Gadamer (1960/1994) *Truth and Method*. Second, Revised Edition trans Joel Weinsheimer and Donald G. Marshall New York. Continuum.
12. Nathaniel Philbrick (2011) "The Road to Melville" *Vanity Fair*, October 20.
13. O. W. Riegel (1931) "The Anatomy of Melville's Fame" in *American Literature*, Vol. 3, No. 2 (May). 203.
14. Ibid, 199.
15. Donald Weeks (1950) "Two Uses of Moby Dick." *American Quarterly*, vol. 2, no. 2, 155–64. https://doi.org/10.2307/3031452.
16. Gabrielle Bellot (2019) "The Literal (and Figurative) Whiteness of Moby Dick." *Literary Hub* (August 1).
17. Merrill D. Whitburn, (1976) "'Moby-Dick' and the Sublime." *The Comparatist* (Vol. 3) 32–39. http://www.jstor.org/stable/44366653.
18. Riegel, "The Anatomy of Melville's Fame," 196.
19. The Commonwealth fund (2022) "The State of U.S. Health Insurance in 2022" September 29. https://www.commonwealthfund.org/publications/issue-briefs/2022/sep/state-us-health-insurance-2022-biennial-survey.
20. Barry, "Spherical Justice and Global Injustice," 72.
21. Cohen, "Review of Spheres of Justice," 464.
22. Michael Specter (2021) "How ACT-UP Changed America" *The New Yorker*, June 7 https://www.newyorker.com/magazine/2021/06/14/how-act-up-changed-america.
23. Jemima McEvoy (2021) "Operation Warp Speed Head Says Trump Administration Responsible For 90% Of Vaccine Rollout" *Forbes* (March 22) https://www.forbes.com/sites/jemimamcevoy/2021/03/21/operation-warp-speed-head-says-trump-administration-responsible-for-90-of-vaccine-rollout/?sh=69e5d16e1848.
24. Michael F. Cannon and Jeffrey A. Singer, (2022) "Health Care" https://www.cato.org/publications/healthcare.

25. Robert Moffit, "The Truth About Government-Controlled Health Care," https://www.heritage.org/article/the-truth-about-government-controlled-health-care.
26. RLC Staff (2016) "Liberty Rights vs. Welfare Rights" https://rlc.org/liberty-rights-vs-welfare-rights (August 18). David Kelley, 2010 "Is There a Right to Health Care" https://www.atlassociety.org/post/is-there-a-right-to-health-care (April 10.)
27. Ben Shapiro (2017) "Health Care Is a Commodity, Not a Right" in *National Review* (January 11): https://www.nationalreview.com/2017/01/health-care-markets-government-commodity-human-right.
28. Milton Friedman (2010) "Take It to the Limits: Milton Friedman on Libertarianism," Interview with Peter Robinson on "Uncommon Knowledge"(December 20) https://www.hoover.org/research/take-it-limits-milton-friedman-libertarianism.
29. Michael F. Cannon (2022) "Medicaid and the Children's Health Insurance Program" in *Cato Handbook for Policymakers* https://www.cato.org/cato-handbook-policymakers/cato-handbook-policymakers-9th-edition-2022/medicaid-childrens-health-insurance-program. See also https://www.heritage.org/health-care-reform/report/the-state-childrens-health-insurance-program-20-reform-agenda-congress and https://www.heritage.org/medicaid.
30. Rahel Jaeggi (2018) *Critique of Forms of Life* (Trans. Ciaran Cronin) Cambridge MA. Harvard University Press. 185.
31. Ibid, 185.
32. Ibid, 186.
33. Walzer, Michael, 'Response', in David Miller, and Michael Walzer (eds), Pluralism, Justice, and Equality (Oxford, 1995; online edn, Oxford Academic, 1 Nov. 2003), https://doi.org/10.1093/0198280084.003.0013.
34. Walzer, 1995/2003 "Response" in *Pluralism, Justice, and Equality*, 287.
35. Statista Research Department (2024) https://www.statista.com/statistics/207579/public-approval-rating-of-the-us-congress/#:~:text=The%20most%20recent%20polling%20data,which%20began%20in%20January%202023.

36. Gallop (2022) "Supreme Court Trust, Job Approval at Historical Lows" September 29 https://news.gallup.com/poll/402044/supreme-court-trust-job-approval-historical-lows.aspx#:~:text=Line%20graph.-,Americans'%20trust%20in%20the%20judicial%20branch%20of%20the%20federal%20government,expressed%20this%20level%20of%20trust.
37. Marquette University News Center (2024) "New Marquette Law School Poll National Survey Finds Approval of U.S. Supreme Court Falls To 39%, Second Lowest Since 2020. (May 22) https://www.marquette.edu/news-center/2024/new-marquette-law-poll-national-survey-finds-approval-of-supreme-court-falls-to-39.php.
38. Megan Brennan (2023) "Media Confidence in U.S. Matches 2016 Record Low" (October 19) https://news.gallup.com/poll/512861/media-confidence-matches-2016-record-low.aspx.
39. Pew Research Center (2024) "Americans' Views of Government's Role: Persistent Divisions and Areas of Agreement June 24 https://www.pewresearch.org/politics/2024/06/24/americans-views-of-governments-role-persistent-divisions-and-areas-of-agreement.
40. Pew Research Center (2023) "In Divided Washington, Americans Have Highly Negative Views of Both Parties' Leaders" April 7 https://www.pewresearch.org/politics/2023/04/07/in-divided-washington-americans-have-highly-negative-views-of-both-parties-leaders.
41. Clay S. Jenkinson, 2023 "What would a National Divorce Look Like" (March 12.) https://www.governing.com/context/what-would-a-national-divorce-look-like.
42. Michael Walzer, *Interpretation and Social Criticism* (Cambridge: Harvard University Press, 1987) 31–2.
43. Herman Melville 1851/2003, *Moby-Dick*. New York: Bantam Books. 211.
44. Evan Mandery (2019) "What Teaching Ethics in Appalachia Taught Me About Bridging America's Partisan Divide" *Politico Magazine* October 13. https://www.politico.com/magazine/story/2019/10/13/america-cultural-divide-red-state-blue-state-228111

CHAPTER 4

Maybe Even Souls: The Moral Basis of Socialism in *Spheres of Justice*

Geoffrey Kurtz

Michael Walzer addressed *Spheres of Justice* to "us who are committed to equality." Who are these people? Where do they come from? Why would, or should, they have such a commitment? Questions about the roots of our political commitments never have easy answers. But, at least regarding commitments to a solidaristic principle like Walzer's vision of sociability without domination, such questions may be more puzzling and more pressing today than they were forty years ago, when *Spheres* was published.[1]

Those years have seen a measurable increase in American disconnection: the decline of large-scale membership organizations, from labor unions to civic clubs to political parties to religious denominations, has been accompanied by the rise of professionally-run public relations groups, service providers, and media platforms.[2] In 1979, as these changes were beginning, Walzer wrote that "the shift from organizing

G. Kurtz (✉)
Borough of Manhattan Community College, City University of New York, New York, USA
e-mail: gkurtz@bmcc.cuny.edu

J. T. Reiner (ed.), *Walzer and Justice: Spheres of Justice in the 2020s*,
https://doi.org/10.1007/978-3-031-87809-1_4

to advocacy has to be reversed."[3] It hasn't been. Whether as cause or consequence of this political transformation, the moral world that Americans share has changed in ways harder to measure but no less palpable. Social critics like Robert Bellah, with his idea of "expressive individualism," or Charles Taylor, with his account of an "age of authenticity," have described a new mood of skepticism toward enduring obligations and common goods. Little wonder, then, that in the past decade Walzer has begun to worry in public about the "cultural reproduction of the left."[4]

Spheres of Justice is an argument for democratic socialism, and these political and cultural changes pose special problems for socialists. During the 1970s and early 1980s, the period when Walzer conceived of and wrote *Spheres*, democratic socialists in the United States pursued a strategy of "realignment," seeking to convene within the Democratic Party a left-leaning electoral majority anchored by a coalition of labor unions, civil rights organizations, and middle-class liberal groups—the coalition that had made its debut with the 1963 March on Washington.[5] Yet within a few years of the publication of *Spheres*, the realignment strategy had reached an impasse, and people in Walzer's political circles worried openly that recent defeats suffered by left-wing coalitions represented more than a short-term setback. Reflecting on Ronald Reagan's re-election to the presidency in 1984, Michael Harrington, a leading proponent of the socialist strategy of realignment and a frequent contributor to *Dissent*, wrote: "There had been, we and others realized, a certain *dealignment*. In America, which was in an even more individualistic mood than usual, organizations per se were less important than political commercials on television that treated candidates like breakfast food."[6] Similarly, Walzer's fellow *Dissent* editor Irving Howe wrote that the 1984 elections revealed a "degeneration of the democratic process" through which "public life grows emptier and emptier."[7]

In an America deprived of what Walzer calls "a politics of parties, movements, meetings, and public debate"[8] and suffused with new degrees or kinds of individualism, those who try to think about solidarity and equality, let alone pursue them, are more likely than ever to find themselves either uncertain and inarticulate or impatient and strident. And so readers of *Spheres of Justice* today may find themselves lingering at points in the text where Walzer, in writing the book, may not have anticipated lingerers. I want to show what it is like for a reader to linger at one such point. In *Spheres*, as elsewhere, Walzer writes a great deal about what follows from a commitment to equality but little about where such a commitment might come from in the first place. Yet, whether or not he intended this, what Walzer writes in *Spheres* suggests a certain way of understanding such a commitment. I want to follow those suggestions farther than Walzer does, to draw out ideas that he implies or invites but doesn't quite say. In doing so, I will argue that he gives his readers reason to think that his aversion to addressing fundamental questions is not, after all, a necessary part of his political project.

Authority

In a recent interview, Walzer remarks: "I have never tried to write about the foundations of ethics...The metaphor I have always used is: we are living in a house. We assume the house has a foundation, but I've never gone down there. I am trying to describe the living space."[9] Walzer's reasons for declining to visit the foundation of the house are in part about what one can't know and in part about what one shouldn't do and always about his commitment to pluralistic and democratic politics.

Political thinkers who begin from the premise that "there is one human nature" will find themselves driven to argue that there is "one good society that 'fits' human nature," Walzer has warned. This "singular" conception of justice begs for "some world-historical agent—the messiah, the communist vanguard, the enlightened despot" to enact it.[10] Walzer worries about political thinkers who found the authority of their ideas on an explicit claim to understand human nature, because he expects them to claim that any moral argument lacking this foundation is to be ruled invalid and that all reasonable people are obliged to accept that ruling. This way of understanding the relationship between politics and its foundations does not necessarily generate authoritarian politics. Yet its practitioners, we might say, are likely to find themselves dreaming authoritarian dreams. However humane their political theories may purport to be, political thinkers who seek an authoritative foundation can be democrats only on the surface.

As if inverting Leo Strauss's worry about the persecution of the philosopher by the city, Walzer suggests an ethic of self-limitation for political theorists: those who do not want vanguards or despots ought to keep their political thinking within certain bounds. Declining the quest for a singular political authority means resisting the temptation to say too much about the foundations, especially the anthropological foundations, of their political ideas. Better, Walzer writes, to do political theory "in the cave, in the city, on the ground."[11] Better, we might say, not to explore the foundations of the house.

This reluctance to explore the foundations of his politics limits what Walzer can say in *Spheres of Justice*. In the preface to that book, he ventures near the foundations of his egalitarianism but draws back; he asks an important question and almost, but not quite, evades answering. This passage strikes me as being crucial, and well worth pondering. I will quote part of it now and a little more of it later. Walzer writes:

> It is not my immediate purpose to ask the conventional philosophical questions: In what respects are we one another's equals? And by virtue of what characteristic are we equal in those respects? This entire book is an answer of a complicated sort to the first of those questions; the answer to the second I don't know, though in my last chapter I shall suggest one relevant characteristic. But surely there is more than one: the second question is more plausibly answered with a list than with a single word or phrase.[12]

Walzer's first answer to his question about the foundations of equality may seem simple: "I don't know." Perhaps he doesn't know because he hasn't been able to find out, or perhaps because he hasn't tried to find out. If the question about the anthropological basis of human equality "is more plausibly answered with a list than with a single word or phrase," however, it would seem that his reasons for not knowing are not so simple as either of these possibilities would suggest. Lists are, of course, plural. They are also open-ended: a list of four items suggests the possibility of a fifth. And if the items on a list are different in kind from one another—as is the case with Walzer's list, as we will see—they cannot be known through the same method or with the same degree of certainty. When Walzer says "I don't know," he is acknowledging that he has an incomplete anthropology. When he proposes that what we can know is likely to take the form of a list, he is also calling for an uncompletable anthropology, an account of human personhood that resists closure because it refuses singularity.

Yet answering a question with a list is unsatisfying. Are all the items on the list equally important, or important for the same kinds of reasons? Walzer does not ask those questions about his list of human characteristics. Thus his "I don't know," in addition to reflecting the open-ended character of a list, also reflects his intellectual self-restraint. His point here seems to be at once epistemological and political. If human persons shared only one kind of commonality, if human personhood were fully scrutable, then only one recognizing agent would be needed for the personhood of each to be acknowledged, and a single political actor, a vanguard or despot, might indeed be appropriate. If the best account of human personhood were a list, however, then no single recognizing agent could be adequate, and authoritarian politics would be self-evidently inappropriate. In that case, neither Walzer nor any other political thinker could claim to know, finally and completely, on what basis human persons deserve (or do not deserve) to be equal to one another—and so it is for the best if no one pursues this kind of knowledge.

In *The Company of Critics,* a book he wrote in response to "reviewers and commentators" who objected to his avoidance, in *Spheres of Justice,* of "a universal and transcendent standpoint," Walzer proposes a name for what political thinkers typically seek when they look to the foundations of their politics. They want, he writes, "warrants" that give their arguments "authority." A warrant for one's arguments, if it is to be authoritative, must have an intellectual or moral force that is easily recognizable; it must be the sort of idea that can be made plain in public, because it is only operational when the critic "displays" it.[13]

When Walzer declines to write about the foundations of his own politics, as when he says that he doesn't know the basis on which human persons deserve equality, he is declining the search for a foundational warrant of authority. If finding an unassailable warrant for one's authority were the only reason to explore the foundations of ethics, Walzer would have sound anti-authoritarian reasons for declining that exploration. Yet gaps and openings appear as Walzer works out the implications of his "I don't know," and from them emerges another way in which political thinkers might conceive of moral foundations.

Mystery

The significance of those gaps and openings becomes clearer if we read *Spheres of Justice* in light of *Thick and Thin*, a book Walzer published about a decade after *Spheres*, further refining some of the refinements to his thinking that he had made in intervening works. In *Thick and Thin,* Walzer distinguishes between "minimal and maximal meanings" or "thin and thick accounts" of moral ideas. A thick account of justice is social and contextual, "culturally integrated" and thus "fully resonant" within its home context. The closer to universality a concept, the thinner the account we are able to give of it. Moral reasoning, Walzer proposes, does not in practice begin with thin concepts which are then "adapted" or "elaborated" in thick, culturally-specific ways. Instead, we begin with thick accounts and resort to thin accounts only on occasion. The fact that the possibility of mutual human recognition is reiterated across cultures should not be taken to mean that I can only recognize another as human if I have a fully worked-out and universal theory of what it means to be human. Rather, it means that any such concept of the human is a by-product of the real experiences that I (or you or anyone else) might have when I (or you or they) recognize the humanity of another in the particular way that my (or your or their) culture provides for such a recognition. Accordingly, Walzer's examples of thin and universal moral arguments have mostly to do with negative claims, prohibitions on violations of life and liberty.[14] A political vision derived from them would be more suited to framing limits than to generating substantive commitments, and thus would be a poor guide to political action or to determinations of distributive justice.

Echoing his discussion of the critic's search for authority in *The Company of Critics*, Walzer writes in *Thick and Thin* that "philosophers commonly look for" what he calls "governing principles" with "universal reach." Critical of that overweening desire for authoritative arguments, he also doubts that thin concepts can sustain such expansive visions.[15] Both the criticism and the doubt make sense. But it is important to note what the contrast between thick and thin leaves out.

Walzer derived this distinction from the work of his Institute for Advanced Study colleague Clifford Geertz, an anthropologist who distinguished between "thin" and "thick" descriptions of culture.[16] A thin description states facts or notes events; a thick description explains what those facts or events mean to their participants. A thick description does not necessarily use more words than does a thin description, but it *says* more. In Walzer's sense of the term, accounts of human nature or of "the human" are necessarily thin, and we can recognize their thinness because we know that even if what such accounts equip us to say is at times important, they nevertheless equip us to say very little.

But surely there is more than one reason why one might have little to say about something. Thin description is not the only alternative to thick description. There might be little to say about something because there is little substance there to talk about, as Walzer expects to be the case with thin accounts of moral claims. But it might also be that there is little to say about something—at any rate, little that can be said in prose—because words are inadequate to a subject's gravity, or because attempts to directly explain the subject's meaning falter. A subject may be of such overwhelming significance, or its significance may so surpass our capacity for explanation, that indirect language or reticence or even silence is fitting.

Obliquely, Walzer makes room for this possibility. In the last chapter of *Thick and Thin*, he offers a "picture of the self...consistent with [his account of] equality."[17] A pluralistic theory of politics, Walzer proposes, fits well with an image that he calls the "divided self." The divided self is like a "thickly populated circle" from which a person's many memberships and values speak, in the midst of which a "listening self," distinct and "perdurable," attends to them all "like a newly elected president, summoning advisors, forming a cabinet."[18]

Walzer's image of the divided self may well help us understand some features of our inner lives: that we are "complex," canny about our complexities, capable of self-criticism and "worried" by it; that we experience ourselves as being unfinished, "not finally this or that."[19]Walzer's complex account of inward matters helps make sense of his pluralistic and democratic theory of outward matters. Attending to our dividedness does not help us much, however, in understanding another feature of inner life that is at least as important in Walzer's political theory: namely, commitment, as in that of "us who are committed to equality." Walzer's recent remark about himself is telling: "I often thought that I was boringly consistent. I started as a social democrat, I will end as a social democrat."[20] To make sense of the consistent commitment on which Walzer's theory of justice depends—his own commitment, or anyone else's—requires attention not so much to the dividedness of the self as to its still center, the cohering quiet that makes the self a self and not merely a set of affinities.

What makes the many-sided self a self? How, within this plurality, does personhood arise? Walzer declares, flatly: "I don't know the answers to these questions." But a few sentences later he offers an answer of sorts: "[T]he production and reproduction of selves, and even of self-critics, is a great mystery."[21] The curious thing about this passage is that if we read it alongside the passage in *Spheres of Justice* in which Walzer asks how we come to recognize one another's equal personhood, we are likely to notice a suggestive parallel. I have already quoted from that passage but now need to add more. In *Spheres*, shortly after his other "I don't know," comes Walzer's list of characteristics relevant to the principle of equality: "The answer has to do with our recognition of one another as human beings, members of the same species, and what we recognize are bodies and minds and feelings and hopes and maybe even souls."[22]

The words "mystery" and "souls" play corresponding roles in these two passages. Walzer tells us, in both instances, that he doesn't know the answer to a question about how we recognize a human person as a person, and then he goes on to tell us what little he thinks he can say about such recognitions, in one case culminating with the notion of mystery and in the other with the notion of souls. Either term could serve simply to mark the limits of what can be transparently explained. But when we read them in tandem, they open toward additional meanings.

The word "mystery" could indicate something we cannot understand or communicate; it could signal a philosophical dead-end, as if to say: You can't get anywhere from here, so retrace your steps. Yet the oldest layers of meaning in the word, as in the Latin *mysterium* and Greek *mustērion*, suggest that at times something not fully understandable or communicable may be such precisely because it is the sort of thing we ought to recognize as being sacred. The Psalmist writes: "Behold, thou desirest truth in the inward parts: / and in the hidden part thou shalt make me to know wisdom."[23] Using the word "mystery" in a way parallel to how he had earlier written about "souls," Walzer invites his readers to understand the mystery of selfhood as just such a hidden thing—to see the mystery he refers to in *Thick and Thin* as an intimation of sacred matters and to see the souls he refers to in *Spheres* as mysteries.

The biblical notion of "soul" is closely associated with God's breath or spirit: "And the Lord God formed man of the dust of the ground, and breathed into his nostrils the breath of life; and man became a living soul."[24] "Soul," in this account, is a trace of the divine. Understood as a sacred mystery, the soul cannot be just another item on the list of characteristics that human persons share; it becomes fundamental to our way of understanding what it is to be human. Yet, as a trace of the divine, a soul must be, like God, beyond human comprehension. Since the soul is a mystery that resists explanation, our accounts of it will be neither thick nor thin. We may be able to know or say something about it, but neither our knowledge nor our speech will involve direct or full access to its meaning. If we recognize human persons as ensouled creatures, then, we have arrived at a foundation for moral claims about human commonality, a "general principle" with "universal reach." But it is a foundational principle that cannot be put on display in the manner of a warrant of authority.

Especially if they have in mind Walzer's invocation of "mystery" in *Thick and Thin*, readers of *Spheres of Justice* might notice a seemingly extraneous word in the phrase that ends Walzer's list of shared human characteristics: "and maybe even souls." Walzer could have written "and maybe souls." A wording like that might have achieved some of the things that Walzer was aiming for in this passage: such a phrase would have broached a possibility without insisting on it, extending Walzer's list of human features beyond the empirical to include among those who deserve recognition as human those whose bodies or minds are dissimilar to others'.[25] Yet he writes "and maybe *even* souls." The word "even" introduces a hope, a stretch toward the limit of what might be. Walzer's wording—ever so slightly more evocative than it might seem to have needed to be—nudges his readers to go farther, to seek for something more. Here, he evokes ideas that remain at the edges of his political thought. I would like to bring some of those ideas into the open so that I can say something about why they matter.

Ideas Offstage

The Fall 1981 issue of *Dissent* featured a "Notebook" section consisting of two articles, one by each of the journal's editors, Irving Howe and Michael Walzer. Howe's contribution was the text of a talk he had given at the May 1981 convention of the Democratic Socialist Organizing Committee, an organization of which both he and Walzer were prominent members.[26] In it, he relates a "luminous sketch" in which the Italian Christian socialist Ignazio Silone tells a story from his childhood, an anecdote that gives Howe occasion for reflections on what he calls "the moral basis of socialism." Silone's story, Howe writes, "yields a moral perspective that sustains a politics of socialism."[27]

Walzer's "Notebook" entry had a similar purpose. It consisted of a set of excerpts from the journals of the British historian R.H. Tawney.[28] Introducing the excerpts, Walzer writes:

> In the early 1970s, I taught a course at Harvard on the moral arguments for capitalism and socialism...I had real difficulty finding any serious philosophical defenses of, even statements of, socialist values. Marxist historicism long ago replaced moral philosophy among committed socialists. On one level, Marxism was a science; on another level, it was a tactics. And in the (connected) worlds of scientists and tacticians, any sort of moral reflectiveness became an object of disdain. It suggested a lack of confidence in historical development or an unwillingness to do what had to be done to help that development along.
>
> In Anglo-American political life, moral argument survived most clearly among the Christian socialists, the greatest of whom was R.H. Tawney. By the time I finished putting my reading list together, I had decided that Tawney was also the most important socialist moralist of the 20th century.[29]

The Harvard course Walzer mentions here was the genesis of *Spheres of Justice*, as he would explain in that book's acknowledgements. At the time he published this *Dissent* piece, he was partway through the writing of *Spheres*; it seems that he was revisiting Tawney's writings as part of his project. Reading *Spheres* with this *Dissent* piece in mind, we can think of Tawney's writings as standing just offstage from Walzer's 1983 book, not always prominent but always present.[30]

Walzer writes that Tawney came closest to a "clear statement of basic principles" not in his books but in the private journals he kept between 1912 and 1914, published posthumously as *R.H. Tawney's Commonplace Book*. In the *Commonplace Book* excerpts which Walzer selected for publication in *Dissent*, Tawney argues that views common to English people in his time—for example, condemnation of slavery—provide a basis for seeing the "industrial problem [as] a moral problem." Moral principles that are already widely accepted, that have become "the common property of Christian nations," are like legal doctrines that can be "applied to particular sets of social conditions," and so Tawney writes that he wants to bring "new economic cases under some of the rules of conduct generally accepted by civilized men." Those rules of conduct need to be articulated forthrightly: "The fact is that what we want is a restatement of principles."[31]

Socialist politics, for Tawney, is a moral enterprise; it depends on the precepts of a common culture—in the case of his society, a Christian culture. Tawney sees values or principles, rather than science-like confidence about history or social structure, as the crucial factor in political thinking and political argument, and he believes that values are worth appealing to when they are shared, when they are generally-acknowledged "common property." In Tawney's writings, Walzer finds a model for his own social criticism, a style of political thought that derives its authority not from foundations but, so to speak, from within the living spaces of the house.

But Tawney, an Anglican writing in an era when the Church of England permeated and stabilized English public life, finds it unnecessary to distinguish two things that Walzer (and his readers today) cannot help but distinguish: religion as the common vocabulary of a culture and religion as the grammar of a fundamental commitment the importance of which does not depend on how widely it is shared. Walzer extracts from Tawney's journals passages that speak to the former, trimming his excerpts so as to just miss those that speak to the latter. The first of the four journal excerpts in Walzer's *Dissent* selection ends with this sentence: "They have seen human souls sacrificed so often to money that they have ceased to believe in any other motive except personal gain." Then, as if his thoughts have been nudged in a new direction by his use of the word "souls," Tawney writes the following, which Walzer does not quote:

> One of the things which strikes me as I grow older is the extraordinary truth and subtlety of the religious dogmas at which, as an undergraduate, I used to laugh. "Original sin" that what goodness we have reached is a house built on piles driven into black slime and always slipping down into it unless we are building day and night. "Grace" that wickedness in oneself is not overcome by willing: every day of one's life one learns this, and I at least forget it every day. Religious people say that one [sic] grace enables one to overcome sin. What seems to happen to one is this. As long as one is making an effort to overcome bad temper, one does not get on at all; at least I don't. Bad temper simply gets put on its metal [sic]. But if one relaxes the effort and so to speak, throws oneself flat and lets whatever power there is take possession of one and do with one what it likes, one's mind gets peaceful and smoothed out without a conscious effort. In fact "grace" does what "will" can't—all the discoveries worth making are as old as the hills.[32]

The fourth of the passages that Walzer excerpts—ending with the sentence I have already quoted about the need for a "restatement of principles"—is followed, half a page later, by a passage that seems to be exactly the sort of "clear statement of basic principles" that Walzer says he found in Tawney's writings.

> In order to believe in human equality it is necessary to believe in God. It is only when one contemplates the infinitely great that human differences appear so infinitely small as to be negligeable [sic]. To put it [an] other way, the striking thing about man is that he is only a *little* lower than the angels themselves. When one realizes this it is absurd to emphasize the fact that one man is, even so, lower than another. One can't look a gift cherub in the mouth. What is wrong with the modern world is that having ceased to believe in the greatness of God, and therefore the infinite smallness (or greatness—the same thing!) of *man*, it has to invent or emphasize distinctions between *men*.[33]

Walzer does not include this passage among his *Dissent* excerpts, either. Although it answers the need that he says Tawney's writings answer, here, as elsewhere, Walzer declines to quote Tawney's musings on his own religious life. But notice what Tawney does with this reference to his belief in God. His concern here is not with how he might make an egalitarian argument in public or with how he might discover a warrant of authority for his political ideas. A passage like this might seem to be irrelevant to Walzer's concern, in *Spheres of Justice*, with the articulation and interpretation of a society's shared moral world. Yet the argument of *Spheres* depends on there being people who already hold egalitarian commitments. And exploring the ground on which a person—himself or another—can come to "believe in human equality" is precisely Tawney's purpose here. Tawney introduces something that Walzer's writings allow for but do not directly affirm: a confidence that in speaking of the sacred mystery of ensouled personhood one might find grounds for holding a commitment to human equality. Tawney's theological musings turn out to be not so much private as pre-political, the condition that makes possible his public stances.

Irving Howe's talk on Silone, the companion piece to Walzer's excerpts from Tawney, suggested that socialist politics needs moral grounding and that the way to meet that need is (at least in part) to alter one's own "perspective." Inviting *Dissent* readers to read Tawney, Walzer directed them toward, even if he did not quote, passages with a similar import. It is as if Walzer has assembled a company of ideas and has directed only some of them to appear on stage. Nevertheless, the whole company remains. The milieu from within which Walzer makes his circumscribed arguments draws larger meanings than Walzer avers from the little he says directly about the moral basis of socialism.

Orientation

Rejecting the quest for unassailable warrants of authority, Walzer has nevertheless shown another way of depending on moral foundations. I want to propose a name for that alternative: Walzer, it seems to me, has equipped his readers to see moral foundations as a source of orientation.

By an orientation, I mean a compelling basis for the sort of commitment that can give direction to a person's life (or to a part of a person's life—say, the political part). An orientation is a source of sustainable motivation and guidance that one can depend upon whether or not others join in recognizing that moral foundation as compelling. An orienting foundation might, in principle, be universally valid, but for a particular person to find it compelling it need not be universally, or even widely, acknowledged as valid.

The distinction I want to make between authority and orientation is not quite the same as the distinction between reason and passion: although an orienting foundation may be a source of deeply felt commitment, it is also a matter for thought and argument. The distinction is also not quite that between public and private: although the power of an orienting foundation does not come from its display, recognition of its compelling power may well be shared by many. Nor is the distinction quite that between objective and subjective: we can distinguish orientation from authority while being agnostic regarding whether, or even while believing that, the compelling power of an orienting foundation has a basis more certain than the feelings or perceptions of individuals. Walzer has distinguished between the "knowledge of a poet," which can be "communicated" (if mostly by "intimation") but "never directly implemented," and that of a philosopher, which "can be implemented" because it "lend[s itself] readily to legal embodiment."[34] An orientation is somewhere in between: like the knowledge of poets, it does not lend itself to legal embodiment, but at the same time it is not irrelevant to the quest for ideas to implement; it can be an inspiration for, or an end defining, that quest.

Orientation is a good name for what Tawney finds when interpreting "religious dogmas" with "subtlety" and when thinking about the relationship between belief in equality and belief in God, or for the grounding that Howe finds in Silone's "moral perspective." *Spheres of Justice* does not directly address Tawney's and Howe's concerns with accounting for one's own moral and political orientation. Yet readers of *Spheres of Justice* might nevertheless notice, in and around that book, signs of something like an orientation for egalitarian politics.

At the edges of Walzer's writings, allowed for but not endorsed, emerges an account like the following. At the hidden center of our experiences of selfhood, we can recognize a mystery, or a point of receptivity to mystery, that could be called a soul. In other human persons, we can (somehow) recognize the same. Recognizing ensouled personhood as a (or perhaps the) fundamental thing that human beings have in common, we adopt a moral perspective that directs us toward a politics of solidarity and equality. Doing so, we root our egalitarian commitments in a commonality that can be intimated but that resists explanation or display, like what Wendell Berry has called "connection / Outreaching understanding."[35]

A moral foundation of this sort answers a need that Walzer's works assume and avoids a problem that he fears. Because this kind of moral foundation depends on a mystery rather than on knowledge, it need not be shaken by incomprehensible events or political defeats. Thus it can orient its adherents in their political activities and sustain their enduring political commitments. An orienting mystery can provide the moral basis for a political commitment, but not in the sense that it provides authoritative warrants for public argument. Quite the contrary: a mystery cannot serve as a warrant of authority, precisely because those who recognize it do not claim to understand it. They are certain of the mysterious object of their belief, but they are not able to give a full or precise account either of their certainty or of its object. You can communicate a mystery, but you cannot claim to have come to the end of what can be said about it, and what you are able to say may need to be indirect, more evocation (or invocation) than display. You cannot credibly draw a definitive conclusion from a premise that resists definition. Thus a mystery can be compelling for many people—perhaps even for all—without inviting a singular epistemic authority for its recognition or a singular agent of transformation to enact the politics that follow from it.

Walzer comes close to saying something like this in a coda to the set of interviews from which I have already quoted:

> Perhaps the oldest argument against inequality is the assertion by the writers of the Hebrew bible that all human beings are created in the image of God. This simple sentence resonated in medieval peasant revolts, among radical Protestant reformers, in the American Declaration of Independence, and in the civil rights movement of the 1960s. It still a line that calls upon Americans to live up to what we say we believe. We should keep repeating it, even if some of us have to revise the biblical sentence: all human beings are created in the image of God, *whether or not God exists*.[36]

To find grounds for the principle of equality, Tawney looks to the gulf between God and humanity, Walzer to the likeness between divine and human, the "image." They appeal, in other words, to different texts: for Walzer, the lesson of human equality is taught by Genesis 1 (and perhaps 2) and for Tawney by Genesis 3 and 4. This is a difference worth exploring, but for now I want to focus on what these two readings of Genesis have in common. Walzer, like Tawney, seems to be searching for a teaching about equality that "resonate[s]" with or "calls upon" its hearers. Like Tawney, in other words, he admits here a concern with orientation. And in pondering how one might become oriented, like Tawney he turns to a teaching that, as he recognizes, resists understanding, even to the point of inviting paradox. God appears here not as a ruler whose authority precludes space for politics, but as the source or instigator or guide who makes possible a politics worth pursuing—not a self-evident figure casting an imposing shadow, but someone far more elusive, someone who might seem both a pillar of cloud and a pillar of fire, both a still small voice and a roar.[37]

Reflecting on our creation in the image of God, Walzer nods toward ideas that he has never worked out in public. But what Walzer begins to say in those brief reflections fits within the field of meanings evoked by his remark in *Spheres* about souls and by the texts from Tawney that stand offstage from that book. Walzer makes room for the idea that those committed to equality can speak of the moral foundation that orients their political commitment without claiming to derive authority from that foundation, as long as that foundation is itself a mystery. Must a mystery that orients a commitment to equality be a *sacred* mystery? If I may say so: I don't know. But it seems to me that an egalitarian politics as radical as Walzer's cannot be utterly closed to the sacred; it cannot be strictly and dogmatically secular.[38] That Walzer allows for a link between egalitarian politics and sacred matters is not in itself surprising; others have made similar links.[39] What is noteworthy is that where religious socialism, social gospel theology, and liberation theology have often sought sacred warrants of authority, Walzer instead points to an orienting mystery.

Reviving Socialism

What do we see differently in *Spheres of Justice* if we decide that we can, after all, describe a foundation that fits Walzer's conceptual house? More precisely, what do we see differently if we suppose Walzer's arguments to rest on an anthropology in which the mystery of our ensoulment by God grounds the claim that we should be one another's equals? These questions deserve long and complicated answers. Here, I will simply suggest two places from which to begin: a theme within *Spheres of Justice* that needs more emphasis, and an observation regarding the politics that follow from Walzer's argument for complex equality.

Walzer's list of the features by which we might recognize one another as human ("bodies and minds and feelings and hopes and maybe even souls") moves from things seen to things unseen; each item is less accessible to our senses than the one before. If we take ensoulment to be our most morally consequential common feature, recognizing one another as human will require us to look beyond what is easy to see about one another. Reading *Spheres of Justice* with the soul in mind, we find that if we are to think through the politics of equality, we have to understand the experiences through which we come to recognize one another's humanity.

If, as Walzer writes, "self-respect…is a function of membership," especially of "some substantial connection to the group of members," then respectful recognition of one another must also be a function of such memberships. "In a democratic society," Walzer writes, recognitions of excellence or differences of rank "are easiest at a distance" and are especially easy when those recognitions are "[s]udden and temporary," as in our acknowledgement of "the celebrities-for-a-day created by the mass media."[40] This rings true. But what he implies here is even more interesting than what he says. A contrary sort of recognition, we should expect, will be easiest in contrary circumstances: we will best recognize what we have in common, what makes us equals, when we are up close, in contexts where we can know one another well and for a long time.

Thus Walzer is too even-handed when he writes: "Political community for the sake of provision, provision for the sake of community: the process works both ways…Mutual provision breeds mutuality. So the common life is simultaneously the prerequisite of provision and one of its products." Community is indeed one of our needs, but it is not like other needs. I need community in a sense like that in which I need food or shelter or security or education: to allow for my continued and flourishing life as an individual. But membership in community, especially small and stable (and thus knowable) community, has a meaning that goes beyond the meanings of those other needs. Such membership challenges my tendency to see my own needs as central. It allows, maybe even pushes, my attention beyond my own neediness. Thus it is a condition for my full appreciation of others' humanity, a means of recognition. Ensconced in a close community, I am apt to find intimations of the reality of others' souls. Walzer is no doubt correct to write that since "individual choice is most dependent upon local mobility, this would seem to be the preferred arrangement in a society like our own."[41] Yet our society's preference for mobility undermines our chances of knowing more of one another than what we can see. Even if not a preference they should try to abolish, mobility turns out to be a dynamic that egalitarians must criticize and resist. Membership, mutuality, human-scaled sociability: these things need cultivation and defense, and the need is urgent.

Still, although it is through social encounter that we are best prepared to recognize one another as ensouled creatures, this does not mean that ensoulment is itself a social good. Walzer writes: "All the goods with which distributive justice is concerned are social goods[,] objects of cultural assessment….God's goods, to be sure, are exempt from this rule—as in the first chapter of Genesis: 'and God saw every thing that He had made, and, behold, it was very good' (1:31)." If the human person, made in God's image, is among those divinely-valued goods, and if our recognition of one another as ensouled persons depends, in the end, on God's acts and valuations, then our mutual recognition comes, in the end, from outside the (human) social world. We may learn the meaning of one another's humanity through that social world, but its meaning isn't produced there. Walzer writes in *Spheres of Justice* that his argument there is "radically particularist."[42] But his later notion of a "reiterative universalism" comes closer to accounting for the egalitarian commitment behind or beneath his arguments.[43] With a reiterable approach to the universal as an orienting foundation for moral arguments, we should expect there to always be a gap and a friction between the shared and public valuations of any particular social world and the universal or divinely-acknowledged value that we come to know through those particular approaches, the meaning on which the meanings generated by the social world depend. Perhaps this gap explains those few inches of critical distance that even a connected critic needs.[44]

And that little bit of critical distance does need explanation. Walzer's recent worry about the cultural reproduction of egalitarians seems to me to be well founded: it marks how different the present is from the period in which Walzer developed the ideas of *Spheres*. The kind of political movement appropriate to his vision of complex equality is not the kind most conveniently adapted to the contours of American politics and culture today. Certainly some Americans today are, or are trying to be, egalitarians. But on the whole they have little access to the rudiments of civic life; they are likely to have been acculturated as much by placeless and faceless "social" media as by real meetings and memberships; they are less likely, with each passing decade, to be comfortable thinking outside the confines of secularism. I fear that would-be egalitarians in such a context are likely to be drawn to the idea that Walzer calls "simple" equality: to the extent that they have been formed by a culture devoted to self-expression and individual authenticity, today's egalitarians are likely to treat individual preferences, and thus the meanings of goods, as unquestionable. Whether or not I am right to fear this, it is clear that the political era in which Walzer wrote *Spheres*—one in which the realignment socialists' "coalition strategy" remained an available vehicle for egalitarian politics—is no more. American public life today is not promising soil from which to grow an egalitarian movement capable of what Irving Howe called "steady work."[45]

Spheres of Justice is an invitation to think about equality; it is also an invitation into a way of doing politics. Taking up that dual invitation today means working for a revival of politics per se, for a reversal of the erosion of civic life. It means engaging in the slow, patient, uncertain work of organizing groups capable of bringing members into contact with one another and of coalescing with other groups. This work, in turn, depends on the health of cultural or pre-political life, and tending those things is steady work, too. I suspect that if they are to keep at this work, and if they are to find one another, egalitarians in our time will find it urgently necessary, as perhaps their predecessors did not, to learn how to describe the foundations of their shared political commitments, so that they can comprehend their own critical distance from the society to which they are connected and orient themselves by something more fundamental than themselves. Thus the work that follows from *Spheres* today is not a merely political project: it involves a return to the sources of and background conditions for egalitarian politics. And it may be that better discerning our moral orientations will require us—that is, us who are committed to equality—to acknowledge that at the root of our egalitarian commitments we find a mystery. If this indeed turns out to be the case, we may find ourselves entertaining disruptions to secular habits of thought about what politics is and how it works.

Somehow, we must be able to speak about the moral basis of socialism. What I have tried to show here is that *Spheres of Justice*, read carefully, can help us to do so.

Competing Interests The author has no conflicts of interest to declare that are relevant to the content of this chapter.

Notes

1. Michael Walzer, *Spheres of Justice: A Defense of Pluralism and Equality* (New York: Basic Books, 1983), xi. On equality as non-dominating community, see ibid., xiii.
2. Robert Putnam, *Bowling Alone: The Collapse and Revival of American Community* (New York: Simon and Schuster, 2000); Theda Skocpol, *Diminished Democracy: From Membership to Management in American Civic Life* (Norman: University of Oklahoma Press, 2003). These changes are hardly unique to the United States, but I will focus here on American life.
3. Michael Walzer, "The Pastoral Retreat of the New Left," in *Radical Principles: Reflections of an Unreconstructed Democrat* (New York: Basic Books, 1980), 185.
4. Robert Bellah et al., *Habits of the Heart: Individualism and Commitment in American Life* (New York: Harper and Row, 1985); Charles Taylor, *A Secular Age* (Cambridge: Harvard University Press, 2007); Charles Taylor, *The Ethics of Authenticity* (Cambridge: Harvard University Press, 2018); Michael Walzer, "The Political Theory License," *Annual Review of Political Science* 16:1–9 (May 2013), available at https://www.annualreviews.org/doi/10.1146/annurev-polisci-032211-214411.
5. On the realignment socialists, see Paul Le Blanc and Michael D. Yates, *A Freedom Budget for All Americans: Recapturing the Promise of the Civil Rights Movement in the Struggle for Economic*

Justice Today (New York: Monthly Review Press, 2013); Sam Rosenfeld, *The Polarizers: Postwar Architects of Our Partisan Era* (Chicago: University of Chicago Press, 2018), 224–263; Maurice Isserman, *The Other American: The Life of Michael Harrington* (New York: Public Affairs, 2000), esp. 188–190. I borrow the image of anchoring from Daniel Schlozman, *When Movements Anchor Parties: Electoral Alignments in American History* (Princeton: Princeton University Press, 2016).

6. Harrington, *Long Distance Runner*, 116. I imagine that some of *Spheres*' first readers thought of Harrington when reading the book's first paragraph, which mentions, among other types of egalitarian political leaders, "a popular and inexhaustible speaker who tours the local branches and 'builds the base.'" (Walzer, *Spheres*, xi.)
7. Irving Howe, "Four More Years," *Dissent*, Winter 1985, 6–7.
8. Walzer, *Spheres*, 318.
9. Michael Walzer and Astrid von Busekist, *Justice is Steady Work: A Conversation on Political Theory*. (Cambridge: Polity Press, 2020), 117–118.
10. Michael Walzer, "What Is 'The Good Society'?," *Dissent*, Winter 2009. See also Michael Walzer, "Philosophy and Democracy," in *Thinking Politically: Essays in Political Theory*, ed. David Miller (New Haven: Yale University Press, 2007 [1981]), 1–21.
11. Walzer, *Spheres of Justice*, xiv.
12. Ibid., xii. The "relevant characteristic" Walzer suggests later is that "[w]e are (all of us) culture-producing creatures; we make and inhabit meaningful worlds" (314).
13. Michael Walzer, *The Company of Critics: Social Criticism and Political Commitment in the Twentieth Century* (New York: Basic Books, 1988), ix, 14.
14. Michael Walzer, *Thick and Thin: Moral Argument at Home and Abroad*, 2nd edition (Notre Dame: University of Notre Dame Press, 2019 [1994]), 2, 4, 8.
15. Ibid., 26.
16. See Walzer, *Thick and Thin*, xiii n.1, and Clifford Geertz, "Thick Description: Toward an Interpretive Theory of Culture," in *The Interpretation of Cultures* (New York: Basic Books, 1973), 3–30, esp. 6–7, where Geertz introduces the distinction and notes that he in turn borrowed it from the philosopher Gilbert Ryle. On

Geertz's influence on Walzer, see J. Toby Reiner, *Michael Walzer* (Cambridge: Polity Press, 2020), 12 and 69–71; J. Toby Reiner, "Social Meanings and the Cultural Theory of Goods in Michael Walzer's Ethical Anthropology," *Polity* 48:3 (July 2016), 359–386; Walzer and von Busekist, *Justice is Steady Work,* 145. Geertz is among the people Walzer mentions in the acknowledgements of *Spheres of Justice*, and is quoted once in the book: xvii, 110.

17. Walzer, *Thick and Thin*, xiii.
18. Ibid., 85–104; quotations here are from 98–100.
19. Ibid., 96, 98, 99, 103.
20. Walzer and von Busekist, *Justice is Steady Work*, 133.
21. Walzer, *Thick and Thin*, 100, 101.
22. Walzer, *Spheres of Justice*, xii.
23. Psalm 51:6. I am quoting (both here and below) from the King James Version of the Bible, Walzer's preferred translation: see Michael Walzer, *In God's Shadow: Politics in the Hebrew Bible* (New Haven: Yale University Press, 2021), xvii. Note that this verse is among those for which the Jewish Publication Society Bible (which numbers this verse as Psalm 51:8) adds the footnote "Meaning of Heb. uncertain."
24. Genesis 2:7. Note that in Genesis 2 the living human created by God *is* a soul. Walzer's is the more typical modern usage: a human person *has* a soul. I will follow Walzer's usage here, although I admit to being intrigued by the political implications of the biblical phrasing.
25. I was able to ask Walzer about the phrase "maybe even souls" during a June 2019 conversation. He told me that his purpose in writing it had been to include those with severe mental disabilities among those who are counted as being fully human. Appreciating his purpose, I hope I have made it clear that my interest here is less with Walzer's intentions than with his readers' experiences—especially, his readers forty years after he wrote these words.
26. Irving Howe, "On the Moral Basis of Socialism." *Dissent* (Fall 1981), 491–494. On the 1981 DSOC convention, see "Delegates OK Unity Steps," *Democratic Left,* June 1981 (Vol 9, No 6), 1–5, available at https://www.dsausa.org/files/2019/07/DL-1981-Convention-Coverage.pdf. Walzer had been among the announced speakers at DSOC's founding convention several years

earlier: *Newsletter of the Democratic Left*, October 1973, 6, available at: https://dlarchive.dsausa.org/wp-content/uploads/2019/01/DL_1973_V001_06_final.pdf.

27. Howe, "Moral Basis of Socialism," 491. For Silone's story—which is indeed luminous, but which I won't recount here—see Ignazio Silone, "Visit to a Prisoner" in *Emergency Exit*, trans. Harvey Fergusson II (New York: Harper & Row, 1968 [1965]), 1–7. Howe had also reprinted the story in *Dissent* as a tribute following Silone's death; see Ignazio Silone, "Visit to a Prisoner," *Dissent* (Winter 1979), 26–29.
28. Michael Walzer, "From R.H. Tawney's Commonplace Book," *Dissent* 28: 4 (Fall 1981), pages 487–490. For the original texts, see *R.H. Tawney's Commonplace Book*, ed. and with an introduction by J.M. Winter and D.M. Joslin (Cambridge: Cambridge University Press, 1972), pages 12–15, 30, 34–35, 52–53.
29. Walzer, "From R.H. Tawney," 487.
30. The Harvard course was co-taught with Robert Nozick during the 1970–1971 academic year. Walzer wrote *Spheres* between 1977 and 1983. See Walzer, *Spheres of Justice*, xvii, and Reiner, *Michael Walzer*, 12. Walzer cites Tawney's writings several times in *Spheres of Justice*: see the index to that book, 344.
31. Tawney, quoted in Walzer, "From R.H. Tawney," 488–490.
32. Tawney, *Commonplace Book,* 15. Insertions of "sic" and other bracketed words or letters in quotations from Tawney are those of his editors.
33. Ibid., 53–54.
34. Walzer, "Philosophy and Democracy," 4–5.
35. Wendell Berry, "1979 II. Another Sunday morning comes," in *A Timbered Choir: The Sabbath Poems, 1979–1997* (New York: Counterpoint, 1998), 6.
36. Walzer and von Busekist, *Justice is Steady Work*, 169.
37. Walzer, *In God's Shadow*, xi; Exodus 13:21–22, 1 Kings 19:12, Amos 1:2.
38. Read in this way, Walzer's writings harmonize with the work of his longtime intellectual ally Charles Taylor, who writes of remaining "open to something beyond." See Taylor, *A Secular Age*, 544. On Walzer and Taylor's ties, see Walzer and von Busekist, *Justice is Steady Work*, 29.

39. Note Walzer's own list of those (Tawney among them) who have made such links: Michael Walzer, "Drawing the Line: Religion and Politics," in *Thinking Politically: Essays in Political Theory*, ed. David Miller (New Haven: Yale University Press, 2007 [1999]), 147–148.
40. Walzer, *Spheres*, 278, 254.
41. Ibid., 65, 39.
42. Ibid., 7, xiv.
43. Michael Walzer, "Nation and Universe," in *Thinking Politically: Essays in Political Theory*, ed. David Miller (New Haven: Yale University Press, 2007 [1990]), 183–218.
44. Walzer, *Company of Critics*, 41.
45. Irving Howe, *Steady Work: Essays in the Politics of Democratic Radicalism, 1953–1966* (New York: Harcourt, Brace and World, 1966).

CHAPTER 5

Complex Equality, Political Participation, and Democracy in the Workplace

J. Toby Reiner

The subtitle of *Spheres of Justice* (Walzer 1983) is "a defense of pluralism and equality." Walzer dubs the theory that he advances "complex equality," which is also the title of the book's first chapter (3–30). Given that, many readers—especially those used to the Anglophone political theory of the 1970s and early 1980s—would expect a detailed exploration of the roots of equality and of the conceptualization of it that Walzer advances that considers, among other things, how and in what ways human beings are each other's equals. However, Walzer tells us in the preface to *Spheres* that he cannot answer the question as to which characteristics make us equals,[1] and that the only answer he can give about the respects in which we are equals is the whole book (xii). As a result, many readers have found this aspect of Walzer's work opaque or perplexing, and a substantial literature has developed on the topic of Walzer's egalitarianism. Some critics have denied that Walzer's theory is in fact egalitarian at all. This is because he rejects the notion of equal distribution of money,

J. T. Reiner (✉)
Dickinson College, Carlisle, US
e-mail: reinerj@dickinson.edu

J. T. Reiner (ed.), *Walzer and Justice: Spheres of Justice in the 2020s*,
https://doi.org/10.1007/978-3-031-87809-1_5

or any specific good within a sphere, as "simple equality," (13–17, 95–128), and because these critics believe that his suggestion that political theory proceed by critical interpretation of the shared understandings of particular societies (6–10) has conservative, inegalitarian implications.[2] These claims strike at the heart of Walzer's position, given both that he wrote *Spheres* to defend a version of equality, and that he intended the book as a social-democratic corrective to the liberalism that predominated Anglophone theory.[3]

Other readers have been more sympathetic to Walzer's argument. These readers have often held that complex equality is at root a form of advocacy of equal citizenship and have sought to reconstruct the theory in a way that responds to the critics and establishes Walzer's egalitarianism on a firmer footing.[4] That is, what makes us equals is neither equal or near-equal ownership of resources nor equality of welfare – nor, indeed, entitlement to any particular communal good, for on Walzer's account inequality in any one sphere is compatible with complex equality so long as those inequalities do not mount up across the spheres (Walzer 1983: 10–17; for discussion, Miller 1995: 206–07)[5]—but equal status as members of a political community.

In this paper, I argue that although these readers succeed in establishing Walzer's egalitarian credentials, their accounts tend to lose some of the distinctive flavor of Walzer's social-democratic brand of egalitarianism. I will hold that Walzerian equality is primarily about shared or joint participation in a project of collective self-governance, rather than about status. It is not for nothing that Walzer begins *Spheres* by considering whether egalitarian movements betray their ideals when they elect secretaries, press attachés, and speakers (Walzer 1983: xi). After all, in the years in which Walzer developed the argument of *Spheres*, he was not only an academic, but also a committed participant in the civil-rights movement and a regular contributor to public-intellectual magazines, most notably *Dissent*, which he edited from 1975 until 2013. Indeed, one of his first books was a guide to movement politics.[6] Thus, central to Walzer's vision is that equality emerges out of participation, or at least opportunities for participation, in communities determining collectively the decisions by which they shall live. This is because of the social-democratic principle that, "*What touches all should be decided by all*" (Walzer 1983: 292; see also Walzer 1980: 279–94). Walzerian equality is primarily about decision-making power, whereas equality of status is a function of the way in which individuals are treated by society and the state and treat each other. For example, Miller notes that the egalitarian ideal is that "people's behavior toward one another is not conditioned by differences of rank" and that inequalities within spheres "do not crystallize into judgements of overall personal worth" (Miller 1995: 208). This is certainly an important aspect of egalitarianism, but for Walzer's theory what is more important than the way in which people treat each other is how that treatment affects our ability to act—to avoid "bowing and scraping, fawning and toadying" (Walzer 1983: xiii)—and how it contributes to the creation of democratic communities.

To demonstrate the last point, I argue that Walzer's defense of workplace democracy is fundamental to understanding his conception of equality and the underlying principle that decisions should be made collectively. In *Spheres*, Walzer argues for the extension of principles of political democracy beyond the sphere of the state to workplaces—and on to industrial organization as a whole—to ensure that workers have rights to participate in decision-making within the firm to prevent authoritarian government at work (Walzer 1983: 291–303).[7] By insisting that corporations cannot be personal property because they are political organizations in which power is exercised and must thus be shared, Walzer shows that we abolish relations of domination and subordination, and bowing and scraping, by granting to all rights to participate in the common life of society as it makes collective decisions through its political institutions. For Walzer, "democracy and socialism are, roughly speaking, the same thing," (Walzer 1980: 17) because both ensure that all members of a political community can participate as equals in the governance structures of their common life, if they so choose. Equal citizenship is not merely a question of social status or of treatment, but of opportunities for participation in projects of collective self-governance.

This reconceptualization of Walzer's argument showcases the contribution that *Spheres* makes to theorizing equality in two ways. First, although Walzer himself states that the "root meaning of equality is negative" and that "egalitarianism in its origins is an abolitionist politics," (Walzer 1983: xii), and his account has thus been understood as "n-equality," or the removal of hierarchies,[8] there is a positive or activist vision alongside or underneath this. Where n-equality works to abolish subordination, "p-equality" helps it to do so by replacing hierarchy with egalitarian, democratic communities that enable and actualize both the self-respect and the mutual respect of their citizens and members (Walzer 1983: 276–77). Moreover, this is a vision of equality not based on any sort of metric—be that metric welfare, resource ownership, need, or desert—for equality is not an "objective condition,"[9] but a "complex relation of persons" (Walzer 1983: 18).

Second, it shows how Walzer's social-democratic vision of equality is distinct from both analytical liberalism and much of the post-Marxism and post-modernism of contemporary theory. In understanding equality in participatory or communitarian terms, Walzer breaks with the vision common to many liberalisms of people as equal by virtue of their ownership of possessions and that sees equality as compatible with a private life that is withdrawn from the community. However, his account retains liberalism's sense of the importance of personal life, for Walzer breaks with "participatory democracy" in emphasizing the importance of people's rights *not* to participate politically if they do not wish to do so.[10] Social-democratic equality is a communitarian liberal conception that emphasizes more than does the liberalism of the Rawlsian tradition and many other liberalisms the values of public, collective life. Bearing in mind Walzer's most recent work on liberalism as an adjective, it is better to call social democracy "liberal communitarianism" or "liberal social democracy" rather than "communitarian liberalism."[11]

Walzer on Equality

The starting point for Walzer's analysis of equality is the claim that most philosophical egalitarians defend what he calls "simple equality" (Walzer 1983: 13–17), to which his complex equality is a corrective. Walzer considers a conception of equality to be simple if it argues for the redistribution of some good that is widely valued socially such that more citizens have access to the good in question and ownership of it is more widely shared. Egalitarians in a capitalist society often focus on redistributive taxation such that the state ensures a more equal (or less unequal) distribution of wealth than would occur in an unregulated market economy. Similarly, egalitarians in the old communist regimes in Eastern Europe tried to break the power of party apparatchiks by democratizing political processes such that power was more widely distributed (15–16).[12] 'Walzer accepts that some forms of redistribution of both wealth and political power will be necessary for the development of complex equality, but he insists that redistribution cannot ensure equality, and that this holds even if it is extended to some small set of social goods, rather than focusing on a master good. Moreover, he argues that *some* inequality in the holding of goods is compatible with an egalitarian society and with distributive justice.

This is because, Walzer holds, inequality is not, at its core about the monopolization of goods, but about the domination of people that ownership of goods entails. Domination occurs when a social good becomes the key good in a particular society, as capital or wealth is the foremost good in capitalism, and leadership positions within the ruling party were in Soviet-era communism. If a good is dominant, then those who possess it, who may indeed have a legitimate claim to more of that good, are able to dominate others, using possession of the dominant good to ensure access to other goods to which they have no such entitlement. For example, nepotism and cronyism occur when someone entitled to a particular office uses their influence to help their relatives or friends obtain similar positions to which those recipients are not entitled. Walzer argues that the gravest threat to equality is dominance, not monopoly, because when goods are dominant, their possession enables the sort of overall domination that permits the establishment of relations of oppression and subordination. Moreover, preventing monopolization is an unending task that requires perpetual state action: any redistribution of money that ensured equal ownership would be undone within moments by people's use of their money (Walzer 1983: xi; for discussion, Reiner 2020: 60–70).

Walzer's argument echoes the libertarian critique of equality advanced by his friend Robert Nozick. Nozick argued that equal possession of money is a condition that cannot last, because people will use the money redistributed to them in different ways, and that ignores people's relationships with particular goods to which they have special entitlement.[13] Nozick claimed that egalitarian theories are thus incompatible with a free society, because they require perpetual government action to uphold egalitarian distribution, and that they cannot account for individual merit (Nozick 1974: 149–50, 161–64).[14] However, Walzer counters that, while periodic redistribution to prevent the gravest forms of monopolization will aid the egalitarian project, perpetual redistribution to ensure exactly equal holdings is unnecessary if we can prevent goods from becoming dominant. This will happen if goods are distributed for reasons internal to the good themselves, and that reflect the good's social meaning. Walzer's argument draws on Bernard Williams,[15] who, in considering the question of what equality means between people whose circumstances are unequal, argued that differential treatment is compatible with equality, provided reasons are given for the difference that are both relevant and socially operative.[16] Walzer applies this argument to the distribution of goods, and develops a principle of distribution for right reasons, based on the claim that, "If we understand what [a good] is, what it means to those for whom it is a good, we understand how, by whom, and for what reasons it ought to be distributed," with each social sphere emphasizing different reasons because of the different relationships developed therein (Walzer 1983: 9). Thus, Walzer argues, healthcare should be distributed on the grounds of need—that is, of ill health—offices to the qualified, love to those able to inspire it, and so on. Reasons that might be entirely appropriate to the distribution of one good will be inappropriate to that of others, which means that inequalities in each sphere should not carry over into others. Walzer formulates the principle in characteristically negative terms: "*No social good x should be distributed to men and women who possess some other good y merely because they possess y and without regard to the meaning of x*" (Walzer 1983: 19–20). Those with a capitalist green thumb may legitimately own more commodities than do others, so long as they do not for that reason also control political power, avoid hard or dirty work, claim free time that is unavailable to others (especially when they are the ones denying time off to others), and buy what passes for love and respect. When goods are distributed for reasons related to their meaning, Walzer claims, inequality in relation to any particular good does not affect equality overall because it is unlikely to mount up across the goods. If it did so, that would be the best reason we could have for believing that a society of equals is not a live possibility (Walzer 2007:90–92). That is, when talents appear to be unequal overall, that is *probably* the knock-on effect of possession of society's dominant goods (83–85). Jane Austen's Emma might be "handsome, clever and rich" (Austen 2003: 1),[17] but her intelligence and her looks are probably at least in part byproducts of her family's ability to pay for her education, cosmetics, and the time to apply them. Even if some individuals are preternaturally gifted, social equality can still ensue so long as there is neither a dominant class, nor an underclass (Walzer 2007: 87–90).

What underlies these arguments is that, for Walzer, equality is not about possession of goods, but about the nature of the relationships between citizens. Possession matters where it affects the tenor of that relationship. Redistribution of wealth is necessary in a capitalist society because vast inequalities enable the wealthy to exercise undue influence on the electoral process and to make a mockery of equal citizenship.

Thus, Walzer argued both before and after *Spheres* that until the dominance of money is seriously challenged, wealth must be roughly equal (Walzer 1980: 248; Walzer 2007: 74–75). However, equality of wealth is necessary as a precondition of equal citizenship and is less important in and of itself. Walzer argues that ownership of commodities – those things for which we would use money in a world of complex equality (Walzer 1983: 103–08), while the purchase of many other goods was "blocked" (100–103)—*must* be unequal if we are to allow people to choose their own version of a pleasant life (106–08). This makes it an open question whether redistribution of wealth would be necessary at all in a world of complex equality, in which only commodities were for sale. What is more important than redistribution is preventing the use of money to purchase things outside the sphere of commodities or the marketplace, because on Walzer's notion of distribution for right reasons, those are goods that should be distributed for different reasons than ability to pay. Nepotism is one such example, but Walzer's favorite is medical care, the meaning of which is health and longevity, and the distribution of which should thus be according to need (Walzer 1983: 86–91).[18] Ensuring that goods that are not commodities are not bought or sold requires a series of "blocked exchanges" preventing the sale of such things as people, political power, basic welfare, and exemptions from civic service (Walzer 1983: 100–03). The purpose of blocking certain transactions, even if they are ostensibly freely exchanged,[19] is to reduce the dominance of money and so to undermine the ability of the wealthy to use their wealth to dominate others. Similarly, Walzer argues that certain uses of political power should be blocked to prevent domination by the inner caucus of a ruling party (Walzer 1983: 282–84).

The point is that equalization within any one sphere is neither necessary nor sufficient to ensure equality on Walzer's account, nor is it desirable, for if goods are distributed according to their meaning, the different ways in which we stand in relation to goods and other people mean that some must have more than others. In some spheres, Walzer claims, simple equality is a "bad joke" (Walzer 1983: 255). For example, we cannot envisage a society in which all are equally famous and worthy of recognition, and Walzer thus rejects egalitarian liberal arguments against merit or desert in theories of justice (Walzer 2007: 304).

Equal Citizenship and "N-Equality"

The reason that, in a capitalist society, wealth should be equalized is not that everyone ought to possess the same bundle of resources but that it is a prerequisite politically if "we are to stand to one another as *fellow* citizens" (Walzer 2007: 74). Citizenship is indeed therefore integral to Walzer's conception of equality, as noted by the commenters discussed above (see endnote 4). It is foundational to citizenship status, at least on contemporary conceptions of citizenship, that it be in at least some important respects equal. When the United Kingdom granted two votes to university graduates, that meant that some voters had less than full citizenship status and were subject to the political domination of the educated classes.[20] That is, on Walzer's logic, a university degree should not grant its holders extra political influence (but should grant its holders some privileges, such as access to events at the university).

Likewise, the emphasis on what Mayer calls "n-equality" (Mayer 2002)—the removal of hierarchical relations—is central to Walzerian equality. Indeed, we saw that the notion of distribution for right reasons is best formulated in negative terms, for its purpose is not to outline any definite set of distributive principles that are relevant to a particular good, but, rather, to insist that extraneous reasons not intervene. Walzer holds that the range of social meanings is extremely wide[21]; even a good with a meaning that seems to be both obvious and natural, such as bread, may in fact be not only "the staff of life" but also "the body of Christ, the symbol of the Sabbath, [and] the means of hospitality" (Walzer 1983: 8). Even that list considers only those meanings drawn from the parts of the world in which the influence of Judaism, Christianity, and Islam is considerable. Yet while formulating the doctrine in positive terms might not give us much yield as to whether to treat bread as food stuff, religious symbol, or means of social lubrication, formulating it in negative terms helps to clarify that bread should not be a means of extracting political influence in a way that subverts democratic processes. In Walzer's account, all that a theory of justice can do is clarify the terms of public debate—any more determinate intervention within it would violate democratic prerogative.[22]

Hence, those readings of Walzer that see complex equality as fundamentally about removing barriers to equal citizenship point to something crucial to the political vision of *Spheres*. However, there is a positive vision that sits alongside n-equality. The starting point for uncovering it involves noting that Walzerian citizenship is not only about equality but also about *fellowship*. Thus, in considering what complex equality might look like in the contemporary United States, Walzer's first requirement is "a shared economic, social, and cultural infrastructure, a public sector that both enlarges the scope of and gives determinate shape to our private lives" (Walzer 2007: 69; see also Walzer 1983: 318). Simple equality—that is, equalization of ownership within any particular sphere that ends the monopolization of the goods within that sphere—is appropriate in some spheres and inappropriate in others, but it cannot produce overall equality because it does not contribute to the greater fellowship that is an integral aspect of citizenship. Simple equality is also insufficiently pluralistic, for it fails to allow different goods to be distributed for reasons internal to themselves that reflect social relationships not prevalent across society. Equalizing wealth in American society without enhancing the shared infrastructure would fail to encourage "participation within a familiar world; [with] institutions...built to a human scale" (Walzer 1980: 272).

Participation is crucial for the complex egalitarian project, because people are not autonomous individuals whose highest-order interest is in framing, pursuing, and, if necessary, revising a vision of the good life[23] that is theirs to define privately, unless they wish to do so in collaboration with others. As a result, an egalitarian vision that does not promote political participation cannot achieve complex equality, because such a vision would leave a "benevolent elite" organizing social distribution (Walzer 1980: 17). This is why Walzer says at the start of *Spheres* that most theories of distributive justice wrongly describe the process of distribution thus: "*People distribute goods to other people.*" His preferred description is "*People conceive and create goods, which they then distribute among themselves*" (Walzer 1983: 6), because this foregrounds the importance of active participation in communal life, emphasizing both that goods are social products and that we are all involved in the processes of social distribution. Fellowship and participation are necessary, on Walzer's account, because "[People] live in groups and always find that they have limited choices, and share, without having chosen, social standards. If they are ever to be free to choose new limits and standards, they must do so in some cooperative fashion, arguing among themselves, reaching a common decision. But to do this...they must share political power" (Walzer 1980: 37). Without argument within the group, new standards will not be chosen but imposed. Without participation, then, we can have the same amount of money—or, as Walzer quips, the same number of hats (Walzer 1983: 18)—but not equality, for relations of domination and submission may continue, as those with political power determine distributive principles for those without. Walzer's conception of equality is thus reliant on a defense of democracy. Moreover, this applies not only to the institutions of the state but to any sphere of human life in which people exercise power over others.

Democracy in the Workplace: Citizenship as Equal Rights to Participation

Walzer has argued for the extension of democracy from the institutions of the state to other spheres in which power is exercised, most notably the workplace, on several occasions (Walzer 1983: 291–303; 1970a: 24–45; 1980: 273–90; 2007: 76–79; 2009). In *Spheres*, his discussion of workplace democracy is the heart of his account of the sphere of political power. His fundamental argument on power is a defense of limited government. Arguing that an overbearing state "makes for the subordination of [all] other companies," Walzer holds that limited government is, along with blocked exchanges, one of the crucial means of ensuring the realization of complex equality (Walzer 1983: 282–84). He thus advocates a series of blocked uses of political power, including standard liberal-democratic principles such as bans on the sale of political power, on nepotism and cronyism, and on state control over religion, marriage, and belief systems. Walzer's argument extends these liberal principles beyond the state to the workplace, on the grounds that failure to make sure an extension makes possible "private government" in the firm (293). Walzer later claimed that failure to make this extension is where "the leftist complaint against liberalism properly begins" (Walzer 2007: 59). The left notices that liberalism tends to operate with a formal conception of equality, rather than a substantive one, and aims to complete the liberal project by extending the liberal "art of separation" to the economic sphere, thus ensuring that the liberal limitations on political power extend to limits on economic power (Walzer 2007: 59–61). Thus, although Walzer situates his account of workplace democracy—and the broader industrial democracy of which it is a part—within an account of political power, rather than within the sphere of money and commodities (Walzer 1983: 95–128), it is in fact about what we usually understand as economic issues. This is because Walzer's crucial point is that decision-making within the workplace and within industrial organizations are matters of power and, so, that economic power is ultimately political in nature.

This is because politics is about decision-making power, especially those decisions with significant impact on people's lives. Given that people spend a substantial proportion of their lives at work, questions of allocation of time, or project management, or benefits, or pay are among the most important issues to workers, and many of them also affect people's lives outside work. This makes them political. Thus, Walzer insists that capitalism is not merely exploitative but also involves the establishment of private government, by which he means a situation in which managers command, workers obey, and unequal power makes a mockery of the claim that managers and workers are equal citizens (Walzer 2007: 77–8).[24] This is especially so within the modern corporation, where owners and their agents make decisions that determine costs and risks for their workers and that prompt the formation of trade unions to represent those who are subject to this corporate power. Authoritarian rule in the workplace makes equal citizenship a chimera because it easily slips over into domination outside work. When workers and managers attend meetings of their local town council, for example, and the manager gives a powerful speech expressing her view of an issue, the worker is easily put under pressure to vote in accordance with the manager's wishes. Moreover, he can be further induced by carrots or sticks at work.

To illustrate the operation of workplace power and its similarity to power usually recognized as political, Walzer discusses the case of railroad entrepreneur George Pullman and the town he created: Pullman, Illinois (Walzer 1983: 295–303).[25] In Walzer's account, Pullman bought up land that surrounded his business venture, and used that land to build a city that he designed down to the last detail and that he treated as his property. This meant that he owned all businesses in the town and set the rules for both them and the entire town. For example, he controlled the ability of tenants to renovate their homes and gave leases that he could terminate at ten days' notice. In addition, he regulated the ways in which inhabitants dressed and behaved, and if new residents did not live up to these expectations, took steps to compel them to do so, including fining them for breaches. He regulated religious worship, allowing just one church in the town, though permitting religious minorities to rent private rooms for their own religious services. Pullman maintained the city to a high standard of repair, and he kept rents low and wages high, while making relatively low profit margins. However, Walzer comments, "Pullman was an autocrat," who viewed government as "a property right," and made all decisions as governor-owner of Pullman (Walzer 1983: 296–97).

Walzer argued that because Pullman's ownership of the town was undemocratic, it denied its residents rights of citizenship, instead treating them as guest-workers (297). Walzer had argued earlier in *Spheres* that the guest-worker programs of states such as Sweden and West Germany in the 1970s were undemocratic, because the guest workers lacked political rights (56–61). He also notes that the Illinois Supreme Court ordered the Pullman Company to divest itself of all non-manufacturing businesses in 1898 on the grounds that towns must be run democratically because ownership forced residents to fight for the rights that their American citizenship already granted them (297–98). Concurring with the decision, Walzer argues that "political foundation and public service [do] not give a man the right to tyrannize over others" (Walzer 1980: 283). Ownership of land does not entail the right to decide how residents live, because if it did there could be no local self-government.

However, where the Court held that similar principles do not apply within firms, Walzer dissents, holding that power in factories is importantly analogous to power in cities. What makes firms like polities is that both are collective endeavors, places "not of rest and intimacy but cooperative action," such that domination within those endeavors makes for "the displacement of collective decision making, by the power of property" (Walzer 1983: 300). This means that the extent and entailments of property rights are important political issues. If we are to keep property rights within their rightful sphere—that of money and commodities – we must ensure that they do not infringe on politics; that is, on collective decision-making. This requires that "property should have no political currency" (298), and that requires democracy within the workplace such that owners and their managers do not dominate decision-making processes. Moreover, workplace democracy must extend beyond the firm to the local and even to the national level. Examples of such institutional structures include the former Yugoslavia, Catalonia in the 1930s, and contemporary conglomerates such as Mondragon.[26] This also suggests that arguments for workplace democracy can extend to critique of private property rights per se, with worker-owned cooperatives replacing corporations and businesses owned by a small group of shareholders or listed on stock exchanges.[27]

To put this argument in the terms of the theory of complex equality, Walzer argues that the exerciser of power is a political act. If so, then given the thesis that the distribution of a good should depend on the meaning of that good, it follows that entrepreneurs should not exercise power because they own property without regard to the meaning of, and therefore the appropriate distributive principle for, political power. For Walzer, power exists to safeguard a community, and to enable its inhabitants to govern their common life in accordance with their preferred interpretation of the shared understandings or social meanings of their community (Walzer 1983: 281–85). Power in the workplace must thus be arranged for the benefit of the workplace community, not that of owners and managers alone. Structuring workplace power in such a way helps avoid the domination of workers and their reduction to the status of clients or vassals. Walzer's argument is a core part of his social-democratic theory in that it seeks to convert liberalism's formal conception of equality into a more substantive version by extending the liberal art of separation to all parts of social life and completing the project of limited government. Workplace and industrial democracy, including space for worker-owned cooperatives, are thus a core part of Walzerian "strong democracy" (Walzer 2007: 76–79).[28]

We gain greater purchase on Walzer's account by considering his earlier statement of the argument in *Obligations* (1970). That book was set against the backdrop of emerging advocacy of civil disobedience during the civil-rights movement and the campaigns against the American war in Vietnam.[29] Walzer compares industrial action such as strikes to civil disobedience to insist that the former be non-revolutionary (though not necessarily non-violent) in that such action must respect the rights of owners to property and profit but deny that those rights entail absolute power in the workplace, instead advocating democracy as the means of ensuring worker dignity (Walzer 1970: 26–30). Because "ownership of property always entails governmental powers," owners and their officials must be "responsible to the larger community" (32–33). For example, Walzer holds that, in the General Motors strike of 1936–37, strikers could legitimately object to the absolute authority that corporate officials held over hiring and dismissal, work conditions and speed, and pay, and insists that because the power structure was nondemocratic, workers could legitimately disobey any order (41).

It is important to note that Walzer's position does not rest primarily on the exploitative nature of working conditions in the General Motors factories, but on the non-democratic nature of decision-making therein. Whereas if the issue were the working conditions, government regulation might suffice as a solution, because the key question is decision-making power, regulation will not suffice. Regulation would reduce exploitation but leave workers in a position of clientage, rendering them fortunate recipients of state largesse, rather than enabling them to become participants in a scheme of collective self-government that helps them to seek their own good together with others. Regulation, that is, cannot ensure political equality in the absence of worker voice. Voice and participation are necessary because "action is the crucial language of moral commitment" (Walzer 1970: 98). Equality is achievable only through the long-term, committed, public-spirited activity of groups of citizens trying to improve their shared life by finding particular solutions to particular problems. The sort of action that Walzer has in mind is what his *Dissent* predecessor Irving Howe called "steady work," which involves a long series of incremental changes mounting up over time into a systemic overhaul that could effectively constitute revolutionary change.[30]

However, while active participation is an essential tool for the achievement of complex equality, and while liberalism's argument for limited power needs the supplement of social-democratic commitment to the view that economic power is political, these are supplements to, not replacements for, representation. Thus, Walzer is ambivalent about the "participatory democracy" of the student movement in the 1960s, which he believed to be insufficiently accepting of the need for representation. Supporting the rights of citizens to choose *not* to participate, he suggests that Oscar Wilde's quip that socialism would take too many evenings is the key criticism of it (Walzer 1980: 128).[31] Forced participation would replace commitment with coercion. There is a tension here, for if people do not participate politically, they cannot ensure their status as equal citizens because they are at the whim of powerful actors. Yet people are always free to deny themselves their status as equals. As Walzer later put it, there are circumstances in which people may use their agency to deny their own status as agents and to insist on their subordinate status—but because their subordination depends on their choice, they are always partially free subjects who can reject their subordination whenever they choose (Walzer 2007: 47–50, discussing female subordination). That said, this tension does point to a significant feature of complex equality: it is always a project that is in the process of being made and can never be completed. As equality depends on people's active participation as citizens in a project of collective self-governance determining the shape of a common life, and as people have the right to act as kibitzers who refuse to participate, we can always move closer to equality but never finally reach it, once and for all (compare with Walzer 2018: 115, which makes the same point about the achievement of justice).

Walzer's Critics

Walzer's argument on workplace democracy has received significant criticism, even from some generally sympathetic to *Spheres*. Michael Rustin notes that the argument for limiting power in the workplace seems at odds with contemporary shared understandings, especially in the United States, where an "overwhelming consensus" favors property rights over the political rights of workers.[32] Moreover, Rustin argues, talk of separate spheres is misleading here, while blocking exchanges and uses of power would not establish greater parity between political and economic power (Rustin 1995: 34–35). Robert Mayer develops a version of the claim about spheres in the fullest criticism of Walzer, arguing that workplace democracy constitutes a form of simple equality at odds with the theory of complex equality, because it would allow the logic of the political sphere to dominate the economic sphere by interfering with the marketplace.[33] Mayer argues that government regulation of the firm is legitimate but that it should not interfere with the structure of workplace decision-making, as that would constitute interference with property rights and thus an illegitimate boundary crossing between spheres.

I think that the argument that workplace democracy is at odds with contemporary beliefs points to something important, but also misinterprets Walzer's appeal to common understandings. What it offers is a partial explanation of why the decades since *Spheres* have drifted even further away from worker rights and ownership in the direction of an unregulated workplace, leading to ever increasing profit margins for owners, larger salaries for managers and executive officers, and lower pay and more contingent work for most workers. This is especially the case in recent years, with the development of a "gig economy," in which workers do not have just one full-time job, but several part-time contracts, often lacking such benefits as pensions or retirement contributions and, in the United States, healthcare insurance. From a Walzerian perspective, these developments showcase the ever-increasing importance of curbing corporate power to prevent domination. However, they also raise vexed questions about his case for workplace democracy and employee ownership, both because it is especially difficult to imagine what democracy might look like in a workplace in which people have different stakes and because it is increasingly difficult to claim that workers value political community in the workplace and thus that employee rights are in accord with contemporary shared understandings.[34]

Yet Walzer's claim is not that goods should be distributed in the way in which people currently believe that they should be distributed, but that they should be distributed in accordance with their social meaning.[35] That is, Walzer does not argue that contemporary Americans believe that workplaces ought to be organized democratically, but that such organization is an implication of what Americans do believe about the nature of political power combined with his claim that workplace authority is a form of political power. If that is so, then the crucial issue is the second one, for Walzer's case does not in fact hinge on what people currently think about workplace power. Moreover, Walzer's argument for the importance of social criticism as a path to complex equality leans on the argument about hegemony of the Italian socialist Antonio Gramsci, which recognizes that popular beliefs often reflect the interests of the ruling class and thus point in inegalitarian directions.[36] However, Walzer argues, it is possible for social criticism to uncover a deeper, more egalitarian interpretation of our set of social meanings, including one in which workplaces are political and should be organized democratically.[37]

The crux of the debate, then, is whether workplace power is political or economic. Since Walzer wrote *Spheres*, scholars such as Elizabeth Anderson have extended his case that it is political by noting how employers continue to control the lives of employees both inside and outside the workplace.[38] When employees have to wear adult diapers to work because they are not allowed toilet breaks during 12-hour shifts, and when employees can be fired for their political speech on Twitter and other social media, the claim that employers rule their employees' lives seems on firm ground. Critics suggest that even if workplaces are political, power therein is also consensual: by joining an enterprise, workers agree to its decision-making structures (Mayer 2001: 250). Walzer counters that we do not accept such an argument for towns or polities, and that as the danger of oppression and exploitation is present in firms, too, it must be rejected there as well (Walzer 1980: 285–86). It is of course the case that the costs of leaving a firm are not the same as those of leaving a polity, but the difference is not necessarily one of degree, given the dependence of workers on income for their continued existence.

I cannot, of course, resolve the debate about the relationship between political and economic power, but the point is that Walzer's arguments for workplace democracy help us gain purchase on complex equality and, thus, of Walzer's contribution to the political-theory debate about egalitarian justice. For, on Walzer's account, what makes both individual wealth and, especially, corporate power forms of political power that ought to be subjected to the same distributive limitations as are governmental prerogatives is that they are all social forces (Walzer 2007: 59). Wealth creation is never an individual accomplishment alone but always something dependent on social structures. Moreover, market success enables capture or cooption of government in the strict sense. This is integral to Walzer's account of social democracy as a corrective of forms of liberalism that do not provide similar emphasis on the social nature of market power, for characteristic of social democracy is, in Walzer's account, its grounding in the group nature of political and moral life (Walzer 1980: 37). This is the crux of his criticisms of those forms of liberalism dominant in political theory when he wrote *Spheres*, which Walzer views as insufficiently grounded in communal traditions and as aspiring to too great a degree of universality. The upshot is that they treat individuals as more atomized than they in fact are,[39] and downplay the importance of opportunities for political participation. That is why, while Walzer's theory of complex equality does indeed have at its heart the notion of equal citizenship, I think we understand it better if we call it equal participation. Citizenship is in its origins, and in many contemporary understandings, an active status, but today it tends to be understood as referring primarily to our status as private individuals, insisting on our equal rights, and, withdrawn into our own little orbits, wanting simply to be left alone by the state and other social institutions rather than seeking to influence our common life.

Conclusion

Although complex equality is in part about abolition of hierarchies, Walzer's vision also include a positive depiction of active participation in a society of equals deliberating about a common life. It is because of the importance of members determining their own understanding of the good life that Walzer's views are indeterminate at points, and why political projects are in his account always being worked out and never completed. The theory of *Spheres* is, like much of Walzer's work, "perhaps best understood as a defense of politics" against the "traditional philosophical dislike for politics" shared by utilitarianism and rights theory alike.[40] In 1983, the latter was dominant among theories of justice. More recently, numerous scholars often dubbed "realist" have echoed Walzer's call for a more politically engaged approach that leaves greater room for democratic decision-making and does not seek to resolve political debates.[41] I am not sure that the label is fully applicable to Walzer's position, and it is certainly an unfortunate moniker, given that one of his most famous arguments is a critique of realism in just-war theory.[42] But to the extent that there is overlap between the positions, Walzer's insistence that democracy extend beyond the state to the workplace foreshadows important developments in insisting that many decisions that we do not often take to be political ought in fact to be seen as revolving around questions of the distribution of political power. This is one of many examples of the way in which Walzer's socially situated approach, rooted in the attempt to answer pressing political concerns, leads him to consider important topics years and often decades before they become part of mainstream Anglo-American political theory.[43]

Competing Interests The author has no conflicts of interest to declare that are relevant to the content of this chapter.

Notes

1. Walzer does note that he will suggest one relevant characteristic in the conclusion. This turns out to be that we are all "culture-producing creatures" who "make and inhabit meaningful worlds." See Michael Walzer, *Spheres of Justice: A Defense of Pluralism and Equality* (New York: Basic Books, 1983), 314. The claim that the production of culture is perhaps the only universal human characteristic is certainly integral to the argument of *Spheres*. I have elsewhere called it the "social-meaning thesis" at J. Toby Reiner, *Michael Walzer* (Cambridge: Polity Press, 2020), 64–65, 69–75, and defended it against Walzer's critics at J. Toby Reiner, "Social Meanings and the Cultural Theory of Goods in Michael Walzer's Ethical Anthropology," *Polity* 48 (2016): 359–86. A fuller account of Walzer's egalitarianism would consider this topic at

greater length than I do here. Because I think it relates mostly to Walzer's pluralism, it is not the crux of this paper.

2. Influential critics who make these points include George Kateb, "Walzer's Radicalism," in *Reading Walzer* [RW], ed. Yitzhak Benbaji and Naomi Sussmann (New York: Routledge, 2014): 196–221; Richard Arneson, "Against 'Complex Equality'," in *Pluralism, Justice, and Equality* [PJE], ed. David Miller and Michael Walzer (New York: Oxford University Press, 1995): 226–52; Nancy Rosenblum, "Moral Membership in a Postliberal State," *World Politics* 36 (1984): 581–96; Ronald Dworkin, "To Each His Own," *New York Review of Books* 30 (1983): 4–6; Joshua Cohen, "Book Review: *Spheres of Justice: A Defense of Pluralism and Equality*," *Journal of Philosophy* 83 (1986): 457–66; Brian Barry, "Social Criticism and Political Philosophy," *Philosophy and Public Affairs* 19 (1990): 360–73; Lawrie Balfour, "The Appeal of Innocence: Baldwin, Walzer, and the Bounds of Social Criticism," *Review of Politics* 61 (1999): 373–401; and Norman Daniels, "Book Review: *Spheres of Justice: A Defense of Pluralism and Equality*," *Philosophical Review* 94 (1985): 142–48. For references to other texts that make points in this vein, see Reiner 2016, 2020.
3. Walzer 1983: xviii; see also Michael Walzer, "In Defense of Equality," in his *Radical Principles: Reflections of an Unreconstructed Democrat* (New York: Basic Books, 1980): 237–56, and "Liberalism and the Art of Separation" and "Justice Here and Now," both in his *Thinking Politically: Essays in Political Theory* (New Haven: Yale University Press, 2007): 53–67 and 68–80, respectively.
4. Influential versions of this argument include David Miller, "Complex Equality," in Miller and Walzer 1995: 197–225; Tim Scanlon, "Plural Equality," in Benbaji and Sussmann 2014: 183–95; Govert Den Hartogh, "The Architectonic of Michael Walzer's Theory of Justice," *Political Theory* 27 (1999): 491–522; Robert Van der Veen, "The Adjudicating Citizen: On Equal Membership in Walzer's Theory of Justice," *British Journal of Political Science* 29 (1999): 225–58; Adam Swift, "The Sociology of Complex Equality," in Miller and Walzer 1995: 253–80; and Marcus Agnafors, *Justice Among Us: A Philosophical Analysis of Michael Walzer's Theory of Justice* (Linkoping: Linkoping University Press, 2010). However, see Margo Trappenburg, "In Defence of Pure

Pluralism: Two Readings of Walzer's *Spheres of Justice*," *Journal of Political Philosophy* 8 (2000): 343–62 for an account that rejects the view that equal citizenship is a master norm underlying Walzer's division of social life into separate spheres of justice.

5. Walzer elaborates on this claim in "Exclusion, Injustice, and the Democratic State" in Walzer 2007: 81–95. For Walzer's response to the equal citizenship reading, see his "Response" in Miller and Walzer 1995: 281–97.
6. Michael Walzer, *Political Action: A Practical Guide to Movement Politics* (Chicago: Quadrangle Press, 1971).
7. Walzer has made this argument in several other places, too. See Walzer 1980: 273–90; Michael Walzer, *Obligations: Essays on Disobedience, War, and Citizenship* (Cambridge, MA: Harvard University Press, 1970): 24–45; "Justice Here and Now" in Walzer 2007: 68–80 at 76–79; and "What Is 'The Good Society;?" *Dissent* 56 (2009): 74–78.
8. See Robert Mayer, "A Walzerian Theory of Exploitation," *Polity* 34 (2002): 337–56.
9. Walzer, "Response," in Miller and Walzer 1995: 283–84. For Walzer's critique of metric conceptions of equality, see *A Foreign Policy for the Left* (New Haven: Yale University Press, 2018): 98–115. I discuss this in Reiner 2020: 123–26.
10. On this, see Michael Walzer, "A Day in the Life of a Socialist Citizen," in Walzer 1980: 128–38 and in Walzer 1970: 229–38. Walzer argues that citizens are free to be kibitzers who participate rarely, if at all. However, as I discuss below, kibitzers ought not to be considered the equals of participating citizens, given Walzer's conception of equality.
11. Michael Walzer, *The Struggle for a Decent Politics: On "Liberal" as an Adjective* (New Haven: Yale University Press, 2023). For the label "communitarian liberalism," see Mark Cladis, *A Communitarian Defense of Liberalism: Emile Durkheim and Contemporary Social Theory* (Stanford: Stanford University Press, 1992), Philip Selznick, *The Communitarian Persuasion* (Baltimore: Johns Hopkins University Press, 2002), and Thomas Spragens, "Communitarian Liberalism," in *New Communitarian Thinking: Persons, Virtues, Institutions, and Communities*, ed. Amitai Etzioni (Charlottesville: University Press of Virginia, 1995): 37–51.

12. Some years after the publication of *Spheres*, Walzer argued that one important means of distributing power more widely is via strengthening the secondary institutions of civil society such that ordinary citizens are more involved in what, in statist societies, are bureaucratic decisions. See his "The Idea of Civil Society: A Path to Reconstruction," *Dissent* 39 (1992): 293–304. For application to bureaucratic capitalism, see Michael Walzer, "Socializing the Welfare State," in *Democracy and the Welfare State*, ed. Amy Gutmann, (Princeton: Princeton University Press: 1988): 13–26.
13. Robert Nozick, *Anarchy, State, and Utopia* (New York: Basic Books, 1974): 61–64.
14. Egalitarian liberals such as John Rawls and Ronald Dworkin do indeed reject appeal to merit or desert in theorizing about distributive justice. See John Rawls, *A Theory of Justice* (Cambridge, MA: Harvard University Press, 1971): 86–93.
15. However, as Walzer notes in *Spheres*, Williams seems to take it that goods have "essential" meanings, whereas Walzer believes that the meaning of a good is always social (Walzer 1983: 9). In arguing that meanings are social, Walzer draws on Clifford Geertz, *The Interpretation of Cultures* (New York: Basic Books, 1973). For Geertz's influence on Walzer, see Reiner 2016.
16. Bernard Williams, "The Idea of Equality," in *Philosophy, Politics, and Society*, ed. Peter Laslett and William Runciman, (Oxford: Blackwell, 1967): 110–31 at 120–25.
17. Jane Austen, *Emma* (Penguin: London, 2003 [1815]).
18. Walzer reiterated this argument in *Thick and Thin: Moral Argument at Home and Abroad* (Notre Dame, IN: Notre Dame University Press, 1994): 26–31 and in "The Long-Term Perspective," *Bulletin of the New York Academy of Medicine* 62: 8–14. For discussion, Reiner 2020: 72–75. See also my introduction to this volume and Georgia Warnke's contribution to it.
19. Stephen Mulhall and Adam Swift, *Liberals and Communitarians* (Oxford: Blackwell, 1996) criticize Walzer's argument about blocked exchanges at 151–54, on the grounds of freedom of exchange.
20. This is a development of twentieth-century conceptions of citizenship. See, for example, Mill's defense of plural voting in "Considerations on Representative Government," [1861] in John

Stuart Mill, *On Liberty and Other Essays* (Oxford: Oxford University Press, 1998): 205–467 at 302–25. For a reading of Mill that stresses the importance of political participation to his view, while accepting that it seems at odds with equality, see J. Joseph Miller, "J. S. Mill on Plural Voting, Competence, and Participation," *History of Political Thought* 24 (2003): 647–667.

21. The classic statement of this point is Michael Walzer, "Objectivity and Social Meaning" in Walzer 2007: 38–52. See also Walzer 1994: 21–40.
22. On this, see Michael Walzer, "Philosophy and Democracy" and "A Critique of Philosophical Conversation" in Walzer 2007: 1–21 and 22–37, respectively.
23. This is Rawls's characterization of one of the two moral powers that, he holds, individuals share (the other being a capacity for a sense of justice). See John Rawls, *Justice as Fairness: A Restatement* (Cambridge, MA: Harvard University Press, 2003): 18–19.
24. For this reason, Walzer sometimes limits his argument for workplace democracy to organizations that are above a certain size (e.g. at Walzer 1980: 287) and frequently talks of the argument as applying to the internal politics of "corporations" (e.g. at Walzer 2007: 77–78). I am not sure that this limitation is a sound one. Employees within small businesses may well experience their lives at work as being just as authoritarian as do those in larger corporations, albeit they are at the whim of a smaller number of overlords. This may well make the exercise of power less *bureaucratic*, but not necessarily less *authoritarian*. Rather, I think, the experience of workers in a small business is more like that of those subject to personalist dictatorships rather than that of citizens of a bureaucratic state. However, it probably is true that the spillover effects of workplace authoritarianism are less far-reaching when the workplace is smaller – Nike and Amazon exercise power across the world, small businesses only locally. However, that effect might be very large within the small towns or suburbs in which the small business is located.
25. See also the earlier discussion in Walzer 1980: 279–94, although there Walzer fictionalized it, calling the entrepreneur J. J. and the town J-town.
26. For discussion of these examples, see Charles Derber et al., *What's Left? Radical Politics in the Postcommunist Era* (Amherst, MA:

University of Massachusetts Press, 1995): 168–95. See also Henry Tam, *Communitarianism: A New Agenda for Politics and Citizenship* (Basingstoke: Macmillan, 1998): 85–97, 105–14; Pat Conaty and Philip Ross, "Worker co-operatives and economic democracy," in *Tomorrow's Communities: Lessons for Community-Based Transformation in the Age of Global Crises*, ed. Henry Tam (Bristol: Policy Press, 2021): 71–90; and Charles Derber, "Corporate Power in the New Gilded Age," in *Progressive Politics in the Global Age*, ed. Henry Tam (Cambridge: Polity Press, 1998): 182–92.

27. I am grateful to David Miller for this point. Walzer's argument suggests the desirability of growth of worker cooperatives at various points (e.g. Walzer 1983: 291, 301). For reasons of space, I focus on the case for democratic management within a privately owned firm.
28. The classic work on "strong democracy," is Benjamin Barber, *Strong Democracy: Participatory Politics for a New Age* (Berkeley: University of California Press, 2004 [1984]).
29. For discussion of the arguments for civil disobedience, see Katrina Forrester, "Citizenship, War, and the Origins of International Ethics in American Political Philosophy," *Historical Review* 57 (2014): 773–801.
30. On steady work, see Irving Howe, *Steady Work: Essays in the Politics of Democratic Radicalism, 1953–1966* (New York: Harcourt, Brace, & World, 1967); for discussion, Michael Walzer, "Which Socialism?" *Dissent* 57 (2010): 37–43. See also Walzer 1971: 125. For the argument that incremental change can eventually become revolutionary, see Walzer 1980: 201–23.
31. For discussion, Marc Stears, *Demanding Democracy: American Radicals In Search of a New Politics* (Princeton: Princeton University Press, 2010): 198; Michael Kazin, "Two Cheers for Utopia," in *The Port Huron Statement*, ed. Richard Flacks and Nelson Lichtenstein (Philadelphia: University of Pennslyvania Press, 2015): 39–49.
32. Michael Rustin, "Equality in Post-Modern Times," in Miller and Walzer 1995: 17–44 at 34–35. See also Brian Barry, "Spherical Justice and Global Injustice," in Miller and Walzer 1995: 67–80 at 74.
33. Robert Mayer, "Michael Walzer, Industrial Democracy, and Complex Equality," *Political Theory* 29 (2001): 237–61.

34. I discuss the gig economy in J. Toby Reiner, *Community* (Cambridge: Polity Press, forthcoming in 2025): chapter 4.
35. I develop this point in Reiner 2016.
36. Michael Walzer, *Interpretation and Social Criticism* (Cambridge, MA: Harvard University Press, 1987): 33–66.
37. On social criticism, see Michael Walzer, *The Company of Critics: Social Criticism and Political Commitment in the Twentieth Century* (New York: Basic Books, 1988).
38. Elizabeth Anderson, *Private Government: How Employers Rule Our Lives (and Why We Don't Talk About It* (Princeton: Princeton University Press, 2017). See also Sarah Jaffe, *Work Won't Love You Back* (Bold Type Books, 2021).
39. On this, see especially Michael Walzer, "The Communitarian Critique of Liberalism," in Walzer 2007: 96–114.
40. Michael Walzer, "The Moral Standing of States: A Response to Four Critics" in Walzer 2007: 219–36 at 234.
41. For example, Bernard Williams, *In the Beginning Was the Deed: Realism and Moralism in Political Argument* (Princeton: Princeton University Press, 2005); William Galston, "Realism in Political Theory," *European Journal of Political Theory* 9 (2010): 385–411. See also my discussion in the introduction to this volume.
42. Michael Walzer, *Just and Unjust Wars: A Moral Argument with Historical Illustrations* (New York: Basic Books, 1977): 3–30.
43. For other examples, see my introduction to this volume.

CHAPTER 6

Michael Walzer on Immigration: A Critical Analysis

David Miller

I

Michael Walzer hasn't written much about immigration, but his longest discussion of the issue in the second chapter of *Spheres of Justice* has made a considerable impact on the debates in political philosophy about it that have occurred since.[1] This is partly to be explained by the fact that no mainstream theorist before Walzer had thought of it as a topic worthy of attention—Rawls, in particular, deliberately excluded it when developing his theory of justice, and this embargo was inherited by those of his followers who wanted to extend the theory globally.[2] So when Joseph Carens wrote the first of the papers that together have made him into the leading contemporary political philosopher of immigration, Walzer featured prominently as the person who defends the state's right to exclude migrants—the position that Carens wanted to attack.[3] And this is the position he has occupied throughout the subsequent debate, without himself further contributing to it in any significant way.[4] Jacob

D. Miller (✉)
Nuffield College, University of Oxford, Oxford, UK
e-mail: David.miller@nuffield.ox.ac.uk

J. T. Reiner (ed.), *Walzer and Justice: Spheres of Justice in the 2020s*,
https://doi.org/10.1007/978-3-031-87809-1_6

Levy sums the position up accurately, I think: 'Walzer has not become invisible to the debate that he helped spark, but rather his is the position that every reformist theorist begins by distancing him or herself from'.[5]

That position, however, has not been well understood. Those who now write about immigration see Walzer as the main advocate of a simple closed borders view which holds that political communities have an unrestricted right to determine their own membership, implying that they can select among immigrants in any way they choose, including for example on grounds of race—a reading that Walzer encouraged when he appeared to defend a modified version of Australia's notorious 'White Australia' policy from the first half of the twentieth century (pp. 46–48). There has been rather little by way of detailed scrutiny of Walzer's argument. After Carens's early engagement, it has been given a short qualified defence by Toby Reiner and an unsympathetic critique by Phillip Cole (aspects of which I will consider below).[6] My aim here is to give a sympathetic, yet critical, reconstruction of that argument, indicating where there appear to be gaps and inconsistencies and suggesting what might be needed to fill or correct them.

II

I start with the question: is immigration policy a matter of justice? Do principles of justice apply to states' decisions to admit or refuse entry to particular migrants? I start with this question because there are places in which Walzer appears to answer it in the negative. He appears to say, in the opening section of *Spheres*, ch. 2, that although 'the primary good that we distribute to one another is membership in some human community', questions of distributive justice arise only *after* that initial distributive decision has been made. He says that 'the idea of distributive justice presupposes a bounded world within which distributions take place: a group of people committed to dividing, exchanging, and sharing social goods, first of all among themselves' (p. 31). From this it seems to follow that although states' admission policies might be criticized in various ways, as misguided, counter-productive, inhumane, and so forth, they could not be criticized as unjust—or at least not as *distributively* unjust (perhaps Walzer intended to leave it open that they might be unjust in some other, non-distributive sense).

On the face of it, this view looks very implausible. Consider a state that discriminates on racial or religious grounds when admitting migrants, reflecting widespread prejudices among its citizens. This immediately looks like a distributive injustice—one group being treated worse than another on grounds that are irrelevant to the good that is being allocated. Interestingly, in the original version of that chapter published as a free-standing article, Walzer appears to be more hesitant. After asking the key questions that also appear in *Spheres* ('Whom should we admit? Ought we to have open admissions? Can we choose among applicants? What are the appropriate criteria for distributing membership?'), he continues:

> These are hard questions, and perhaps they are not questions of justice at all. Perhaps, indeed, the positive obligations presupposed by theories of distributive justice exist only within established groups, among men and women already members of a single political community (however they came to be members), while toward outsiders we have only negative obligations – not to kill them, rob them, defraud them, and so on.[7]

I draw your attention to the 'perhapses' here. The paragraph is not included in *Spheres*, and with it goes Walzer's expressed uncertainty as to whether immigrant admissions really fall outside the scope of distributive justice. I hazard the suggestion that because Walzer wanted to emphasize the main theme of *Spheres*—the bounded character of distributive justice, and the way in which its principles rely upon shared social understandings of the goods being distributed—when he came to rewrite the chapter for the book he felt compelled to eliminate the uncertainty he had previously expressed. According to the later text, principles of distributive justice apply only within, but not across, the boundaries of the relevant political communities.

But was Walzer right to harden his position in this way? Is it really the case that principles of distributive justice only apply within groups whose membership has already been settled in advance? Consider as a counter-example university admissions. It seems clear that these are subject to considerations of distributive justice. When, for example, students complain that the legacy admissions policies practised by Ivy League universities are unfair because access to university should be determined by academic potential and not by who your parents were, they are appealing, correctly, to a principle of distributive justice. But that principle is a principle of membership: if applied, it will determine who becomes a member of the university. Of course it presupposes a pool of applicants among whom the selection is going to be made. But then so do states' admissions policies: they select among the many potential immigrants who apply to enter. In neither case is the principle applied only to those who are already members of the relevant institutionally-defined group.

Perhaps Walzer might argue here that university admissions are different because they take place *within* a political community whose members agree on what it means to join a university as a student, and therefore what criteria should govern the selection process (in reality, of course, universities often now recruit students internationally, but set that complication aside). But is there really disagreement, between the host societies and the immigrants themselves, about what it means to be admitted as an immigrant? The host society will of course fix the precise bundle of rights and obligations that accrue to each category of immigrants, and the immigrants themselves might or might not approve of the way in which that package has been put together. But there is no disagreement about what is being distributed when admissions decisions are made, nor, at a more general level, about what it means to be an immigrant.

There is a second suggestion in the passage I have quoted from the chapter in *Boundaries*, namely that obligations of distributive justice are *positive* obligations, while we only have *negative* obligations towards those outside our political community. But Walzer goes on to say that although it is tempting to draw such a clear line, the temptation must be avoided, since there are widely recognized Good Samaritan obligations towards those in urgent need of help, and these (positive) obligations apply between strangers regardless of community membership. This applies not only to individuals but also to collectives, and he suggests that 'the collective version of the mutual-aid principle might generate a kind of distributive justice'.[8] This is relevant when we consider the claims of refugees, to which I will turn very shortly.

Before doing so, however, it is worth making the point that the distinction between negative and positive obligations—between the obligation to refrain from inflicting harm, and the obligation to provide some good—is actually unhelpful when we are thinking about which admissions criteria it is permissible for a political community to use. Return again to the case of a racist admissions policy. This could be represented either as unfairly assisting the favoured whites or as unfairly harming the disfavoured blacks. What matters is the unfairness between the two groups, not whether either of them has a pre-existing right to be admitted. A state might be committing no injustice by choosing to exclude everyone, but if it decides to admit some and not others, it commits an injustice if it discriminates on the grounds of race.

Walzer's overall aim is to argue that political communities should be allowed a great deal of latitude in deciding who should be permitted to join them, since 'admission and exclusion are at the core of communal independence. They suggest the deepest meaning of self-determination' (p. 62). But allowing states this latitude over how many immigrants they should take in, and how in general they should select them, is consistent with requiring that the selection criteria used should not breach core principles of distributive justice, such as those that prohibit discrimination on grounds of race or gender.

What now of the cases in which admission is required (or almost required? Walzer does not say explicitly whether people in the following three categories have a *right* to be admitted, or instead something like a strong claim). The first comprises the near relatives of existing citizens. Their claim is derivative from the claims that can be made by those already admitted. Walzer doesn't mention husbands and wives, who presumably can make the strongest claim, but he notes that 'since laborers are men and women with families, one cannot admit them for the sake of their labor without accepting some commitment to their aged parents, say, or to their sickly brothers and sisters' (p. 41).

The next group are those who count as 'kinfolk' in an extended sense. Walzer includes in this category both co-ethnics and those he describes as ideological kin. The context in which this applies is that the groups in question have been forced to abandon their previous countries of residence either because they have been expelled (ethnic Germans expelled by Poland and Czechoslovakia after World War 2) or because it is no longer safe for them to remain (Greek communities relocating from Turkey after World War 1, Hungarians fleeing Stalinism after the Revolution of 1956). There is some overlap here with the category of refugees, discussed below, but what Walzer is highlighting is the bond of affinity that he thinks gives such groups a special claim to enter a particular country, as in the case of displaced ethnic Germans being admitted to East or West Germany. He says that it illustrates a way in which states are more like families than like clubs. I return to the question of the kind of bond that (according to Walzer) holds political communities together in section III.

The third group are refugees, understood in *Spheres* in the conventional way as people who face the threat of being persecuted in their home countries on grounds such as race or religion.[9] Their claim is a claim of necessity, and the grounds for admitting them are Samaritanism/ mutual aid. So long as the numbers seeking asylum remain small, those grounds are sufficient, but, Walzer says, 'when the number increases, and we are forced to choose among the victims, we will look, rightfully, for some more direct connection with our own way of life' (p. 49). Such a connection might exist either because the state has indirectly contributed to making them into refugees (say by taking part in a war of intervention), or because of some ethnic or political affinity between citizens and those seeking refuge. This indeed describes how states usually behave when setting priorities as between different classes of refugees, but it is a further question whether they are justified in doing so. If a refugee's claim is essentially one of vulnerability—the harm that they will suffer if forced to remain in their present country of residence—it may seem that the only defensible selection criterion must be the extent of that vulnerability.[10] Critics have challenged Walzer's assertion that choosing on the basis of affinity, in particular, can be 'rightful'.[11]

Setting priorities also assumes that there is some limit to the number of refugees that a given state is required to accept. Walzer does not discuss directly how this limit might be established. He presumably sees it as justified by the general reasons that states have for controlling immigration, reasons that will be discussed in the following section. He says that 'the principle of mutual aid can only modify and not transform admissions policies rooted in a particular community's understanding of itself' (p. 51). But at the same time he wants to recognize an asylum-seeker's claim not to be returned to the place where he is liable to be persecuted. He says he has no adequate answer to the question 'why be concerned only with men and women actually on our territory who ask to remain, and not with men and women oppressed in their own countries who ask to come in?' (p. 51). Such questions are admittedly difficult. But they point towards the need for a theory of justice in immigration that would draw a clearer line than Walzer is able to draw, through his appeal to 'mutual aid', between what a state can be required to do in this area, and what it might wish to do for reasons of benevolence or humanity.

III

Having outlined Walzer's position on the admission of immigrants (and some of its uncertainties), I turn in this section to the general justification he gives for immigration control. As we have seen, he invokes 'the deepest meaning of self-determination' to explain why political communities must have the right to decide who joins them. It is tempting to pre-empt further discussion by saying that control of its own membership is simply part of what it means for a community to be self-determining. But that is too quick. We need to be told how membership control contributes to other aims that a community might have. Suppose that a golf club were to announce that, having already admitted 100 members, it was essential that they should admit no more. We could reasonably ask them for an explanation. They might tell us that, given patterns of play, the course would be overcrowded if more members were allowed in. Or they might say that one of their key aims was to be a *friendly* golf club, and having consulted Professor Dunbar, they have decided that anything beyond 100 would be stretching the limits of friendship.[12] These reasons may be good or bad, but at least they are reasons. They explain what would otherwise appear to be an entirely arbitrary decision to set limits on admission to the club.

Walzer's general reason for thinking that self-determination requires control over admissions is that this is necessary if political communities are to continue to be '*communities of character*: historically stable, ongoing associations of men and women with some special commitment to each other and some special sense of their common life' (p. 62). But this much-cited phrase needs a good deal of unpacking, since the self-determining units in question are *states*, which with all their internal diversity are very unlike, say monasteries, to which (with the reference to women removed) Walzer's description would most readily apply. Moreover this has to be done with one eye on Walzer's later typology of regime-types, in which the nation-state is presented as only one of four possible ways of arranging a domestic political order.[13] In other words, we cannot simply cash 'community of character' out as 'nation', unless we are going to limit the scope of his argument about immigration to nation-states in particular.

It is nevertheless helpful to begin with the case of the nation-state, because it is there that the argument seems to apply with greatest force. What, then, is a nation? According to Walzer it is 'a historic community, connected to a meaningful place, enacting and revising a way of life, aiming at political or cultural self-determination'.[14] 'A way of life' is further spelt out in terms of some of its main cultural constituents: 'language, religion, historical memory, the calendar and its holidays, the sense of place, a specific experience of art and music'.[15] A state is a nation-state when most of its members share a nationality in this sense, and when the state's purposes are understood to include protecting and developing these elements of culture—a nation-state does not aspire to be culturally neutral.

What kind of immigration policy should a nation-state adopt? The answer that springs immediately to mind is that it should seek immigrants whose cultural formation corresponds mostly closely to that of the existing nation, because these are people most likely to preserve its way of life, or to develop it in ways that respect its historical memory. And this is what happened in one of the specific cases that Walzer discusses, 'White Australia'. Australians at the turn of the twentieth century saw themselves as Britons abroad and they therefore adopted an immigration policy whose aim was to ensure that new arrivals should come almost exclusively from the homeland—a policy that was so effective that in 1947, 87.8% of the Australian population were of British descent.[16] The policy did not formally select either by race or national origin—although some of its advocates were undoubtedly motivated by racist beliefs—but a strategically administered language test produced the desired outcome.[17]

Walzer discusses White Australia when he is examining states' claims to territory, and his verdict is that the White Australia policy that was actually adopted was indefensible given the amount of land at Australians' disposal and the urgent claims of desperate people driven by famine from South-East Asia (pp. 46–48). However this does not settle whether it would have been acceptable if motivated entirely by a desire for cultural homogeneity, rather than racial purity, and if Australia had already been densely populated (or there had been no desperate people seeking admission). The issue of principle is whether the desire to preserve a homogenous culture can provide sufficient grounds either to exclude immigrants entirely, or to select only those who match the prevailing cultural stereotype. Walzer's critics have been very sceptical, both about whether homogenous cultures actually exist (at state-wide level), and about the need for immigration restrictions as a means to preserve them if they do exist.[18] Such critics argue that in order to remain dominant, a societal culture doesn't have to be embraced by everyone on the territory: it is enough that most people living there embrace most of it (different people grasping different cultural threads). Moreover we should expect immigrants progressively to embrace (a large part of) that shared culture as well, as they live among people who already do. States can and do encourage the process by adopting proactive immigrant integration policies.[19]

Walzer might reply here that although national cultures can indeed survive by these means, it is still within a people's right of self-determination to choose to remain completely homogenous—so long as they are indeed homogenous to begin with.[20] Suppose then we leave to one side the problem caused by the presence in Australia of an Aboriginal population, and consider the claim that Australians were entitled in the name of self-determination to remain culturally a carbon copy of Britain, and therefore to exclude all non-British immigrants. The problem with this claim is that it sounds too much like the golf club insisting on limiting its membership to 100 and giving no reason for the limit, other than 'we want to be a golf club with 100 members'. Given that outsiders also have an interest in playing golf, the club's self-determination claim only becomes weighty enough to justifying their exclusion when it rests on stronger reasons than this. Similarly, Australians would need to show that their interest in preserving a common culture could only be met by the highly restrictive immigration policy that they chose to adopt—and for empirical reasons this claim is very implausible, as the later history of migration to Australia, after the policy was abandoned, demonstrates. Given that there were many outsiders with good reasons for wanting to move to that country, a self-determination argument for refusing them entry has to be based on stronger reasons than just a wish to remain exclusively British.[21]

In fact, it is not clear that Walzer's permissive view about the immigration policy appropriate to a nation-state extends as far as White Australia. Elsewhere he argues for the much weaker position that cultural majorities have a legitimate interest in remaining majorities, which would allow for *some* limits to the number of culturally different immigrants being admitted, but nothing like their complete exclusion: 'no one expects the Dutch or the Danes, say, to take in so many immigrants that they become a minority, one group among many, in their own country'.[22] But if we call this the 50% + rule, and White Australia the 100% rule, the right answer, with a view to preserving the cultural integrity of a nation-state without shutting the door, may lie somewhere between the two. It is not that there is some magic number—80%, say—that applies in all cases, since the impact of a 20% immigrant minority on national culture will depend on who the immigrants are, how far they belong to a small number of already consolidated groups, how amenable they are to being integrated, and so forth.[23] So all we can reasonably say is that in any specific case there will be an upper limit to the number who can be admitted, if preserving their national culture is an important aspect of self-determination for the host community.

What about the other regime types on Walzer's list? Nothing that he says about multinational empires gives us much of a clue about the immigration policies he thinks would be appropriate for these polities, but the answer may be that empires do not need immigration policies as such, since they exist as loose conglomerates ruled from the centre, and any control of cross-border movement is likely to be left in the hands of the subordinate communities. The empire itself has an interest in controlling territory and extracting resources, but no particular interest in the character of the people it rules. There is more to be said about consociations. These are states made up of two or more peoples that operate by maintaining a constitutional and political balance among their component parts – Belgium and Lebanon are two of the examples that Walzer gives, and I will include Canada here, though Walzer labels it a 'complicated case', partly because it has some of the properties of an immigrant society, and partly because of the presence of indigenous peoples in significant numbers. Although Walzer does not address the point directly, it seems that consociational partners each have a strong interest in controlling immigration. On the one hand, not having states of their own, they are culturally vulnerable (e.g. to language loss) to an extent that nations with states are not. So they will be keen as far as possible to admit immigrants who already display their favoured cultural attributes. A good example is Quebec's insistence on controlling its own immigration policy, one result of which is that between 50 and 70% of new arrivals have French as their first language, while those who do not are given strong incentives to learn it.[24] On the other hand, they have an interest in stabilising the demographic balance that lies beneath the consociational political arrangements, so each has an interest in matching the other's immigration rate. Lebanon's constitution, for example, assumes that the country's population is divided roughly equally between Christians and Muslims, so although there are several reasons why Lebanon is no longer held up as a good example of a consociational democracy,[25] the arrival of a million refugees from Syria, joining those from Palestine, is one cause of its recent political instability.

With some adjustments, therefore, Walzer's central claim that control over immigration is necessary if states are to continue to exist as 'communities of character' can be applied to consociations. But what finally about 'immigrant societies' of which the US is cited as the leading example? These are not merely societies that contain a large proportion of immigrants, but societies for whom immigration is a defining feature of membership: their citizens see themselves as people displaced from somewhere else, voluntarily or involuntarily, far in the past or more recently. How is it possible, then, for societies formed in this way to refuse entry to new immigrants on the grounds that this is necessary to preserve their character? It seems as though Walzer's argument for immigration control collapses when applied to immigrant societies such as his own.[26]

Before reaching that conclusion, however, we need to look more closely at how Walzer understands American national identity, or as he puts it 'What it means to be an American'.[27] His major theme is that America is neither a nation nor a 'nation of nations' but simply an association of citizens. Its identity is political, not cultural, which makes it possible to live one's cultural life entirely within one of the many groups that compose American society without feeling any sense of being less than a full American. Walzer recognizes that at various points in the country's history some Americans have wanted to create a thicker sense of American nationality, and he doesn't rule out that this might someday come about, but the cultural diversity of successive waves of immigrants has so far blocked attempts at 'Americanization'. What holds America together are its political creed and its symbols, not a national culture.

However there is also a minor theme, tentatively introduced in the same essay, which partially retracts the major. This concedes that America does after all have some of the features that we associate with nationhood on the European model. First, when Americans travel abroad 'we carry with us artefacts of a quite distinctive sort'.[28]Walzer's example is Gene Kelly teaching French children tap-dancing in the film *An American in Paris*, but there is no shortage of contenders for the list of cultural items that the rest of the world thinks of as distinctively American: jazz, westerns, baseball, hamburgers, Coca-Cola..... Second, Americans have an historic sense of belonging to a distinct community; they 'recognize one another, take pride in the things that fellow Americans have made and done', just as do the members of other nations (Walzer rather surprisingly doesn't refer here to the shared experience of participating in two World Wars and many subsequent conflicts). So although the strongly pluralist character of American society enables him to draw a clear contrast with a republican and assimilationist nation such as France, overall his view seems to be there *is* such a thing as American national identity, over and above common citizenship. It is primarily political rather than cultural, it celebrates the success of immigration and has no wish to discourage the resulting ethnic and religious pluralism, but it has content nonetheless. So although America as an immigrant society deserves to be distinguished from a nation-state, the distinction seems to be one of degree, not kind.

Walzer, then, can argue that there are a least *some* identity-related grounds for an immigrant society like the US to limit the inward flow of migrants. But he says very little about what immigrant policy the US should adopt in general—i.e. leaving aside the three special categories of migrant discussed in the previous section. What he does say suggests that he thinks the control should be minimal:

> Don't shut the gates. This is not Europe; we are a society of immigrants, and the experience of leaving a homeland and coming to this new place is an almost universal 'American' experience. It should be celebrated. But the celebration will be inauthentic and hypocritical if we are busy building walls around our country. Whatever regulation is necessary – we can argue about that – the flow of people, the material base of multiculturalism, should not be cut off.[29]
>
> If we are faithful to our own traditions, we will welcome immigrants like the desperate people marching north from Central America; we won't build a wall; instead, we will reproduce the institutions of the Ellis Island that was – only better now and more humane, since we are a richer country. I am not arguing for the open borders favoured by cosmopolitan leftists and libertarian rightists. I am willing to listen to arguments for setting limits on the number of immigrants in any given year – for reasons of political prudence or to prevent any weakening of our (radically incomplete) welfare state. But these are only cautionary arguments. The pull of our history and culture is in the other direction: Let them in! It is the patriotic thing to do.[30]

These passages suggest that in the American case the only reasons for setting *any* limits to immigration are practical/prudential (Walzer mentions the welfare state, so he is perhaps thinking that it might be impossible to provide huge inflows of migrants with education, health care, housing and so forth, and also that the attempt to do so might provoke a political backlash). Moreover in this case the appeal to national identity points in the other direction, towards reinvigorating multiculturalism by injecting new cultural minorities through inward migration. But this leaves us with a puzzle about how to read the much-cited second chapter of *Spheres*. For it seems now that the communitarian-sounding language used there to explain why control of membership is so important for political communities ('The restraint of entry serves to defend the liberty and welfare, the politics and culture of a group of people committed to one another and to their common life', p. 39) doesn't in fact apply to immigrant societies such as the US, only to nation-states and consociations. It begins to look as though this part of *Spheres*, at least, is really written with Europeans, rather than Americans, in mind.

But perhaps Walzer was aware that there might be more than just practical reasons why limiting immigration may be necessary if we wish to have a strong and inclusive welfare state. Although the precise mechanism at play can be debated, it seems that the ethnic and racial diversity that immigration tends to create has the effect of constricting public expenditure on welfare services. One estimate is that 'the typical industrial society might spend 16 or 17% more than it does now on social services had it kept its foreign-born percentage where it was in 1970'.[31] If we ask why the US has failed to follow the other liberal democracies in creating an effective welfare state, racial fractionalisation (in this case, however, only partly the result of immigration) is a main explanatory factor. Looking comparatively at expenditure on social services in the US and across Europe, Alesina and Glaeser conclude that 'about one-half of the US–Europe gap can be explained by European homogeneity. As such, American racial heterogeneity stands, along with political institutions, as one of the two critical factors explaining the absence of a welfare state in America'.[32] The substantive theory of social justice presented in *Spheres* is social democratic in character, and in the third chapter makes the argument for 'an expanded American welfare state' (p. 90). This does not sit easily with the position on immigration to the US that Walzer appears to take in the passages cited above, where it seems that the only reason to restrict inward flows is prudential in nature.[33] The underlying issue is whether a society radically divided along ethnic and/or racial lines can ever build a public consensus in support of the provision of welfare services on a universal basis. In other words, there may simply be a trade-off between allowing mass immigration and creating or maintaining an expansive welfare state.[34]

IV

Up to this point I have been discussing Walzer's position on the admission of immigrants: who states must admit and who they have the right to exclude. But he has also influenced later thinking about immigrant integration and admission to citizenship. He is widely credited with having pioneered what has become known as 'the social membership argument'—the argument that once immigrants have become socially embedded in their new society, they cannot legitimately be denied access to citizenship.[35]

Walzer develops his view about what immigrants can claim once admitted through reflection on the position of people who historically have been denied access to citizenship—in the first place those classed as noncitizen metics in ancient Athens. He claims that by living among the Athenians but having no political rights, they were subject to a form of tyranny (pp. 53–5). Something similar, he argues, was true of the guest workers who had been encouraged to migrate to European states such as West Germany from the mid-1950s onward, but who were then disbarred from acquiring citizenship and as a result suffered from economic vulnerability and social exclusion. Reflecting on these experiences, Walzer maintains that all immigrants must be allowed to become full members of the political community, with the opportunity to gain rights of citizenship in due course. As he puts it:

> Men and women are either subject to the state's authority, or they are not; and if they are subject, they must be given a say, and ultimately an equal say, in what that authority does. Democratic citizens, then, have a choice: if they want to bring in new workers, they must be prepared to enlarge their own membership; if they are unwilling to accept new members, they must find ways within the limits of the domestic market to get socially necessary work done. And those are their only choices (p. 61).

Taken at face value, this categorical statement entails that no scheme of temporary labour migration that denies migrants access to citizenship, and requires them to leave once their work permit has expired, is acceptable. Walzer was certainly correct to condemn the guest-worker programmes that several European states had introduced in the post-war period, but should this condemnation be extended to all such programmes? In a footnote he concedes that his argument 'doesn't plausibly apply to privileged guests: technical advisors, visiting professors, and so on' (p. 60), and also concedes that he needs to explain what distinguishes these visitors from the metics and Gastarbeiter whose position he finds intolerable. Since *Spheres* was published, a number of countries have introduced temporary migration schemes for lower-skilled workers such as agricultural labourers and live-in caretakers, and so we should ask whether the position Walzer takes would apply to these schemes too.[36] In particular, is it essential, normatively-speaking, that they should offer temporary migrants the opportunity to become permanent residents and/or citizens if they so choose?

Walzer's critique of the guest-worker system has in fact two partially-separable elements. He points first to the very poor living conditions experienced by guest-workers, their lack of social rights, and their exposure to exploitation by their employers. Then, second he points to their lack of political voice—they are ruled over without having a chance to rule in turn: that is why 'the government of guest workers looks very much like tyranny' (p. 59). Of course, it is the lack of voice that partly explains their poor living conditions historically. But what if a temporary migration programme were established that gave migrants a full set of civil and social rights, with access to the legal system when necessary to protect these rights? By virtue of their temporary status, they might not have exactly the same rights as permanent residents and citizens, but they would be guaranteed security of the person, access to housing and health care, protection against dangerous working conditions, and so forth. Under these circumstances, would it necessarily count as tyranny to deny them political rights?

The requirement that anyone who lives under the state's authority must be given a say in what it does cannot be absolute, otherwise it would apply to every visitor who for a moment steps on to the country's soil, thereby becoming subject to the law until she leaves. In such a case, it is usually assumed that the visitor tacitly consents to abide by the law when she chooses to visit. Temporary migrants should not however be assimilated to holidaying visitors, since in many cases they may be moving in response to dire circumstances at home. So it would be wrong to appeal to consent to explain why they are legitimately subject to the state's law. Instead what matters is that they are being offered a fair deal when they arrive. They are not full members of the receiving society: the assumption is that they remain citizens of somewhere else, and will continue to enjoy rights there once they return. Their primary purpose in migrating is to work and earn money which they can send or bring back home.[37]

They are exempted from some of the burdens that citizens may have to carry, such as being liable to conscription or to undertake jury service. So as long as the terms of the temporary migration programme adequately protect their rights, as set out above, it does not seem unfair that they are denied the right to vote. Many of the effects of an electoral vote will not be felt until years after the migrants have departed.

There remains the question of whether all temporary migrants must be permitted to stay permanently and become citizens if they so choose. For programmes of one or two years' duration, the social membership argument as developed by Carens does not really apply—the time period isn't long enough for migrants to claim that they have become deeply rooted in the receiving society. Nonetheless various reasons have been given why temporary migrants' interests will not be adequately protected unless they are given this opportunity. For example Lenard and Straehle argue that:

> First, the knowledge that these workers are entitled (in time) to citizenship will decrease the receiving society's willingness to permit them to work under abusive and exploitative conditions (since doing so will reflect their failure to protect their citizens and future citizens), and second, it will give temporary workers the authority they need to demand that their rights are respected by their employers, since they no longer need to fear automatic deportation.[38]

In contrast, Ottonelli and Torresi focus on the conditions under which migrants can be said to act voluntarily when joining a temporary migration scheme, and one of these is that there should be adequate 'exit options' that must include the right to remain in the host country. The reason is that return to the society of origin may have become too costly for the migrant:

> This typically happens, for example, because while they are away migrants have been uprooted from their culture, lost connection with the sending society, or have lost the capacity to procure for themselves the means for a decent life once back home.[39]

There is obviously some truth in each of these claims, but I do not think they add up to a compelling reason to grant all temporary migrants the right to stay permanently.[40] The effect of granting such a right would be to undermine the basic logic of temporary schemes, which is that they allow migrants to boost their incomes very considerably in the short term without taking on unnecessary obligations, while providing states with a way of dealing with labour shortages that may also be short term. Both sides would look at such schemes in a different way if they provided a stepping-stone to permanent residence, and one likely consequence is that states would become much more selective, both in adopting them and monitoring who is allowed to join.

Bearing these points in mind, we can return to Walzer's apparently categorical opposition to guest-worker schemes (though, as we saw, qualified by an exemption in the case of 'privileged guests'). Might he continue to argue that even if the interests of temporary migrants are safeguarded (as those of the original Gastarbeiter were not), it still disrupts the integrity of a society (and of its spheres of distributive justice) if it physically includes people whose status is different from, and lower than, that of citizen? Or would this be excessively purist? By way of analogy, does a kibbutz cease to be a kibbutz from the moment that it makes use of hired labour, even on a small scale? Couldn't temporary migration constitute a separate sphere of justice whose main principle is mutual advantage as between migrants and the receiving state? This last question brings us back to one raised earlier, whether principles of distributive justice can only apply within a community whose (permanent) membership has already been settled, or whether they can also apply more broadly.

V

Walzer's treatment of immigration in *Spheres* was pioneering, and we should therefore not expect him to have provided answers in advance to all the questions that have subsequently arisen, both from changes in public policy and from new developments in political philosophy. I have focussed on three main issues. The first is whether immigration policy should be governed by principles of justice, and if so, justice in what form? The second is how we should understand and assess Walzer's claim that immigration control is necessary to protect the common life of citizens, particularly in the case of a country like America. The third is whether temporary migration programmes are always impermissible because they subject those who participate in them to a kind of 'tyranny'. In each case I have suggested ways in which Walzer's stated view might be adjusted to meet objections in a way that respects his overall position, with which I am very sympathetic. Much of the recent philosophical work on immigration is narrowly migrant-focussed, in the sense of being almost exclusively concerned with the harms that migrants suffer as a result of prevailing systems of border control, and the moral or legal rights they can claim as a result. Though this focus is understandable, it remains one-sided if not combined with a wider investigation of the impact that immigration can have on the integrity of political communities and their right to self-determination. This also requires engagement with practical examples, historical and contemporary, that are the hallmark of Walzer's distinctive approach to political theory and feature prominently in his engagement with this issue in particular.

Competing Interests The author has no conflicts of interest to declare that are relevant to the content of this chapter.

Notes

1. M. Walzer, *Spheres of Justice: A Defence of Pluralism and Equality* (Oxford: Martin Robertson, 1983). All otherwise unattributed page references are to this book.
2. Rawls said that his theory was meant to apply to 'an ongoing society, a self-sufficient association of human beings which, like a nation-state, controls a connected territory... a closed system; there are no significant relations to other societies, and no one enters from without, for all are born into it to lead a complete life' (J. Rawls, 'Kantian Constructivism in Moral Theory' in J. Rawls, *Collected Papers*, ed. S. Freeman (Cambridge, MA: Harvard University Press, 1999), p. 323. The followers I have in mind are C. Beitz, *Political Theory and International Relations* (Princeton, NJ: Princeton University Press, 1979) and T. Pogge, *Realizing Rawls* (Ithaca, NY: Cornell University Press, 1989).
3. J. Carens, 'Aliens and Citizens: The Case for Open Borders', *Review of Politics*, 49 (1987), 251–73. Carens deals with Walzer more briskly in J. Carens, *The Ethics of Immigration* (New York: Oxford University Press, 2013), pp. 260–2, but continues nonetheless to recognize the pioneering nature of his discussion of immigration which 'greatly influenced my own thinking' (p. 316, n.3).

4. Walzer has recently returned to it in a short paper, which in the main follows the view set out in *Spheres* though with some adjustments to take account of more recent political developments. See M. Walzer, 'Immigration and Citizenship', *The Tablet*, 30 September 2020.
5. J. Levy, 'What it Means to be a Pluralist' in Y. Benbaji and N. Sussmann (eds.), *Reading Walzer* (Abingdon and New York: Routledge, 2014), p. 119.
6. J. T. Reiner, *Michael Walzer* (Cambridge: Polity, 2020), pp. 102–108; P. Cole, *Philosophies of Exclusion: Liberal Political Theory and Immigration* (Edinburgh: Edinburgh University Press, 2000), ch. 4. Walzer is also discussed in P. Meilaender, *Toward a Theory of Immigration* (New York: Palgrave, 2001), pp. 155–70.
7. M. Walzer,'The Distribution of Membership' in P. Brown and H. Shue (eds.), *Boundaries: National Autonomy and its Limits* (Totowa, NJ: Rowman and Littlefield, 1981), p. 2.
8. Walzer,'The Distribution of Membership', p. 18. Walzer here and in *Spheres* assimilates Samaritanism and mutual aid, but this is unwarranted. Samaritanism is the unilateral giving of aid: the Samaritan cares for the man who has fallen among thieves, but does not expect his care-giving to be reciprocated. Mutual aid, on the other hand, does involve reciprocity: the aid-giver expects that, were their position to be reversed in future, the person she is now helping would help her in return. So its natural home is a community whose members interact with one another over time. Samaritanism, in contrast, can and should be exercised towards perfect strangers as well as towards associates. Jesus was using the parable to upend a literal understanding of what it means to love one's neighbour as oneself.
9. In 'Immigration and Citizenship' Walzer draws the conceptual lines differently. He defines people fleeing persecution as 'asylum-seekers', and applies the term 'refugee' to people fleeing poverty or natural disaster. In extending the term's scope in this way, he follows some recent usage, but it remains a matter of controversy whether the widening is justified. For discussion see D. Miller and C. Straehle, 'Introduction' in D. Miller and C. Straehle, *The Political Philosophy of Refuge* (Cambridge: Cambridge University Press, 2020).

10. However what it means to be vulnerable is less straightforward than it might at first seem. See my discussion in D. Miller, 'Selecting Refugees' in Miller and Straehle, *The Political Philosophy of Refuge.*
11. See Cole, *Philosophies of Exclusion*, pp. 69–70.
12. They are erring on the side of caution, since the 'Dunbar number' – 'the maximum number of individuals with whom we can have a genuinely social relationship' – is estimated by its originator to be 150. See R. Dunbar, *Grooming, Gossip and the Evolution of Language* (London: Faber and Faber, 1996), p. 77.
13. See M. Walzer, *On Toleration* (New Haven and London: Yale University Press, 1997); see also M. Walzer, 'The Politics of Difference: Statehood and Toleration in a Multicultural World' in M. Walzer, *Thinking Politically*, ed. D. Miller (New Haven and London: Yale University Press, 2007). The other three regime types are 'multinational empires', 'consociations', and 'immigrant societies'. In *On Toleration*, 'international society' appears as a fifth regime-type, but for obvious reasons this can be set aside for purposes of the present discussion.
14. M. Walzer, 'Nation and Universe' in Walzer, *Thinking Politically*, p. 214.
15. Walzer, 'Nation and Universe', p. 203.
16. C. Price, 'Australia' in D. Kubat (ed.), *The Politics of Migration Policies* (New York: Center for Migration Studies, 1993), p. 6.
17. The circumstances of the policy's adoption and the arguments used to justify it are recorded in M. Willard, *History of the White Australia Policy to 1920* (London: Frank Cass, 1967). These arguments broadly correspond to those suggested by Joseph Carens when setting out what he takes to be the strongest case that could be made for White Australia, though Carens's conclusion, contra Willard, is that the charge of racism cannot finally be avoided. See J. Carens, 'Nationalism and the Exclusion of Immigrants: Lessons from Australian Immigration Policy' in M. Gibney (ed.), *Open Borders? Closed Societies? The Ethical and Political Issues* (New York: Greenwood Press, 1988). For further discussion, see K. Windschuttle, *The White Australia Policy* (Sydney: Macleay Press, 2004).
18. See, for example, Cole, *Philosophies of Exclusion*, ch. 4; S. Benhabib, *The Rights of Others: Aliens, Residents, and Citizens* (Cambridge: Cambridge University Press, 2004), pp. 114–124.

19. See D. Miller *Strangers in Our Midst: The Political Philosophy of Immigration* (Cambridge, MA: Harvard University Press, 2016), ch. 8.
20. He is therefore highly critical of early twentieth advocates of a similar 'white, Protestant America' policy on immigration, 'as if non-white and non-Protestant citizens were invisible men and women, who didn't have to be counted in the national census' (p. 40). I return to Walzer's treatment of America's immigration policy below.
21. I share Walzer's view that self-determination claims (when supported by substantial reasons) can provide valid reasons for restricting immigration, but several recent scholars have disputed this: see S. Fine, 'The Ethics of Immigration: Self-Determination and the Right to Exclude', *Philosophy Compass*, 8 (2013), 254–68; S. Laegaard, 'Territorial Rights, Political Association, and Immigration', *Journal of Moral Philosophy*, 10 (2013), 645–70; J. Hidalgo, 'Self-Determination, Immigration Restrictions, and the Problem of Compatriot Deportation', *Journal of International Political Theory*, 10 (2014), 261–82; B. Van der Vossen, 'Immigration and Self-Determination', *Politics, Philosophy and Economics*, 14 (2015), 270–90; M. Lepoutre, 'Immigration Controls: Why the Self-Determination Argument is Self-Defeating', *Journal of Social Philosophy*, 47 (2016), 309–31. I have attempted a reply in D. Miller, 'Controlling Immigration in the Name of Self-Determination' in A.S. Campos and S. Cadilha (eds.), *Sovereignty as Value* (London, Rowman and Littlefield, 2021).
22. Walzer, *On Toleration*, p. 50.
23. I have chosen for illustrative purposes a figure that is significantly higher that the proportion of immigrants actually present in nearly all of the European states that are Walzer's leading examples of 'nation-states'.
24. F. Rocher, 'In Canada's French-Speaking Quebec, Immigration Sparks Anxieties about Language and Identity', *Migration Information Source*, June 23, 2023 https://www.migrationpolicy.org/article/immigration-quebec-language.
25. As it was in the period before 1975: see A. Lijphart, *Democracy in Plural Societies* (New Haven and London: Yale University Press, 1977), pp, 147–50.

26. In an earlier discussion of Walzer on self-determination, I noted a similar tension between his defence of the state's right of self-determination, which appeals to the 'common life' of the 'independent community' that the state protects, and the strongly pluralist analysis that he gives of US domestic politics in particular. See D. Miller, 'Toleration, Self-Determination, and the State' in Y. Benbaji and N. Sussmann (eds.), *Reading Walzer* (New York: Routledge, 2014).
27. M. Walzer, *What it Means to be an American* (New York: Marsilio, 1992).
28. Walzer, *What it Means to be an American*, p. 40.
29. Walzer, *What it Means to be an American*, p. 17.
30. Walzer, 'Immigration and Citizenship', pp. 6–7.
31. S. Soroka, K. Banting, and R. Johnston, 'Immigration and Redistribution in a Global Era', in P. Bardhan, S. Bowles, and M. Wallerstein (eds.), *Globalization and Egalitarian Redistribution* (Princeton, NJ: Princeton University Press / New York: Russell Sage Foundation, 2006), p. 278.
32. A. Alesina and E. Glaeser, *Fighting Poverty in the US and Europe: A World of Difference* (Oxford: Oxford University Press, 2004), p. 146.
33. Although in the second passage he mentions preventing the welfare state from being weakened as a possible reason for imposing limits, I am reading this as a practical claim about the stress that rapid and large-scale immigration may place on the provision of social services, rather than a deeper concern about whether a strong welfare state is possible at all in an ethnically divided society such as the US.
34. This is sometimes referred to as 'the progressive's dilemma'. Whether there is in fact such a trade-off may depend not only on the level and type of immigration, but also on the institutions and policies that make up the welfare regime. For an account of how Canada, in particular, had succeeded in avoiding the dilemma, see K. Banting, 'Is There a Progressive's Dilemma in Canada? Immigration, Multiculturalism and the Welfare State', *Canadian Journal of Political Science*, 43 (2010), 797–820.
35. This argument is central to Carens' thinking about immigration: see Carens *The Ethics of Immigration*, esp. ch. 8. See also my

discussion in Miller, *Strangers in Our Midst*, pp. 123–7. I have drawn upon ch. 6 of this book in what follows.

36. For discussion of some of the issues these schemes raise, see J. Carens, 'Live-in Domestics, Seasonal Workers, and Others Hard to Locate on the Map of Democracy', *Journal of Political Philosophy* 16 (2008), 419–45; P. Lenard, 'Why Temporary Labour Migration is not a Satisfactory Alternative to Permanent Migration', *Journal of International Political Theory*, 8 (2012), 172–183; Carens *The Ethics of Immigration*, ch. 6; P. Lenard and C. Straehle, 'Temporary Labour Migration, Global Redistribution, and Democratic Justice', *Politics, Philosophy and Economics*, 11 (2012), 206–30; V. Ottonelli and T. Torresi, *The Right Not to Stay: Justice in Migration, the Liberal Democratic State, and the Case of Temporary Migration Projects* (Oxford: Oxford University Press, 2022).
37. On the importance of understanding temporary migration as a particular kind of life-project, see Ottonelli and Torresi, *The Right Not to Stay*, esp. chs. 1 and 5.
38. Lenard and Straehle, 'Temporary Labour Migration', p. 215.
39. Ottonelli and Torresi, *The Right Not to Stay*, p. 80.
40. See further my discussion of Lenard and Straehle in Miller, *Strangers in our Midst*, pp. 100–1 and of Ottonelli and Torresi in D. Miller, 'Accommodating the Life Plans of Temporary Migrants', *Law, Ethics and Philosophy*, 9 (2023), 129–42.

CHAPTER 7

Whatever Happened to Shared Understandings? Do They Survive?

Steven Lukes

On returning after forty years to Michael Walzer's *Spheres of Justice*, three themes strike me as of considerable interest today. One, most obviously, is its then-innovative and still-compelling interpretation of equality: of what it means to view and treat people as equals. 'Complex equality' is a deep- and wide-reaching idea. It captures the multiplicity of every individual's identities and affiliations, points to the variety of ways in which they can be ranked, each drawing on reasons internal to the various spheres, and it offers a basis for criticizing as unjust the crossing of necessary boundaries—the imposition of inappropriate rankings for being 'dominant' and sometimes 'tyrannical.' The book offers a wealth of telling examples, some of them topical right now, and some that have been the subject of significant subsequent literatures and studies, that display the fecundity of this idea. These examples include affirmative action and positive discrimination, immigrants' entitlement to citizenship, political interventions in education, the protection of religious freedom, dirty work,[1] and more. It

S. Lukes (✉)
New York University, New York City, USA
e-mail: sl53@nyu.edu

J. T. Reiner (ed.), *Walzer and Justice: Spheres of Justice in the 2020s*,
https://doi.org/10.1007/978-3-031-87809-1_7

contributes in precise and graphic ways to our understanding of the bourgeois critique of feudalism when 'rank dominated dress' and 'the meaning of clothing was shaped in the image of the feudal order' (Walzer 1983: 26) and of commodification and 'market imperialism' (120) under capitalism as 'what money can buy' (103–108) evades 'blocked exchanges.' (100–103).[2]

The second theme, of continuing relevance today, is Walzer's critique of excessive abstraction in the practice of political philosophy. His argument, he writes,

> is radically particularist. I don't claim to have achieved any great distance from the social world in which I live. One way to begin the philosophical enterprise—perhaps the original way—is to walk out of the cave, leave the city, climb the mountain, fashion for oneself (what can never be fashioned for ordinary men and women) an objective and universal standpoint. Then one describes the terrain of ordinary life from far away, so that it loses its particular contours and takes on a general shape. But I mean to stand in the cave, in the city, on the ground. Another way of doing philosophy is to interpret to one's fellow citizens the world of meanings that we share. Justice and equality can conceivably be worked out as philosophical artefacts, but a just or egalitarian society cannot be. If such a society isn't already here—hidden, as it were, in our concepts and categories—we will never know it concretely or realize it in fact. (xiv)

This forthright and elegant paragraph marked a clear sense of sharp separation from the approaches of his former Harvard colleagues John Rawls and Robert Nozick (though he engages with both in the course of the book on particular points). The 'analysis I propose,' he wrote,

> is imminent[3] and phenomenological in character. It will yield not an ideal map or a master plan but, rather, a map and a plan appropriate for the people for whom it is drawn, whose common life it reflects. The goal, of course, is a reflection of a specific kind, which picks up those deeper understandings of social goods which are not necessarily measured in the every day practice of dominance and monopoly. (26)

Thus, regarding Rawls, Walzer wrote, there is 'no single set of primary or basic goods conceivable across all material and moral worlds—or, any such set would have to be conceived in terms so abstract that they would be of little use in thinking about particular distributions.' (8) As for Nozick, with whom he co-taught a class on capitalism and socialism at Harvard, Walzer commented that his 'radically individualistic conclusions...seem to me to miss the social character of production.' (323) Nozick's highly abstract and wholly fictionalized theory of rights was, Walzer suggests in his most recent book *The Struggle for a Decent Politics* (Walzer 2023), meant only 'half-seriously' (which has always been my impression. It always struck me as a brilliant, bravura defense of the indefensible). Nozick was, he noted, 'a capitalist revolutionary with no following among the capitalists.' (Walzer 2023: 148)(Rawls's impact has of course been far greater, albeit principally within the walls of academia[4]). It is worth noting that Rawls drew back in later writings from the heroic claim, amounting to philosopher's hubris, on the last page of *A Theory of Justice:* to have achieved a standpoint that is 'objective and expresses our autonomy'—a 'form of thought and feeling that rational persons can adopt within the world' that

> enables us to be impartial, even between persons who are not contemporaries but belong to many generations. Thus to see our society from the perspective of this position is to see it *sub specie aeternitatis*: it is to regard the human situation not only from all social but also from all temporal points of view.... (Rawls 1971: 587).

Nozick, likewise, did not follow *Anarchy, State and Utopia*'s style of reasoning in later work. Perhaps the most extreme version of that philosophical style, to which Walzer was and remains opposed, can be found in a celebrated paper by (of all people) the one-time Marxist G. A. Cohen entitled 'Facts and Principles.' Cohen there departs from what 'most moral and political philosophers are disposed to think'—namely, that 'all principles are sensitive to fact' holding that view to be 'demonstrably mistaken.' Cohen's thesis is that basic principles and basic value judgments are 'fact-insensitive.' More precisely, he writes that 'all principles that reflect facts reflect facts only because they also reflect principles that do not reflect facts, and that the latter principles form the ultimate foundation of all principles, fact-reflecting principles included.' (Cohen 2003: 213–14, 231). The difficulty that I see in Cohen's view is its apparent assumption that one's principles can be arrived at and adopted in a purely abstract fashion, prior to and apart from any factual basis. We surely need to know what it is about our society that calls for action-guiding principles (Rawls calls this a knowledge about 'general facts' about society).

The question, surely, is what *degree* of abstraction is appropriate to the question at hand, what distance to claim from the social world in which one lives? And, indeed, Walzer has written extensively about this in later writings about criticism and interpretation. Criticism, he has observed,

> requires critical distance. But what does that mean? In the conventional view, critical distance divides the self, when we step back (mentally), we create a double. Self one is still involved, committed, parochial, angry; self two is detached, dispassionate, impartial, quietly watching self one. The claim is that self two is superior to self one, at least in this sense, that his criticism is more reliable and objective, more likely to tell us the moral truth about the world in which the critic and all the rest of us live. Self three would be better still.....(Walzer 1987: 49-5).

This discussion reminds me of Adam Smith's 'impartial spectator' (the 'man within the breast') in his *Theory of Moral Sentiments*, to whose judgment we appeal when facing moral questions. But that man in the breast is of course a man of his time and place. But is there a way to stop this regress at a place where all could agree? Is there any prospect that it may culminate in a view that is something like objective and (a different question) universally applicable and acceptable? Is there a place to stop between the 'radical particularism' of *Spheres of Justice* and Cohen's extremism, between the cave and the mountain top from which nothing is to be distinctly seen?

I propose to leave the direct discussion of this set of thorny questions aside in order to focus on the remainder of this essay on the third theme I see as raised in *Spheres of Justice*—a theme that calls for further refinement and exploration. I refer to Walzer's aim to pursue the first two themes by seeking to identify our 'shared understandings' of social goods—which are 'already here—hidden, as it were, in our concepts and categories.' It was not his purpose, he wrote, to

> sketch a utopia located nowhere or a philosophical idea applicable anywhere. A society of equals lies within our own reach. It is a practical possibility here and now, latent already, as I shall try to show, in our shared understandings of social goods. Our shared understandings: the vision is relevant to the social world in which it was developed: it is not relevant, or not necessarily, to all social worlds. (xiv)

The phrase occurs eleven times in the book but the idea is present throughout. The questions to be faced are: how are these to be identified? To what extent did they exist in the United States in 1983 when *Spheres of Justice* appeared? To what extent do they exist there today? And how would we know?

When sitting down to write this essay, I began with the question in my title: 'Whatever happened to shared understandings?' The reason is obvious enough. *Spheres of Justice* appeared in 1983, two years after the inauguration of President Reagan and it was still possible then to write of 'shared understandings' with reference to politics in the United States. Even ten years later in 1993, Rawls, when he published *Political Liberalism* (Rawls 1993), no longer claiming to attain the perspective of eternity, could still write of an 'overlapping consensus.' In the penultimate section of the last chapter of his book entitled 'Justice in the Twentieth Century' Walzer could write of

> a decentralized socialism; a strong welfare state run, in part at least, by local and amateur officials; a constrained market; an open and demystified civil service; independent public schools; the sharing of hard work and free time; the protection of religious and familial life; a system of public honoring and dishonoring free from all considerations of rank or class; workers' control of companies and factories; a politics of parties, movements, meetings, and public debate.

Institutions of this sort, he added, 'are of little use unless they are inhabited by men and women who feel at home within them and are prepared to defend them' (318).

Four years after the January 6 insurrection and after the 2024 Presidential election, with Donald Trump attaining almost fifty percent of the popular vote, it is impossible to address these questions without raising the topic of what has come to be called polarization. In January 2020 Ezra Klein asked why are we polarized? (Klein 2020), drawing on all the relevant research and he came up with a perfect storm of contributory forces across the previous fifty years that intensified and consolidated over the latter thirty and have shown every sign of strengthening in the three years since the publication of Klein's book.

Fifty years ago, the two parties, Democrats and Republicans, were far more similar: they were scrambled ideologically and demographically but with the success of the civil rights movement and the collapse of the Dixiecrats they became ideologically sorted, as southern conservatives joined the Republicans and northern liberals joined the Democrats. But then over time, sorting became polarization–or, if you prefer, issue-based polarization became identity-based polarization–as opinions changed to cluster around the two poles; the poles came to reflect people's identities rather than their opinions. This transformation, Klein writes,

> has taken the two parties from being coalitions that looked alike, lived similar lives and thought only somewhat differently to two warring camps that look different, live different lives in different places, and find themselves in ever deeper disagreement. (36)

Today, he writes,

> the parties are sharply split across racial, religious, geographical, cultural and psychological lines. There are many, many powerful identities lurking in that list, and they are fusing together, stacking atop one another, so a conflict or threat that activates one activates all. And since these mega-identities stretch across so many aspects of our society, they are constantly being activated, and that means they are constantly being reinforced. (136)

In Shanto Iyengar's words,

> The old theory was political parties came into existence to represent deep social cleavages. But now party politics has taken on a life of its own—now it is the cleavage. (Iyengaar quoted in Klein 77).

The suggestion here is that (to use Walzer's vocabulary) people's understandings on more and more issues have increasingly come to depend on their political affiliations. In short, because of polarization the sharing has come to shape the understandings.

Instead of people choosing their party affiliation based on their political views, and changing parties if their views are no longer represented by that party, they shift their views to align with their party identity. As Liliana Mason has written in her remarkable book *Uncivil Agreement: How Politics became our Identity*,

> The American political parties are growing socially polarized. Religion and race, as well as class, geography, and culture are dividing the parties in such a way that the effect of party identity is magnified. The competition

> is no longer between only Democrats and Republicans. A single vote can now indicate a partisan's preference as *well* as his or her religion, race, ethnicity, gender, neighborhood, and favorite grocery store. This is no longer a single social identity. Partisanship can now be thought of as a mega-identity, with all the psychological and behavioral magnifications that implies (Mason 2018: 14).

How does this work? One approach to answering this comes from political psychology. Thus John Jost argues that 'certain ideas are attractive to some people and repulsive to others, and that means, essentially, that ideologies and psychologies are magnetically drawn to each other.' To this Klein adds that

> [a]s the differences between the parties clarify, the magnetic pull of their ideas and demographics become stronger to the psychologically aligned—as does their magnetic repulsion to the psychologically opposed.

This works differently for the more and the less politically engaged. Thus, Klein continues,

> we're taking the magnets and stacking them all on top of one another, so the pull-push force of that stack is multiplied—particularly for the people most engaged in politics. (47)

There is little dispositional sorting among the politically disengaged, but among the highly engaged, the effects are huge. In forming opinions,

> the question for the unengaged citizen is: what will this policy do for me. Among the engaged, however, reactions to economic issues are better understood as expressively motivated signals of identity. The question for the engaged citizen is: what does support for this policy position say about me? (Johnstone et al. 2017: 5).

However, for both engaged and disengaged, their understandings are dependent upon their trusted sources of information, and here there has been a massive transformation over the last forty years. By now all of us live within self-contained informational ecosystems whose impact extends far beyond and far more deeply than is captured by the concept of *bias*—for the very concept of bias presupposes a standpoint from which it can be detected. What we are now contemplating is the threat that *that* standpoint is disappearing from view, and even what is scientifically grounded is seen by one side as partisan. This is the prospect that Rush Limbaugh famously spoke of in terms of our living 'in two universes'[5] which seldom overlap,' that Kellyanne Conway suggested when she talked of 'alternative facts' and that most recently Naomi Klein named the 'mirror world.' The journalist David Roberts has coined the phrase 'tribal epistemology' to characterize what happens when

> Information is evaluated based not on conformity to common standards of evidence or correspondence to a common understanding of the world, but on whether it supports the tribe's values and goals and is vouchsafed by rival leaders.' (Roberts 2017).

This of course raises the question of symmetry: are we not all equally caught up in this relativizing spiral? There is, obviously, motivated reasoning on both sides and it is certainly true that the magnetic attraction and repulsion, and the tribal pressures to conform are at work on both sides of the partisan divide. (I think that Walzer's latest book is his response to this uncomfortable truth). Just as in red states and especially in rural communities, abortion, suspect books, vaccination against Covid and mask mandates are denounced, so in liberal and left circles there is a disturbing equivocation about freedom of speech (de-platforming and canceling) and an illiberal readiness to denounce those who dare to raise questions, for example about gender and especially transgender issues.

And yet there is a real difference between the parties, with respect to the structures of their support, well described by Klein:

> Sorting has made the Democrats into a coalition of difference and driven Republicans further into sameness. As a result, appealing to Democrats requires appealing to a lot of very different kinds of people with different interests. It means winning liberal whites in New Hampshire and traditionalist blacks in South Carolina. It means talking to Irish Catholics in Boston and the karmically curious in California. Democrats need to go broad to win over their party and…the need to reach into right-leaning territory to win power. Republicans can afford to go deep. (231)

They do this by appealing to ideologically and demographically homogenous voters whose views are well to the right of the median voter—voters who feel their power is slipping away, whereas Democrats must construct broad coalitions –a practice that 'cuts against the incentives of pure polarization' (247).

There is also a corresponding asymmetry in their informational ecosystems. As Grossmann and Hopkins, authors of the book *Asymmetric Politics* (Grossman and Hopkins 2016), have shown, only the Republican party has actively opposed society's central information-gathering- and disseminating institutions—universities and the mass media—while Democrats have remained reliant on these institutions to justify policy choices and engage in political debate., considering them both independent arbiters and allies. Although each party's elites, activists and voters now depend on different sources of knowledge and selectively interpret the messages they receive, the source of this information polarization is the American conservative movement's decades-long battle against institutions that it has deemed irredeemably liberal.

***

Has polarization, then, extinguished the hope of discovering shared understandings that, on Walzer's account in 1983, seemed to him to offer the prospect of social justice—understandings that were 'hidden' and 'latent' and a prospect promising greater (complex) equality that was 'within our own reach'? The intervening years have made us ever more aware of the forces that have sustained and accentuated polarization—not least the role of social media, gerrymandering and dark money. Moreover, partisanship has become ever more negative, fueling hatred, where there seem to be no constraints, and mutual incomprehension and stereotyping of the other side. The result, to quote Mason again, emerge

> when partisan identities fall into alignment with other social identities, stoking our intolerance of each other to levels that are unsupported by our degrees of political disagreement (Mason 2018:63).

In this concluding part of this essay I want to push back against the pessimism of the first part by asking whether there may be reasons, first, to doubt the extent and depth of polarization and, second, to seek ways of eliciting shared understandings that polarization conceals.

On the first point, we should reflect on the phenomenon of so-called 'affective polarization' (antipathy towards the opposing party) in which social media have exaggerated the extent of actual polarization, thereby contributing to what political scientists have called 'false polarization' but thereby ending up by making it real. The sociologist Rogers Brubaker has well described this self-fulfilling process:

> The voices of outrage on social media platforms are amplified by our tendency to pay more attention to moral and emotional stimuli when scanning a social media feed, by the fact that people who post frequently on political topics and more partisan, more polarized and more inclined to outrage than others, and by algorithms that boost the circulation of engaging material. The voices of outrage not only *drown* out others, they *drive* out others, as more quiet and moderate voices, disgusted by the toxic atmosphere, drop out of the discussion. Social media therefore yield a distorted picture of the distribution of political views that represents the public as much more deeply divided, and much more clustered towards the extremes, than it actually is. To moderate partisans, this makes the opposing party seem more extreme and threatening, and it can thereby increase antipathy towards that party. (Brubaker 2023: 142).

As for the second point—the prospect for eliciting shared understandings concealed by polarization—I would like to resurrect the dispute between Walzer and Ronald Dworkin occasioned by Dworkin's rather negative, indeed hostile review of *Spheres of Justice* (Dworkin 1983). The debate, which appeared in the correspondence columns of the *New York Review of Books* (Walzer and Dworkin 1983) was exceptional, as such debates go, in displaying a real grappling with the issues dividing author and critic, and in a way that advanced the discussion in a really significant way.

Dworkin is skeptical about the very idea of shared understandings about justice in 'a society like ours, in which questions of justice are endlessly contested and debated.' 'What can it mean,' Dworkin asks,

> to say that people disagree about social meanings? The fact of the disagreement shows that there is no shared meaning to disagree about.' (Dworkin 1983).

To this Walzer replies that 'two kinds of disagreement are possible, which I have probably not sufficiently distinguished.' One is where

> people can disagree within a tradition. They interpret meanings in somewhat different ways. Or they take different positions on boundary disputes and on overlapping and entangled goods (Walzer and Dworkin).

The other occurs in 'divided societies' where,

> people disagree because they come out of radically different cultural traditions, as in many third world states today.

Somewhat scornfully, Dworkin rejects this suggestion, remarking that 'if society is divided on some issue, the tradition runs out where the dispute begins' and 'politics must replace justice,' proposing instead that 'the principles we should struggle to promote politically must be principles we promote because they seem right…'.

Walzer clearly believed that we lived in the kind of society in which the first kind of disagreement prevailed. In such societies we should, in his view, look for the 'right principles,' not by moving into abstract theory but by looking for shared understandings. As he wrote, in contrast to Dworkin,

> Social goods and distributive spheres have first to be found through a process of empirical investigation, and then they have to be understood through a process of interpretation.

In the final section of this essay, I want to look at some recent ethnography and at the recent literature on experiments in deliberative democracy to see whether they can offer any clues as to how such investigation and interpretation can proceed under conditions of ever greater polarization.

***

First, we should note that what look like clashes between opposing values can turn out to be disagreements about what counts as realizing a value that is shared. When that is so, the disagreements may become less intractable insofar as they are amenable to empirical or factual considerations. In the light of her close ethnographic studies in the red states of Louisiana and Kentucky (Hochschild 2016, 2024) the sociologist Arlie

Hochschild observes that beneath the heated public rhetoric of the day, she discovered,

> hidden traffic across what we might call an 'empathy bridge' spanning opposing views on 'stolen' January 6, migration, climate change, sexual identity, and race.

She found that,

> Republicans and Democrats share more views than they think they do, studies show. The average man or woman on the street tends to be more moderate in view than party leaders. At the same time, each side holds an exaggerated view of the other. (Hochschild 2024: 241).

What are often characterized as deeply divergent values can thus be the result of politically generated messaging framed in rhetorical language[6] shaped by powerful elites employing what I have called three-dimensional power, both intentionally through propaganda and rhetoric or unintentionally, and whether the power is overt, covert or latent (Lukes 2021). Disentangling all of this can seem formidably challenging, even hopelessly so, but, remarkably, people can, under certain favorable conditions, do their own disentangling.

In the United States at the present time, according to James Fishkin and his colleagues, 'on some salient issues, division along party lines seem increasingly intractable.' There is 'clear evidence that affective polarization has increased at the mass level and this gap in affect reinforces the division on substance.' On some issues, 'the lock-step choreography of party elites and mobilizable voters (undoubtedly with causal arrows in both directions)…leads to policy deadlock,' endangering 'both process and outcome legitimacy.' Social sorting has accompanied political sorting, and so our division into political tribes, they write,

> has led to a tribalism of social separation. This in turn reinforces political polarization at the mass level and stalemate among policy elites. Affective polarization intensifies political distrust, further fueling the deadlock. (Fishkin et al.: 1464).

As similar processes have developed across the world over the last decades, various models of 'deliberative democracy' have been tried out (see Bächinger et al. 2018) in many countries, including Brazil, Finland,

Taiwan, South Korea and even Mongolia. They have included citizens assemblies, citizens juries, consensus conferences and deliberative polling, and they have met with varying success. Indeed, a recent OECD report states that a 'deliberative wave' of such experiments has swept over the western world in the last decade. In the face of what looks like ever greater alienation from the institutions and the practice of representative democracy, the political theorist Helene Landemore has recommended placing ordinary citizens, rather than elites, at the heart of democratic power by centering political institutions around the 'open mini-public'—a large, jury-like body of randomly selected citizens gathered to define laws and policies for the polity, in connection with the larger public (Landemore 2020). Landemore draws on detailed, first-hand knowledge to present the case of Iceland's redrafting of its constitution in 2012–2013. Instead of officials writing a text behind closed doors and later submitting it to a referendum, Icelanders chose a new format involving a randomly selected National Forum of 950 citizens, an elected assembly of 25 citizens and the use of crowd-sourcing techniques that allowed the public to participate in the drafting of the new constitution. The resulting document was approved in a 2012 referendum by two-thirds of the voting population and is, Landemore writes,

> one of the most inclusive constitutions in history and touts some radically new ideas, such as the nationalization of previously unowned natural resources, the right to Internet access, and the principles of citizen initiative (the right for citizens to propose a law) and the right of referral (the right for citizens to initiate a referendum on an existing law) (xvi).

Most relevant from our point of view, the 950 members of the National Forum interacted in groups of eight at round tables monitored by discussion leaders, all trained facilitators, who did not contribute any personal views but were merely there to ensure that everyone had an equal opportunity to voice their opinions (159). The point was to 'take a snapshot of the Icelandic people's shared values and norms,' to 'facilitate self-clarification rather than problem-solving debates': the 'question was, simply: "What values do we actually share?" (As opposed to "What values should we share?")' (174).

Fishkin and his colleagues, on the other hand, have implemented the 'deliberative polling' model to perform a 'national field experiment in deliberation' (1466) on the eve of the 2020 presidential primary season in the United States, bringing together a random sample of participants in a single place for extensive face-to-face discussions over a long weekend. In randomly assigned groups of about a dozen, they spoke face to face across their divisions with neutral moderators and experts with diverse views who would answer questions. The topics discussed were immigration, the economy (including taxes), health care, the environment (including climate change) and foreign policy. What happened is remarkable. The experiment's results, the authors conclude, offer 'proof of concept that deliberation, with an appropriate design, can dramatically narrow differences between Republicans and Democrats on issues where they are initially deeply polarized.' (1478).

The most polarizing proposals from both left and right generally lost support, and those furthest to the right lost Republicans' support and those furthest to the left lost Democrats' support. On immigrants, for example, Republicans became far more welcoming and less punitive; and on economic issues Democrats became wary of ambitious spending and reluctant to impose uniform policies across the country, while a number of internationalist proposals drew increased support with deliberation. The dynamics included people sometimes responding to corrections where a question of fact was concerned (such as whether undocumented immigrants pay taxes—they do). Most importantly from our point of view, they also involved people entering into the viewpoint of those they disagreed with, enacting empathy for others when stimulated and constrained by face to face discussion.

Here the authors invoke an interesting distinction they take from the social psychologist Ziva Kunda between two varieties of motivated reasoning: 'directional' and 'accuracy based.' The former will increase partisan polarization in natural settings on issues that are already polarized, whereas the latter can be encouraged in an experimental setting. Thus, they write,

> Kunda concluded that subjects were motivated to be accurate when they 'expected to be evaluated, expected their judgments to be made public, or expected their evaluations to affect the evaluated person's life.' When people think their views will matter, and when they have to share the reasons supporting their views, they become more attentive to accuracy goals (1468).

The deliberative poll was designed to foster exactly these motivations—attending, in other words, to the 'second person standpoint' of others in social interaction–by encouraging 'the small groups to seek and weigh relevant information and come to their individual considered judgments'(1468). Finally, the authors consider the experiment to have confirmed the so-called 'contact hypothesis': the hypothesis that under certain conditions (where the parties have equal status, common goals, cooperation and institutional support) working together increases trust, reduces prejudice and yields decreased affective polarization. In sum, they claim the deliberative poll to have shown that the group discussions, moderated to ensure mutual respect and a context of equality, and combined with the common task of formulating questions for the competing experts will lower the temperature of the heated partisan divisions, and change the way the in-group feels about the out-group.

Deliberative polling has been performed in many places across the world, as have the other forms of deliberative democracy involving mini-publics. But however successful they may be, there is always the issue of representativeness: what do they reveal concerning society at large? And there is the challenge of how these processes might be scaled up to larger populations[7].

That they can have a larger-scale impact is shown by the case of Ireland, which first introduced a Citizens Assembly in 2012, consisting of sixty-six randomly selected citizens and thirty-four professional politicians already in power, to deliberate about marriage equality. This experiment succeeded in generating trust among these two categories of actors and beyond that it gained support from the wider political class. Six years later, a second Citizens Assembly was set up, consisting of ninety-nine randomly chosen members of diverse views meeting over five weekends from November 2016 to April 2017. Commissioned by the Irish parliament, this recommended repealing the Eighth Amendment to the Irish Constitution, which banned abortion. The country subsequently held a referendum on exactly this issue on 25 May 2018. Repealing the Amendment was approved by 66.4% of voters—something barely imaginable before the Assembly was convened.

We can think of these various forms of deliberative democracy as experiments that test for the existence of shared understandings by encouraging social interaction, at least for a slice of time, among individuals in their capacity as citizens, in ways that aim to reduce the impact of polarization in shaping participants' interests and values, exposing them to power across its various dimensions. Despite their all-too-obvious limitations, these various experiments are, I suggest, significant indicators. They can render explicit the extent of people's shared understandings about justice and show what the forces are that impede both their expression and their realization. Perhaps, therefore, we should draw the conclusion that the polarization we have experienced need not mean that few shared understandings survive. It is largely driven by the mobilization of power to comfort the comfortable while inflaming the grievances of the disadvantaged. Experiments in deliberative democracy can help to reveal what is hidden, by enabling people by themselves to discover, despite that mobilization, what interests they have in common and what could realize values that they share.

Competing Interests This chapter will also appear as the concluding chapter of the author's book, *The Diversity of Morals* (to be published by Princeton University Press in 2025).

Notes

1. See Press (2021).
2. See Satz (2010) and Sandel (2012).
3. On re-reading this, I wondered whether this was a misprint for 'immanent.' In the light of what I am going on to argue, I now wonder whether what was meant was *both* immanently present, as in 'immanent critique,' and imminently realizable.
4. John Rawls died in 2002. At the year's end, the New York Times published its annual selection of obituaries under the title 'The Lives They Lived.' It included the great jazz singer Peggy Lee, the diplomat Cyrus Vance, the comedian Spike Milligan, the terrorist Abu Nidal and two other Harvard figures: Charles Ditmas, the official keeper of the university's seventy or so antique clocks since the 1940s and David Riesman, author of The Lonely Crowd, whom The Times described as 'the most influential sociologist of the era.' Rawls was not included.
5. Seven years before the election of Trump, Limbaugh spoke of the media, the scientific community, academia and the government as 'the four corners of deceit' and said: 'We live in two universes. One universe is a lie. One universe is an entire lie. Everything run, dominated and controlled by the left here and around the world is a lie.

The other universe is where we are, and that's where reality reigns supreme and we deal with it. And seldom do these two universes even overlap.'

6. Arlie Hochschild discusses this process in her analysis of how Donald Trump 'guided the emotional needle' from "loss" to "stolen"' by gathering together an impressive list of what people have experienced as losses into a 'master narrative,' from the 2020 election to good jobs to 'recognition of one's struggles and accomplishments' to pride. (Hochschild 2024: 223).
7. The research program proposed by Henry Farrell and his co-authors (Farrell et al. 2023) would investigate exactly this: 'how network structure and social influence affect flows of information and opinion between individuals with different perspectives. It might incorporate practical findings about democratic decision making—for instance the circumstances under which juries can form more accurate collective beliefs and how citizen constitutional assemblies and online town halls can support better communication between politicians and public…the circumstances under which epistemic breakdown and misinformation can become established in democracies…[and] how epistemic factionalization occurs among people who do not trust others with different beliefs.' (770).

References

Bächinger, A, Dryzek, J. S., Mansbridge, J. and Warren, M. B. (eds.) The Oxford handbook of deliberative democracy Oxford: Oxford University Press.

Brubaker, R. 2023 Hyperconnectivity and its discontents. Cambridge: Polity.

Cohen, G. A. 2003 'Facts and principles' Philosophy & Public Affairs 31 (3):211–245.

Dworkin, R. 1983 'To Each his Own' (Review of Spheres of Justice) New York Review of Books, April 14 1983.

Farrell, H., Mercier, H. and Schwartzberg, M. 2023 'Analytical democratic theory: a microfoundational approach' American Political Science Review 117,2:767–772.

Fishkin, J., Siu, A., Diamond, L, and Bradburn, N. 2021 'Is deliberation an antidote to extreme partisan polarization? Reflections on "America in one room"' American Political Science Revies 115,4: 1464–1481.

Grossmann, M. and Hopkins, D. A. 2016 Asymmetric politics: ideological republicans and group-interest democrats. New York: Oxford University Press.

Hochschild, A. 2016 Strangers in their own land: anger and mourning on the American right New York: The New Press.
Hochschild A. 2024 Stolen Pride: Loss, Shame, and the Rise of the Right. New York: The New Press.
Johnston, C. D., Levine, H. G. and Federico, C. M. 2017 Open vesus closed: personality, identity and the politics of redistribution. Cambridge and New York: Cambridge University Press.
Klein, E. 2020 Why we're polarized. New York: Avid Reader Press/Simon and Schuster.
Landemore, H. 2020 Open democracy: reinventing popular rule for the twenty-first century Princeton, New Jersey: Princeton University Press.
Lukes, S. 2021 Power: a radical view Third edition. London and New York: Macmillan Internatonal and Red Globe Press.
Mason, L. 2018 Uncivil agreement: how politics became our identity. Chicago: Chicago University Press.
Press, E. 2021 Dirty work: essential jobs and the hidden toll of inequality in America. New York: Farrar, Straus and Giroux.
Rawls, J. 1971 A theory of justice. Cambridge MA: Harvard University Press.
Rawls, J. 1993 Political liberalism New York: Columbia University Press.
Roberts, D. 2017 article in Vox May 19.
Sandel, M. 2012 What money can't buy: the moral limits of markets. New York: Farrar. Straus and Giroux.
Satz, D. 2010 Why some things should not be for sale: the moral limits of markets. New York: Oxford University Press.
Walzer, M. 1983 Spheres of justice: a defense of pluralism and equality. New York: Basic Books amd Oxford: Martin Robertson.
Walzer, M. 1987 Interpretation and social criticism. Cambridge, Mass.: Harvard University Press.
Walzer, M. 2023 The Struggle for a decent politics. New Haven: Yale University Press.
Walzer, M. and Dworkin, R. 1983. Exchange of letters. New York Review of Books July 21 1983.

CHAPTER 8

Spheres of Justice Revisited After 41 Years

Michael Rustin

My reading of *Spheres of Justice*, for the purposes of this paper, is going to be primarily a political one. I shall be interpreting it as having been an intervention in a debate about the nature and feasibility of equality as a moral and political goal. This relates of course to the fact that Michael Walzer has had a lifelong association with the American democratic socialist journal *Dissent*, of which he was co-editor from 1975 to 2013. It is these political connections which I shall have strongly in mind, rather than, for example, the intricacies of Michael's engagement with the long tradition of classical political theory and philosophy some of whose major figures - Plato, Aristotle, Hobbes, Locke, Rousseau, Marx et al.— are often discussed in the text. Michael's advocacy of complex equality is one with which I am broadly in political agreement, and is one which I found of great value when he first put it forward, and have done since then.

I will say something first about the context of political debate in which *Spheres* first appeared, in 1981. This was during a period where there had been a significant support for the idea of enhanced equality in the

M. Rustin (✉)
University of East London, London, England
e-mail: m.j.rustin@uel.ac.uk

J. T. Reiner (ed.), *Walzer and Justice: Spheres of Justice in the 2020s*,
https://doi.org/10.1007/978-3-031-87809-1_8

societies of the United States, Britain and Western Europe. A "welfare state" had been established in Britain, and also in western Europe, after the end of the Second World War. Lyndon Johnson had promulated his Great Society programme in 1964 and 1965, before its implementation was diverted and ultimately aborted by the Vietnam War and the break-up and defeat of the Democratic coalition which was one of the war's outcomes. There had been considerable sociological and social philosophical debate about equality in this period, certainly in Britain, with many researchers and philosophers exploring its dimensions and manifestations. The 1970s was probably the high point of egalitarian advance in several countries of the West, with workers' share-ownership and industrial democracy even gaining a place on the mainstream social democratic party agendas in Sweden and Britain. But the 1970s was also a period of increased social and industrial conflicts, leading to fears of an emerging state of "ungovernability" and "system crisis." (Habermas 1976). One could say that the demands and aspirations which had developed from the post-war condition of full employment and increased prosperity had outstripped the capacity of social and governmental systems to negotiate and contain them.[1] It was such failures of mediation which brought the downfall of Labour governments in Britain both in 1969 and 1979, in both cases through unmanageable conflicts with trade unions from which these governments might have expected support.

John Rawls produced the most influential philosophical advocacy of social justice, to be understood as setting limits on permissible inequalities, in 1971, in *A Theory of Justice. Spheres* can be understood in part as a response to this work. Its purpose was to provide a more persuasive and grounded idea of what a more egalitarian society might be. In the term used by Walzer's anthropologist friend and colleague from the Institute for Advanced Study, Clifford Geertz, *Spheres* sought to be "experience near" in its approach, rather than abstract and deductive. It provided innumerable illustrations from sources in literature, political theory, social science, and observational reports, of different "forms of life" whose attributes could elaborate the nature of complex equality. Michael argued that a case for equality could only be effectively made if it connected with the particular ways in which people understood and found meaning in their particular life-situations. Members of philosophy seminars might be happy to imagine themselves entering a social contract from an "original position" in which they would not know their own starting place. They might, in that situation, choose to identify with those with the potentially worst-off outcome for themselves of an imagined contract, and support only those inequalities from which they, as among the hypothetically worst-off, would also benefit. But, Michael suggested, most people do not arrive at decisions in this way—they start off in their minds from their actual position in society, not from an imaginary one. They may be tolerant of risk (as many people are in capitalist societies) and be willing to take the chance that in the competitive race of an unequal society they will not end up as losers. We know that many citizens are reluctant to see their own incomes reduced even in order to help those much worse off than themselves. This seems to be why the United States does not have a system of universal free health care paid for by progressive taxation.

There was another context to Walzer's argument, namely the limitations and deficiencies of the idea of "equality" as this was often promulgated at the time, both by some of its friends and by its enemies.[2] A problem, from the point of view of its advocacy, was its common confusion with sameness, the idea that an equal society would be one on which identity and uniformity would be the prevailing condition, even liable to be imposed through oppression. Obviously, the State Socialism of the USSR and Eastern Europe was a strong negative example of this situation, and one to which Walzer and his *Dissent* comrades were always strongly opposed. The barracks-like housing blocks to be seen in many Communist cities seemed to be a forceful material representation of their people as uniform masses. But social democrats in the West were not always exempt from such demeaning conceptions of their citizens as passive subjects of their governments. I remember in the early 1960s, just before Labour took office in 1964, the then Shadow Minister Tony Benn (in fact he was Anthony Wedgwood Benn until 1973[3]) speaking to a seminar of socialist students about how appalling it was that local authorities, often Labour ones, did not permit the tenants of public housing to choose the colour of their own front doors. Benn was scathing and entertaining on this subject. Later, one could identify those tenants who had been supported by the Thatcher government in buying their council houses (in its "Right to Buy" scheme) by their differently-coloured doors. Protests from the left during the troubled 1970s were sometimes directed against the paternalistic and authoritarian aspects of State social provision.

Thus what was valuable in *Spheres of Justice* was its defence both of equality *and* of difference, two values which had often been presented as opposed to and incompatible with one another. This was the condition which Walzer formulated as "complex equality", and as his defence of pluralism and equality. In 1985 I published a book myself, with Verso, (that is *New Left Review*'s publishing house), called *For a Pluralist Socialism*.

My intellectual formation is mainly as a sociologist, and for this reason Walzer's characterisation of "spheres of justice" as they are embodied in forms of social life is attractive. One's dissatisfaction with John Rawls' approach to these issues is connected with this. Rawls interprets the freedom he is committed to as a value which, within the constraints of his idea of justice, is by and large individualist, as it in the moral theory of Immanuel Kant which underpins it. As long as what individuals choose is consistent with the moral law, what goods in particular they desire or choose is for them to decide. The central constraints on them are that they should recognise other people's right to a similar freedom (this means treating people as ends and not as means) and that their own actions are those which could be without moral contradiction be carried out by anyone in the same situation. This is the principle or criterion of universalisability. It has been pointed out that for both Kant and Rawls, these principles are largely free from any specific prescriptive content, offering little substantive conception of what attributes a society would have that would be consistent with them.

Spheres of Justice sets out an account of justice which is by contrast rich in real and imagined social particulars of many kinds. Walzer's writing is notable for what Geertz referred to in his advocacy of anthroplogical method as "thick descriptions." As I've said, these are drawn by Walzer from many sources. His point of departure is not the individual seen as a *tabula rasa,* choosing to be what he or she wants, but people inevitably formed to some degree as social subjects, to a degree "made" by the societies and cultures in which they have been, as the sociologists say, socialised.

Sometimes at least even the socialist Marx seemed not fully to recognise this necessarily social dimension of identity. In the *German Ideology* he wrote:

> For as soon as the distribution of labour comes into being, each man has a particular, exclusive sphere of activity, which is forced upon him and from which he cannot escape. He is a hunter, a fisherman, a herdsman, or a critical critic, and must remain so if he does not want to lose his means of livelihood; while in communist society, where nobody has one exclusive sphere of activity but each can become accomplished in any branch he

wishes, society regulates the general production and thus makes it possible for me to do one thing today and another tomorrow, to hunt in the morning, fish in the afternoon, rear cattle in the evening, criticise after dinner, just as I have a mind, without ever becoming hunter, fisherman, herdsman or critic.

This seemed to suggest that the distribution of labour was a problem for humankind, rather than as the sociologist Durkheim saw it largely a benefit, since the "division of labour" as he called it made possible a greater diversity of life forms and modes of exchange. It is false to believe that individuals can encompass through their own choices any significant proportion of possible human activities. There is an immense diversity of these, which only to a small extent be realised in any one person's life. For example, how many subjects can a single student choose to study at the same time, how many different musical instruments can she play, how many sports can she engage in, how many different vocational skills can she hope to acquire? One observes one's grandchildren making their required choices of subjects at school, and is aware even then of the considerable implications these may have for their future lives.

Spheres brought a new theoretical recognition of the value of diversity and plurality when it appeared. That seems to have reflected a broader change in society at that time, where the appreciation of diversity seems to have increased. The aesthetic reaction to modernism in architecture was in part a rejection of its spirit of austere rationalism. The appeal of consumer society was built on the range of goods it could offer. Debates about the environment now commonly focus on the need to conserve or restore "species diversity", among plants, animals and insects. Perhaps this interest in diversity may have in mind not only nature, but may also reflect a view of the preferred condition of human lives.

I will now ask, what else has changed, in the social and political environment since *Spheres* was first published, besides a rejection of uniformity in favour of choice and difference? Walzer is committed to the view that ideas of justice should be related to the meanings which members of society actually hold and share. They should not be debated merely as abstract principles with few roots in the consciousness or common-sense (in Gramsci's terms) of societies' members, still less imposed on them. So, in what ways has our shared body of meanings evolved in these years?

One can perhaps identify some significant shifts in thinking, and also some landmark events which have encouraged these. One important advance in ideas was the promulgation of the United Nations Human Development Index in 1990, in the first of what became its annual Human Development Reports. This was based on the "capabilities approach" set out by Amartya Sen in 1985. This approach has established criteria for evaluating social development among the nations which are broader and more inclusive than the measures of Gross National Product and its growth which formerly dominated the development debate. The Human Development Index is a statistical composite index which combines measures of life expectancy, education (mean years of school completed and expected years of schooling on entering the education system), and per capita income. Its promulgation has itself been a step towards replacing a one-dimensional with a pluralist index of wellbeing. It recognises several different "spheres of justice", and potentially displaces "economic growth" as the primary global measure of development. There are nations which score highly by the criterion of GDP, for example, but less well by other critical indicators. For example, avoidable mortality rates in the United States are higher than in the majority of OECD countries, due in part, but not only, to the limitations of its health care system.

A second development which has been important is the empirical demonstration that inequality is in itself a source of harm. This is not only where it signifies the subjection of some people to the power of others. *Spheres* gave many examples of that state of affairs and its injuries. What recent researches, for example by Richard Wilkinson and Kate Pickett (2010), have added to this understanding is to show that inequality causes harm not only through the powerlessness but also through the disrespect which it imposes on those in lower social positions, more or less in proportion to the steepness of the gradient of inequality in a society. Interesting in this work is its epidemiological evidence that high degrees of inequality are associated not only with worse outcomes (reflected in measures of longevity, ill-health, educational attainment, substance abuse and crime) for those who are located at the lower end of hierarchies of inequaltity but that these outcomes are worse on average for the entire societies in which steep "inequality gradients" exist. The central finding of this research is that inequality is harmful to the wellbeing of entire societies and the populations, and not only to that of their poorest members, as has often been supposed.

A third recognition which is now wider than when *Spheres* appeared concerns the global aspects of injustice, and the events and interdependencies (e.g. famines, civil wars, flows of refugees) which are related to this. Walzer was able to write fairly confidently in 1981 of the nation state as the principal entity within which the claims of justice could reasonably be adjudicated. He asserted that the obligations involved in according with distributive justice should give priority to those who are fellow-members of their own society, which for the most part is taken to mean fellow-citizens of their own nation. "Membership", the question of who belongs to a moral community and who doesn't, has an important place in the argument of *Spheres*. But one wonders today how far a sense of common responsibility and membership has been extending beyond these national boundaries, even as a conservative, populist backlash is in many countries insisting on the prior claims of nationality ever more fiercely. It is possible that this backlash is in fact in large part an active rejection of the claims being made for a broader human kinship and solidarity, for example in regard to the plight of refugees and migrants, and is a defence against them.

The global exposure to the Covid pandemic and to climate change, is surely forcing recognition of the reality that many problems can no longer be seen as located tidily behind national boundaries. The success of the European Union with its conjunction both of the freedom of movement of goods, capital and labour among its Member States, with a high degree of devolution of responsibility for nations to manage their social, welfare and cultural afffairs, is an advance on an earlier phase of nation-centred development. The phenomena of gross breakdowns of govenmental order, and of severe economic backwardness, such as exists most widely on the African continent, indicates that successful nation states such as those of Europe and the North America need to address issues of distributive justice that go beyond their own boundaries, in their own interests as well those of nations and peoples worse off than themselves. The days when social democracy in one nation might have seemed a realistic option have passed.

In 1979 and 1980, just before *Spheres* was published, a seismic change occurred in the governing arrangements and balance of powers in the United States and the United Kingdom (and soon in other countries) with the elections to power of Ronald Reagan and Margaret Thatcher. These elections initiated, not without some uncertainties at least in Britain,[4] what is often described as the era of neoliberalism. (Hall, Massey and Rustin 2015). This term names a period of deregulation of capital, in which many of the constraints, or "countervailing powers" (to use Galbraith's term) which had been placed upon it during the post-war years of the welfare settlement and the New Deal, were stripped away. The power of trade unions was cut back (the defeats of the air traffic controllers strike in 1981 in the United States, and of the coal miners' strike in the United Kingdom were key moments), in Britain a large sector of publicly-owned industries was privatised, and a significant part of the welfare system, notably publicly-owned housing, was sold off. This was initially to their existing tenants under the government's "Right to Buy" scheme, but then into an amorphous private and often then rented housing stock.

But most important of all from the point of view of equality, complex or simple, was the deregulation of the banking and financial system which took place from 1985, in the so called "Big Bang". The effect of this was in effect to establish a "sphere" (to use Walzer's term in an unwelcome context) of financial accumulation. This was significantly separate from the material economy of goods and services, although it came to exercise considerable power over it. The monetary value embodied in exchanges of currencies and speculative assets came, in an extraordinary way, to outweigh the value embodied in the "real" economy. The catastrophic climax to this development occurred in the financial crisis of 2007–2008, when this house of cards came crashing down. Governments have in the years since then sought to repair this system, for example by imposing greater regulatory constraints upon banks and financial agencies to prevent a recurrence of extreme turbulence. Both the US government and the European Union have attempted to restore and rebalance growth in their economies by the kinds of expansions of credit (and budget deficits) once recommended by Keynes, although this is now sometimes specifically oriented to transitions to renewable energy in face of the climate crisis. Thomas Piketty and many others have pointed out that in these years of deregulation, whose proclaimed purpose was to enable market economies to expand more quickly, average levels of economic growth in the west were lower than they had been in the earlier post-war years ("les trentes glorieuses") when the balance of power between capital, labour and governments had been a more equal one, without historical precedent as Piketty has shown. What also took place in these deregulated and finance-dominated years was a considerable increase in inequalities of income and wealth. In terms of *Spheres of Justice*, it can be said that concentrations of financial power, subject to weakened regulation and countervailing claims from governments and other actors (such as unions), have invaded many if not most other spheres of life. In part this has been through the pressure on institutions to place the demands of financial solvency and profitability above all other goals, whether this is in the management of a business (where this was always predominantly the case), or a university, or an elected local authority (the largest city council in Britain, Birmingham, declared itself to be bankrupt in September 2023 and put into commission by central government.)

Another indirectly invasive source of power needs also to be noted as an aspect of unregulated power of capital. This is the field of energy production, in particular that of fossil fuels. The central issue here is the immense "external diseconomies" (in the language of market theory) which the fossil fuel corporations (both public and public) impose on societies world-wide, through the effects of carbon emissions on global warming, with the massive harms and costs that this is already bringing about. Gordon Brown has drawn attention to the immense redistribution of wealth away from the poor which windfall profits from fossil fuel production have recently caused.

In these reflections, I have been considering the economic and political changes which have taken place which have taken place since *Spheres* was first published. In the light of these developments, making progress towards goals of complex equality and enhanced social justice have become in some although not in all respects more difficult than it seemed to be at its original time of writing. It seems now that the political context of *Spheres* when it was written was one in which a good deal of advance had been made, in the context of the post-war welfare settlement and the New Deal, towards a greater measure of equality and social justice. It seems that one could at that time reasonably hope for further advances in that direction, although giving greater priority than was previously recognised to diversity and difference. But these assumptions seem now to be scarcely realistic in the light of changes in the division of economic and political power which have come about during the decades of neoliberal, which is to say capitalist, hegemony. One can say that ground that had been won for greater social equality and justice in those years has been lost in the intervening decades.

Developments over the last forty years surely tell us that there needs to be a substantial advance in the direction of equality simply conceived, in terms of income and wealth, if a future of complex equality such as *Spheres* imagines is likely to come about. What grounds are there for anticipating such a development?

What one can say is that the possibility of the forms of complex equality envisaged in *Spheres* becoming actualised now depends on a reversal of the generally inegalitarian developments of the decades of neo-liberalism. Isn't there now some recognition that the domination of economy and society by deregulated corporate and financial institutions cannot bring stability and development? It seems that governments need to be assigned a larger role if the present challenges to people's well-being are to be overcome. The domestic programme of the Biden administration in the United States was a reflection of this purpose, insufficient as it turned out to be. How does this changed context bear on the arguments of *Spheres of Justice*?

It seems that at the least a very large invasion of many spheres of social life by the unfettered power of global capital and finance needs to be noted as having disrupted the balance of social forces which existed four decades ago. It also has to be recognised (not least in the outcome of the 2024 elections in the United States) that popular responses to the disruptions and harms which have occurred during the decades of hegemony of capital and the free market have by no means taken a social democratic or egalitarian form. These seem to be contextual issues relevant to the consideration of the arguments of *Spheres of Justice*.

However, although it can be said that many material and political obstacles to the achievement of complex equality are now larger than they seemed to be in 1981, there has also been a contrary and more positive development. This lies in the global growth of human aspirations during this period, and the enhanced flows of information and communication which sustain them. These may yet have the potential to outweigh the resistance of the privileged.

The Arguments for Complex Equality

I am in broad agreement with the conception, outlined in *Spheres,* of Complex Equality as charactering a just social order. However, I am not convinced by the specific form of argument by which Walzer has set out his view, and in this part of my paper I will explain why.

At a point in *Spheres,* its author tells just that he is interested to characterise the nature of a just society, but not to outline or defend a particular view of what a good society might be. What is the significance of this conceptual distinction, and why should "justice", with its focus on the distribution of goods, be given priority over a concept of value which would allow us to consider the nature and quality of "goods", and not only the criteria by which they are allocated? Was this choice a legacy of John Rawls' seminal contribution into this field of debate, and a perceived need to respond to this framing in its own terms? Or was it due to the fact that some socialists have historically been very preoccupied with issues of distribution, for example in the English Fabian tradition. This was much concerned with revisions which considerations of justice and equality required to be made to prevailing utilitarian principles which justified whatever actions gave rise to the greatest happiness of the greatest number.[5]

Spheres is rich in its descriptions of different forms of life and their qualities. It is very far in its texture from merely abstract argument which justify who should get or deserve what goods. It argues that the value of particular goods (such as those provided by health care, education, or possessed as divine grace) is part of the inherent meaning of the activities in which they are embodied. *Spheres* proposed that a just society might be one in which such fields of activity might be ones in which their own inherent values would be freely realised. Without invasion or suppression by the demands emanating from other spheres. But one wonders why Walzer did not, at least as it seems, care to compare the nature and value of the "goods" to which each sphere of justice is almost by definition of itself devoted. And consider what different balances and ensembles of these might amount to as connected but necessarily different ways of life.

Considerable attention given in *Spheres* to the role of "blocked exchanges" in disallowing the invasion of some *Spheres of Justice* by the demands and modes of being of others. Critics such as Judith Andre (1995) have argued that this argument from "blocked exchanges" does not bear the weight which Michael places on it. In so far as certain kinds of exchange are or should be blocked, it has been argued that this is not because they are specifically "blocked" or defined as illegitimate, but rather because the acts which characterise them violate certain fundamental rights, or indeed endanger specific goods. The problem with slavery or contract-killing, for example, is not that buying and selling of lives are taking place, but that human life and human freedom are basic human rights which should not be abrogated by <u>any</u> means. It is the fundamental and intrinsic value of human life that is the issue, not the specific injury to it caused by monetary exchange. Slavery was wrong when it was imposed by military conquest and tyrannical decision, even if it were not organised through market exchange, as in European and American slave-trading. The prohibition of the buying and selling of votes (another example of a "blocked exchange) is a similar case. The principle being violated here is that citizens who have the vote should be free to cast it according to their own preference, and that this freedom should not be abrogated in any way whatsoever. The buying of votes is one form of distortion, but many others have existed or can be imagined, such as when fathers control the votes of their families. The idea of "blocked exchanges" singles out one particular and indeed significant form of invasion of a right, that which enacts the power of money, but many other kinds of abridgements of rights can and do occur.

I suggest that a more coherent case for Complex Equality can be made by identifying those rights which all citizens should have equally by entitlement, as a common ground or foundation of life in society. Then upon this foundation may be determined many differences between forms of life which should be determined by individual and social choice, and through the process of political argument which is highly valued in *Spheres*. Perhaps Sen's capabilities approach and the Human Development Index begins a way of mapping the actual existence and achievement of such entitlements and goods. This approach does not imply that nations whose scores are similar by these measures are necessarily similar to each in other respects, or should be.

There will of course be disagreements regarding what such fundamental rights should be taken to be. Because of differences of view regarding the rights of women, for example in regard to education, even the idea of the attainment of literacy as a measure of human development may be contentious. But the fact that what is to be recognised as a universal human entitlement will be a matter of dispute does not mean that agreement upon them should not be sought. One notes, for example, that one area of dispute in the Human Development debate concerns political citizenship. How far are civil and political rights (freedom of speech and association, the election of governments, etc.) to be recognised as universal measure of human development? One can see that the achievement of international consensus in that area will be long in coming, though that is not a reason not to seek it. David Miller pointed out in his introduction to *Pluralism Justice and Equality* (p. 2) that Walzer himself conceded that "some requirements of justice run across all cultures, and may on that account be regarded as a kind of minimal and universal moral code". But of course it is a question of how minimal this code should be.

I will put another question. Why would one not choose an Aristotelian idea of human flourishing, in all its potential variety, and the conceptions of the good which can be derived from this, as a principal measure of value? *However, in effect Spheres* may have gone a long way towards doing this. This is because the domains of justice, or of freely-determined forms of life, in effect assign value to many intrinsic kinds of good, such as those embodied in political life, varieties of work, the pursuit of education, etc. The idea of "complex equality" incorporates within its concept of distributive justice a recognition and endorsement of the many kinds of good there are. I have always found this to be an appealing idea. But does it suffice to frame the social choices which we may wish to make?

Complex Equality and Complex Hierarchy

What does the "complex" in the composite concept of "complex equality" call to one's attention? In what respects is "complex" different from simple "equality"? Perhaps in its recognition that equality is not everything, and that some inequalities may have a positive value. Of course it is a central argument of *Spheres*, that specific inequalities may be acceptable and even desirable as long as inequalities in one sphere do not overdetermine inequalities in others, or spill over into a general condition of inequality.

It seems to follow from this that there are benefits to be obtained from some forms of hierarchy, as well as from some forms of equality. Might relationships of complex hierarchy be differentiated from simple hierarchy (or from tyranny, with which hierarchy is liable to be confused) just as complex equality can be differentiated from simple equality with its own concomitant of uniformity and sameness?

To explore this possibility, I am going to introduce to the argument an additional theoretical approach. This derives from the sociologist Durkheim, and is concerned not primarily with inequalities in societies, but rather with their prevailing forms of social relationship and solidarity. The central issue is how far societies promote individual self-hood, choice and identity, and how far they are organised as or collectivised entities, in which for example families, tribes, clans or sects determine the main pattern of human lives. Durkheim's thesis was that modern societies were evolving in an individualising direction, with the division of labour and market exchange being central causes of this. Durkheim was, however, also social democratic in his sympathies, believing that common social entitlements ("non-contractual elements of contracts") should underpin a system based on an advanced division of labour.

Following Durkheim, the anthropologist Mary Douglas, in *Natural Symbols* (1970) and her later writing devised a theoretical model which classified social forms by reference to the priority they assigned to the roles and powers either of the individuals or of the groups of which they were composed. With remarkable ambition she proposed that this model and the categorical frame it set out was of universal application. She argued that it allowed one to perceive the range of alternatives and choices which existed within any social order. This was because in addition to the extreme or pure kinds of solidarity (or social relationship) which her model posited, a multitude of compromise formations, and dynamic interactions between each form, could also be identified. Douglas's radical sociological determinism asserted that the institutional form which dominated a society determined all the other dimensions of its existence. Especially, she argued, institutional form determined "thought style", or culture, rather than ideas being the determining social force. Although her approach has been named "cultural theory" by some of her associates, Douglas's ideas are anti-culturalist and anti-idealist in their assumptions. "Grid-Group" theory is the term by which these ideas of Douglas are known.[6]

Douglas's argument is that there are four polar or "pure" forms of solidarity in societies. Each of them depends on the degree to which the claims either of group membership or of individual interest and preference dominate behaviours. The possibilities are graphically displayed in her "Grid-Group" diagram, which has various iterations in her and her colleagues' writing. Here is one version of this diagram:

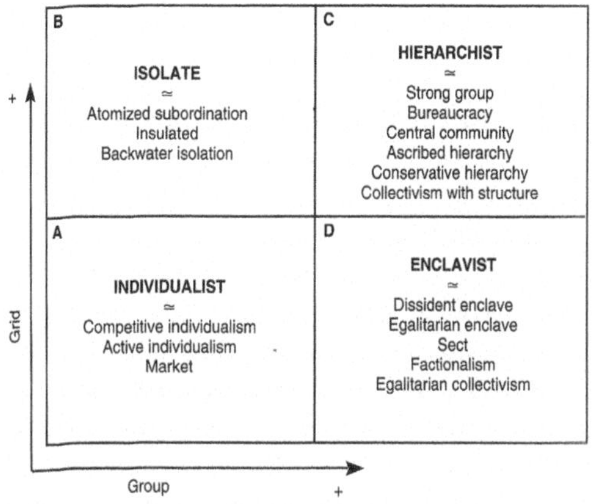

Diagram 6 Some synonyms for the four quadrants of grid and group

Source: 1978a, 1982b,c, 1990d, 1993c, 1994h, 1996b

224

On the right-hand side of the diagram are those locations where the bonds of group membership are strong, on the left side is where they are weak. Towards the top end the definition and regulation of individual roles is strong, towards the lower end they are weak. These two axes generate four quadrants, each representing its dominant form of life. The Individualist quadrant, bottom left, represents a situation in which both group ties and the definition of individual roles are weak. This is the zone of unrestrained individualism. The Enclavist quadrant, bottom right, represents a state of strong group ties and weak definition of individual roles. This represents the most egalitatarian position. The top left quadrant is that of isolates and fatalists, such as incarcerated prisoners who have both weak group membership and weak group ties, but a strong indeed often oppressive framing of their individual roles. (However, Douglas thought the "isolate" position could sometimes be productive of innovation) The top right quadrant is one in which both group ties and individual role definition are strong. This is the location of hierarchy.

The Douglas "school" became interested in the dynamic aspects of this classificatory model. They came to argue that all societies and institutions would be likely to exemplify all of these possibilities in some combination of them, but in different balances. They also recognised probable interactive and feedback effects. For example, an ultra-individualist form of life would be likely to produce losers, casualties and rebels. Its losers might gravitate to the abject, isolate quadrant, e.g. end up sleeping on the street. Its rebels might join an enclaved protest movement, for example escaping from anomie by banding together in a sect hoping for deliverance or as a political movement fighting injustice. The character of the enclave is that its members are deemed to be in a relationship of equality to one another, united against what lies outside their boundary. Douglas, a lifelong Roman Catholic, was herself most drawn to hierarchy. One of the attractions of hierarchy, which is strong in both group ties and in individual role-definitions, that it accords a recognised identity and location in society, to all of its members. The idea of complex hierarchy, elaborated later in this work, distinguishes this from mere tyranny. It is possible in such hierarchies that even those occupying the lowest positions may be accorded respect and dignity, although of course this is often not the case.[7]

The dominant forms of solidarity in democratic capitalist societies are located along the diagonal (in the grid-group diagram) from the top right to the bottom left of the schema. That is, combining in some variable proportions hierarchical with individualist forms. It is possible to locate different varieties of capitalism at different points of this diagonal. By and large, the society of the United States lies further towards the "south-west" in the direction of individualism, and those of Europe are positioned nearer to the "north-east", because of their persisting traditions of hierarchy. Societies of both kinds are likely also to possess smaller but variable zones of enclaved and isolated life. The individualist culture of the United States pushes an unusually large part of its population into the isolated quadrant, in part because of its high rates of imprisonment. The United Kingdom has long been moving in this direction. Each of its recent governments has sought to build more prisons, even though the British prison system is now in a state of crisis, with some of its institutions infested by both drugs and rats.

Douglas combined a personal predilection for hierarchy, especially complex hierarchy, as her preferred social form, with an assertion that ethical and political prescriptions should not be inferred from her theoretical model. Its aim, she said, was to identify that a multitude of potential patterns of social life, in a way which enabled informed choices to be made between them. These could be choices made by individuals, regarding in which social locations and according to what values they should live their lives, or by social groups and institutional thinking and acting collectively.

Spheres imagined that choices would emerge from the different locations of meaning and value in societies, for example those of the practices of education, health care, or science. Douglas locates such choices in a broader institutional environment, where common norms (of individual enterprise or sectarian conviction, or traditions) might suffuse many activities. I am not clear how Walzer's focus on inequalities and their kinds, and Douglas's on different patterns of social relationship, can be brought together in a useful dialogue.

I find it useful however (bear in mind that I believe this is in part a political debate) to be able to formulate an understanding of the properties of different forms of social life, and to justify one's preferences by reference to their respective virtues and deficiencies. For example, I found the view taken by Jon Elster (1995) that one should value efficiency, as imposing one valid constraint on the distribution of goods, a persuasive one. Where would we have been, for example, without the efficiency of the companies which produce and the governments which distribute Covid vaccines? And what is one to make of the fact that 24,855 miles of high-speed railway had been completed in China by the end of 2021, but so far none whatsoever in the United States.

In other words, even if one is a convinced democratic socialist, it is well to remember that choices have to be made between political and social alternatives, and that no single concept of social justice may be able to determine what this choice should be.

I will conclude, perhaps self-indulgently, with a description of one local form of life in Britain. It is always as well to recognise that there are so many forms of life, and that dominant political representations of society are usually in touch with few of them. The RNLI, the Royal National Lifeboat Institution, is an organisation, which operates lifeboat stations all around the British coast. It is supported wholly by voluntary donations, rather than by government and taxation, although it does interconnect with a statutory HM Coastguard service and the NHS (to treat rescued casualties) and it sometimes summons RAF helicopters to its aid. Most of its lifeboat crews are volunteers who live or work near to lifeboat stations since they have to be able to be called to duty on their pagers in what they call "a shout" at short notice, and at any time. Their availability must depend on the willingness of employers to allow crew-members to leave their workplaces whenever they are called, without prior notice. No doubt some kind of complex hierarchy is in place in the operation of the lifeboats. For example there is always a skipper in command—this seems to be a general rule of seafaring—and some of the key staff of lifeboat stations are paid. I have to say that I know about this service mainly from BBC television documentaries which film its call-outs, no doubt, from the RNLI's point of view, providing it with very positive publicity, and I am sure encouraging donations.[8] The element of collective altruism in the provision of this service is striking. It reminds one of Richard Titmuss's famous description and advocacy of the system of voluntary blood-doning by which the NHS in Britain is provided with blood. The lifeboat crews seem to have an ethos of commitment and of mutual respect. Why would they volunteer otherwise? No doubt however there are hierarchies of experience and ability, even on the lifeboats, and no doubt at the higher level from which the instituion is governed, hierarchy has some place.[9]

One was reminded how specific and special the "Sphere of Justice" is in which this service operates by a recent press report. Nigel Farage, the former leader of UKIP, the United Kingdom Independence Party, and the initator of the Brexit campaign, criticised the RNLI for operating what he called a "taxi-service" for refugees and asylum seekers who were attempting to cross the English Channel in small boats, some of which got into trouble or sank, leading to many people being drowned. The head of RNLI responded to this attack on his service by saying that it was the mission of the RNLI to rescue people who were in danger at sea whoever they were, and for whatever reason they were in danger. (One sees how the RNLI crews seem always to refrain from criticising or blaming those they rescue, however careless or irresponsible they have been. Those rescued however often combine expressions of gratitude to the lifeboat crews, with expressions of contrition for having put themselves and others in danger.) After this exchange, it was reported that donations to the RNLI had increased, it seems in respond to this declaration of principle by its chief officer.

Here is a "Sphere" of altruism and social solidarity (no doubt with its particular roots in seaside communities and traditions) which seems to be a healthy state, in these difficult times. This example may not seem to have much connection with the philosophical theme of this volume, but perhaps it is permissible to end this paper with a description of one exemplary and uncontaminated Sphere of Justice, one which seems to embody elements of both Complex Equality and Complex Hierarchy.

Competing Interests The author is grateful to Informa UK for permission to reprint the diagram that appears in this chapter.

Notes

1. This was the case in France in 1968 and Italy, with its "hot autumn" of 1969 as well as Britain.
2. The socialist idea of equality has often been formulated in political discourse as if it were synonymous with the liberal idea of equality of opportunity, of careers open to the talents. These concepts are however different. Except in times when enhanced occupational aspirations are being widely satisfied, the opportunity for some to ascend a social scale must be counterbalanced by the experiences of descent, to make space for them. Such fluidity of movement is most likely to be tolerated when "inequalities of outcome" are limited, in a situation when even those who do less well receive respect.
3. Having given up the title of Lord Stansgate which he inherited in 1960 in 1963.
4. Thatcher's power was only securely established in her second election of 1983, which took place after the breakaway of the Social Democratic Party from the Labour Party in 1981, and after her military success in the Falklands War against Argentina in 1982.
5. Jon Cruddas's *A Century of Labour* (2024) valuably describes the different philosophical currents which have formed the politics of the British Labour Party, noting the disproportionate prominence of the utilitarian tradition.
6. Rustin (2024) describes Douglas's theory with its application an institutional case-study.
7. I have found Douglas's model useful in understanding changes which have been taking place in a particular institution within the NHS. I have seen this as a shift from a long-established form oof complex hierarchy, with different mental health professions at its core, towards a more individualised form of organisation, with enclaved and isolate forms of behaviour as defensive reactions to this change. This is a local instance of a broader shift of culture and organisation in the NHS and elsewhere.
8. One omission I have noted from this film series is of call-outs that have ended in deaths at sea, although these must occur. However, near-escapes are frequent, giving the films their drama.

9. The RNLI does after all have Royal in its title. Its trustees include both former volunteer lifeboat crew-members, and a Rear-Admiral and a peer.

References

Andre, K. (1995) "Blocked Exchanges; a Taxonomy". In Miller and Walzer, op.cit. pp 171–196.

Cruddas, J. (2024) *A Century of Labour*. Polity Press.

Douglas, M. (1970) *Natural Symbols*. Cresset Press.

Elster, J. (1995) "The Empirical Study of Justice", in Miller and Walzer op. cit., pp 81–98.

Habermas J. (1976) *Legitimation Crisis*. Heinemann.

Hall, S., Massey D., Rustin M.J. (2015) *The End of Neoliberalism? the Kilburn Manifesto*. Lawrence and Wishart.

Miller, D. and Walzer, M (ed.) (1995) *Pluralism Justice and Equality*. Oxford University Press.

Reiner, J, Toby (2020) *Michael Walzer*. Polity Press.

Rustin, M.J. (2024) "The explanatory models of Mary Douglas and Melanie Klein compared, in the context of an institutional case study." *Organisational & Social Dynamics* 24(1) 1–25.

Wilkinson, R. and Pickett, K. (2010) *The Spirit Level: Why Equality is Better for Everyone*. Penguin.

CHAPTER 9

Defending the Medical Sphere: Using Walzer in the 2020s

Margo Trappenburg

Introduction

Around the turn of the century, I published two articles in which I used Walzer's *Spheres of Justice* to think about the distribution of health care in Western welfare states (Trappenburg 1997, 2000). I argued that one of the criteria to evaluate a theory of justice should be its usability to guide us when thinking about current policy problems. *Spheres of Justice* did very well in this respect. It seemed the right theory at the right time. In my work as an expert on health care policy and social policy I could use Walzer's insightful ideas on the sphere of security and welfare and the distribution of medical care to think about the best way to distribute benefits to citizens in need and medical care to the sick. In this article I want to find out whether *Spheres of Justice* can still guide us in present-day policy issues. I will use the same policy areas: health and social policy;

M. Trappenburg (✉)
Utrecht School of Governance, Utrecht University, Utrecht, The Netherlands
e-mail: m.trappenburg@uvh.nl; m.j.trappenburg@uu.nl

University of Humanistic Studies, Utrecht, The Netherlands

J. T. Reiner (ed.), *Walzer and Justice: Spheres of Justice in the 2020s*,
https://doi.org/10.1007/978-3-031-87809-1_9

both located in Walzer's sphere of security and welfare (Walzer 1983, ch. 3).

Walzer's theory builds on two important master-principles: (1) social goods should be distributed in accordance with the distributive criterion befitting their meaning in their societal sphere and (2) spheres of justice should be kept apart. I will use the term "master-principle" to distinguish these two principles from "within-spheres principles" such as: medical care ought to be distributed according to medical need. I will reconsider each of the two master-principles. Regarding the first master-principle I will reassess the proper width of societal spheres. In *Spheres of Justice* the division of societal spheres is related to shared understandings about the distribution of social goods. Before, but certainly after *Spheres of Justice* was published, social scientists have written volumes about sectors in society adhering to one or another particular "logic", embodying a certain "professional culture", upholding "professional standards" and "professional norms" (e.g. most notably Freidson 2001; Mol 2008; Jacobs 1992). In political philosophy a broader idea of sphere-specific justice is defended by Sandel in *What Money Can't Buy* (2012). Whereas Walzer bases his division of spheres on different distributive criteria, the later social science-based studies as well as Sandel's account are more encompassing than that, identifying more morally relevant aspects of societal spheres. I will ask the question whether the distribution-based approach offers enough and the right guidance in present-day policy questions. Or do we need the more extended vision of societal spheres advanced by other thinkers?

Regarding the second master-principle—spheres of justice should be kept separate—I will identify two underpinning ideas that make it so appealing, the first related to our image of "moral man", the second related to the use of power in society. I will subsequently confront these underpinning ideas with current insights and present-day policy problems and then evaluate the second master-principle's usability in the sphere of security and welfare.

The article is built up as follows. In the first section, "Interpreting Shared Understandings", I sketch the background and the basics of *Spheres of Justice*, defending my choice to use it in the context of a Western European welfare state. Subsequently, in the section called "Preserving Shared Understandings in Times of Marketization", I'll give an impression of how the arguments in *Spheres of Justice* were used in the era of neoliberalism that unfolded in the decades after 1983. I will then consider whether distributional criteria suffice or should be complemented by broader sphere-related moral criteria. In sections titled "Multi-dimensional Man and the Division of Power in society" and "Identity Activism and Integral Policy Making", I'll reconsider the two ideas underpinning Walzer's second master-principle and reassess its value for contemporary issues. In the final section, "Still Useful After All These Years", I give a final assessment on the usability of *Spheres of Justice* in the 2020s.

Interpreting Shared understandings

When *Spheres of Justice* was first published in 1983 it seemed an answer to a prayer that I didn't even know I had. Amidst the other theories of justice published at that time—Rawls's *A Theory of Justice* (1971), Nozick's *Anarchy, State, and Utopia* (1974), Ackerman's *Social Justice in the Liberal State* (1981), Dworkin's famous articles on distributive justice (1981a, b)—*Spheres of Justice* felt decidedly European. For a European reader the starting point adopted by Rawls, Nozick, Ackerman and Dworkin always felt very American: "let's choose a hypothetical beginning point, be it an original position, a state of nature, an intergalactic journey or a hypothetical island where we end up as shipwreck survivors. We'll develop principles of justice under these abstract, hypothetical conditions and have them guide us in our current political communities." Such musings come more naturally to readers with a national history that actually began afresh at a definite point in time, with founding fathers drawing up a constitution, than to readers whose states of origin had grown organically, starting somewhere in the days of the Roman empire and then gradually evolving from there.

Walzer chose a non-hypothetical starting point. Rather than invent or discover principles for a just society somewhere out there, outside Plato's cave (cf. also Walzer 1987), "sub specie aeternitatis" (Rawls 1971, p. 587), he meant to stand "in the city, on the ground" (Walzer 1983, p. xiv). From there he would interpret to his fellow citizens "the world of meanings that we share". Strictly speaking this would have entailed interpreting American shared understandings to fellow Americans, but Walzer chose examples from the past and from across the globe—metics in ancient Athens, a medieval Jewish community, immigration in Australia, guest workers in Western Europe, the National Health Service in the UK—to make sense of shared understandings in various political communities. Nor did Walzer's final assessment of just institutions (his eventual ideas on a fair distribution of education, welfare, political power, membership in the political community and so on, after the anthropological or historical excursions) strike as particularly American. *Spheres of Justice* outlines the argument that the world of meanings that we share consists of various spheres in which social goods are distributed according to sphere-specific criteria: the entrance to higher education should be awarded according to desert; medical care should be distributed according to need; and consumer goods ranging from yachts to hi-fi sets and rugs (Walzer 1983, p. 108) should be the subject of free exchange. Apart from the sphere-specific distributional criteria, justice consists in keeping the different spheres apart: the entrance to higher education cannot be granted to Hugh rather than Harriet because he needs it more if she is the more talented student. Nor can medical care be awarded to the highest bidder because the meaning of medical care is radically different from the meaning of yachts and rugs. It is up to citizens and to the state to keep the spheres of justice separate. This is not a vision of justice shared globally (at various points in *Spheres of Justice* Walzer points out that it would not hold in a devout caste society, see pp. 27, 314), but it certainly applies to Western welfare states in general, including those in Western Europe. One might even argue that, ironically, Walzer's theory is more at home in Western Europe and Canada than in the US, because of the reigning American consensus that health care should be distributed according to need.

Non-American readers who are convinced by *Spheres of Justice* may adopt Walzer's way of doing philosophy. They would then interpret Canadian, British, or Dutch shared understandings to their fellow citizens in Canada, the UK, or the Netherlands. But in many cases, they may also feel that Walzer's take on the distribution of certain social goods (medical care, benefits, higher education) concurs with the shared understanding regarding these particular goods in their own society. In these cases, their employment of Walzer's theory would go beyond the adoption of his method; it would involve acknowledging his shared understandings as also, even equally applicable in their own political communities. For readers especially interested in the application of Walzer's theory to policy problems the steps to follow would be similar in the US and in other Western states:

- Identify the shared understandings regarding the distribution of, say, political power, higher education, medical care.

- Determine that these would be, respectively: political power should be divided according to citizens' preferences, higher education according to merit and medical care according to medical need.
- Then evaluate or possibly criticize real-existing societal arrangements, for example argue that rich citizens have too much political influence compared to poor citizens in the US, that Oxbridge universities in Britain take in too many wealthy students from elite boarding schools in the South of the country, or that mental care hospitals in the Netherlands spend too much effort on patients who suffer from mild psychiatric conditions and too little on the most seriously ill.

In the next section I will discuss how this type of argument fared during the era of neoliberalism.

Preserving Shared Understandings in Times of Marketization

The decades after *Spheres of Justice* was published are generally described as the epoch of neoliberalism or new public management (e.g. Sandel 2012; Schram 2018; Hood 1991; Diefenbach 2009). In many Western countries public utilities (electricity, telephone infrastructure, postal services, public transport) were privatized and marketized. Market incentives were also introduced in societal spheres like health care and education. The market logic was deemed to enhance efficiency (lowering the price of services rendered) and improve performance (enhance the quality and speed of service delivery). However, marketizing former public goods or introducing market incentives in sectors like health care and education raises distributional questions. Following Walzer's theory it is quite acceptable to sell yachts, hi-fi sets and rugs to the highest bidder. With regard to consumer goods the system of free exchange produces an outcome that is satisfactory in terms of price and quality for both buyer and seller. But with regard to social goods like health care and education our shared understandings suggest that they should be distributed according to need (health care) and desert (higher education). Hence, during the heydays of neoliberalism participants in parliamentary and public debates often posed the question whether marketization of parts of the public sector would go against our shared understandings and the objections against marketization were distributional in nature, like textbook applications of *Spheres of Justice*.

Example 1. Fast Lane Treatment in Health Care

During the 1990s there were long waiting lists for certain medical treatments in the Netherlands. Inspired by the general atmosphere of marketization and neoliberalism policymakers came up with a plan to grant citizens the chance to buy a fast lane ticket to health care, like one can buy from airplane companies when they offer priority lanes. Proponents of the fast lane treatment pointed out that this was bound to increase overall efficiency. Waiting lists would decrease in the regular lane too because the fast lane treatment patients would be siphoned off. It might be even more efficient to allow employers rather than individual citizens to buy fast lane treatment for their workers. Workers would recover sooner and then rejoin the workforce, thus increasing total productivity.

Opponents of the plan pointed out that it would violate our shared understandings of medical care. Medical care ought to be distributed according to medical need. The fast lane proposal would allow lesser afflicted patients to jump the queue (even if they technically joined a different queue); they might be treated before other patients who might need medical care more urgently. Likewise, if workers were to be treated before, say, pensioners suffering from a more serious or more urgent affliction, this would violate a cherished principle concerning the distribution of medical care. It might be more efficient, it might even be more just from a utilitarian perspective, but it would be wrong all the same.

Example 2. Favoring the Young and Healthy

During the era of neoliberalism competition was introduced in the Dutch health care system. Private health insurers buy large quantities of medical treatments from care providers, negotiating a fair price on behalf of potential clients. Subsequently they offer insurance packages to aspiring clients. Young and healthy clients need less care. Health insurers thought they might offer these clients a bargain price. According to the Sickness Insurance Law insurers are not allowed to refuse elderly clients or clients suffering from preexisting conditions; they have to charge these expensive clients a standard premium. But insurers argued it might be acceptable to lure the young and healthy to their company with minimum care packages for a lower price.

Opponents of the bargain price package again used a Walzerian counter-argument. The bargain price proposal would not directly violate our shared understandings of medical care. However, the principle that medical care ought to be distributed according to medical need is based on solidarity between the sick and the healthy, the old and the young: from each according to their ability to pay, to each according to their medical need. The bargain price proposal suggests that people pay for their own health consumption rather than that of others. The young would pay little because most likely they will not fall ill. The elderly would pay a high premium on account of their higher risk. A prominent member of the board of health insurers at the time stated that care was comparable to cars. “Some people want to buy a Mercedes and are willing to pay for that. Others are happy with a Fiat Panda. So why should that be different in health care?” (Trappenburg 2005, p. 26). But his plea went unanswered. In the end the shared understandings regarding the distribution of medical care prevailed. Medical care was to be distributed according to medical need.

Despite the successful preservation of cherished shared understandings regarding the distribution of social goods, marketization and privatization were implemented in large parts of the public sector. What happened may be described in two different ways. The first way builds on a famous article by Hood, entitled “A Public Management for All Seasons?” (1991). Hood argues that governments and policymakers have to reckon with three sets of values. So-called theta values instruct governments to keep their dealings with citizens “honest and fair.” Sigma values admonish them to keep things “lean and purposeful”, that is: effective and efficient. Lambda values instruct them to keep things robust and resilient. Hood argues that it is impossible to honor the three sets of values simultaneously. The dominant values in the era of neoliberalism and new public management were sigma values. The Walzerian shared understandings regarding the proper way to distribute social goods are theta values, relating to fairness. Following Hood’s argument, we might hypothesize that an increasing emphasis on sigma values (marketization) while holding on to theta values (shared distributive norms) would have gone to the detriment of lambda values. And this is indeed an appropriate way to describe what happened to Dutch health care during the era of marketization: numerous incentives were introduced to enhance efficiency, and all slack was squeezed out of the system. When Covid hit Europe in 2020 the Dutch health care system was immediately overwhelmed. Seriously ill patients were transferred to hospitals in neighboring countries because the number of intensive care beds had been reduced to the utter minimum in the previous decades. The system had become much more efficient while staying true to the appropriate distributive principles, but it was no longer resilient; it could not absorb shocks like the Covid epidemic.

The second way to describe what happened to the health care system is to argue that although the changes did not affect patients or health care consumers, they certainly did affect health care staff: nurses, doctors and hospital administrators. In sociological accounts of the health care sector we learn that its employees usually do not possess commercial talents; they tend to be non-entrepreneurial; though they appreciate a good salary as much as any other citizen they do not enjoy thinking about how to maximize profits. In terms of Freidson (2001) the logic of a health care system is based on professionalism. This entails that doctors in different hospitals or practices consider one another as colleagues: professionalism is about monopoly, not about competition (Freidson 2001, p. 3). In the past doctors were forbidden to advertise their services. If a doctor felt that another doctor in a different hospital would be better equipped to cure a patient suffering from a complicated disease, he would refer his patient to that hospital; unlike salesmen selling yachts, rugs and hi-fi sets, who would not dream of sending clients away to other shops where they sell the same product, only cheaper, better or more beautiful. Professionals "place the good of the client, the public, or the development of a discipline over their own economic self-interest" (Freidson 2001, p. 214). Professionals are bound by codes of ethics, which specify how to do that, and disciplinary courts of fellow-professionals hold them to account if they fail to live up to their code. It is this part of the sphere of medical care (or the medical care part in the sphere of security and welfare) that has come under attack because of the advancement of marketization. Doctors now have to think about the long-term profits of the hospital, they are expected to advertise their hospital to potential clients. They are supposed to think along with patients, honoring requests that they do not deem necessary from a medical perspective.

Before marketization, Dutch general practitioners were widely known for being rather strict. One of their tasks was to perform triage. They used to distinguish between patients whose ailments would disappear naturally, patients who could be treated by the GP themselves and patients who needed hospital care from a specialized physician. Except in emergency situations patients could not enter hospital care without a letter of referral from their GP. Legally, this is still the case, but GPs have been encouraged to become client-friendly, more like salesmen. Patients have been encouraged to become assertive consumers and to shop around to get what they want. Doctors, hospitals and GP practices are reviewed on websites, just like hotels, restaurants and campsites. Patients can demand a referral to hospital care and leave a negative review on the public website if the GP refuses their request. Contemporary GPs also perceive opportunities. Before marketization they were opposed to medicalization. People who did not suffer and felt fine were left alone, because they didn't need medical attention. Since the advent of marketization GPs come up with profitable schemes to invite healthy people to come in for a blood pressure check-up or other money-making diagnostic test (Dwarswaard 2011). The fact that GP practices are now bought and sold by hedge fund investors has exacerbated this phenomenon (De Rijk 2024). In terms of Sandel one might say that the marketization of health care has not led to inequality, but it has led to the "corruption" or corrosion (Sandel 2012; p. 8) of professional norms.

In *Spheres of Justice* professional norms get rather short shrift. The topic is discussed most extensively in a section tellingly called "professionalism and the insolence of office" (Walzer 1983, pp. 155–160). Walzer argues that professional men and women lay claim to a particular body of knowledge. They guard the entrance to their profession so that they can "command high fees and salaries" (p. 156) and maintain their status as professionals in a hierarchy. To undergird his argument Walzer refers to the work of Larson (1977) on professionalism. Larson is one of a group of scholars who—mostly during the 1970s—wrote critical, even cynical accounts of professionalism, usually arguing that professionals mystified their expertise so that lay persons would not be able to evaluate their work, and could be charged with a lot of money if they wanted to use their services. Apart from Larson the works of Illich (1975) and Berlant (1975) belong to this group. In his younger years Freidson (1970) whose 2001 book was discussed above also belonged to this group of scholars. The critical approach of professionalism argued that (1) doctors pretend to be dedicated to their patients' best interests but in reality, they are self-serving and money-driven and (2) doctors tend to have a paternalistic attitude toward patients claiming to know what's best for them disregarding patients' own preferences. Neoliberalism (or rather: politicians and policy makers adopting the general mood of the time, expecting all sorts of beneficial effects as a result of marketization) transformed this critical view on the medical profession into a call for marketization: your doctors are just as money-driven as ordinary salesmen, so let us treat them as such. And: you should not let doctors decide what's best for you; you can be an informed and assertive consumer, you should be entitled to choose and to shop around for medical services (Dean 1999; Tonkens 2008; Schram 2018). According to Freidson (2001) something got lost on the road to marketization and this something is "the soul of professionalism". While some doctors may be self-serving and greedy, the profession as a whole embodies the norm that they should be dedicated to their patients' best interests and it is valuable that doctors uphold this norm individually and collectively.

Based on this impression of evidence regarding the health care sector I conclude that spheres of justice contain more morally relevant elements than sphere-specific principles of distribution. It is possible to have the sphere of money and commodities with its market-based principle of free exchange invade another sphere of justice whilst preventing damage to that sphere's distributing principle, but it is quite possible (even likely) that something else will be lost along the way. Walzer (1983, pp. 218–219) discusses a similar scenario when writing about vouchers in education. Granting parents vouchers to find a school for their children that matches their preferences in terms of religious instruction or pedagogical approach is a good way to ensure that schools cannot cater for wealthy children only. But it would lead to "rootlessness and easy mobility"; in terms of Hirschman (1970), it would induce parents to practice exit rather than voice thereby possibly damaging desirable ties between school and neighborhoods. Again, like in the medical care example, there is more to spheres than distributive justice.

Multi-dimensional Man and the Division of Power in Society

To many readers Walzer's interpretation of shared understandings concurred with their own, which made the book very useful for citizens and policymakers grappling with the questions brought up by marketization in the last decades of the twentieth century. But *Spheres of Justice* struck a deeper chord as well; its underpinning image of moral man seemed sympathetic and not overly demanding. If one reads utilitarianism-based books by Singer (2009, 2015), which invariably suggest that one should take the greater good of humanity or even all living creatures on the planet into account in everything one does or considers doing, one ends up feeling either guilty, ashamed and depressed for failing so abysmally or irritated with the author and overstrained by his highly demanding philosophy. By contrast Walzer's portrayal of moral man seemed plausible and appealing. *Spheres of Justice* builds on the assumption that talents are more or less randomly distributed among human beings. Some people were born naturally beautiful, which would benefit them greatly in the sphere of love and affection. Others were good at sports and athletic prowess could lead to medals, world cups, rounds of applause and fame and glory among enthusiastic spectators. Yet others were clever, or avid readers. Their reward was a high grade-point-average at schools and universities and possibly access to prestigious colleges. Some people were naturally kind which would win them affection and friendship. Rhetorical talents could lead to the esteem of one's fellow citizens if one addressed the city council. Entrepreneurial skills would be rewarded with money and market commodities. And so on, and so forth. It seemed very reassuring that one did not have to tick all the boxes: one could be a lazy student but a kind and loving son; a talented television host, but an unfriendly boss or father; an overweight, clumsy woman but a talented academic; a skilled businessman but a bad citizen or party member and so on.

This nuanced picture of man as usually being a mixture of failings and good qualities is the first idea underpinning Walzer's second master-principle: spheres of justice should be kept separate. The multi-faceted picture allows us to evaluate fellow citizens on abilities or failings in one particular sphere at the time: politicians have to be good at politics and advocate beliefs that we endorse. They do not have to be faithful marital partners; that is not relevant for the job. Patients will be treated according to need and here too, their family life, criminal record, or academic performance is irrelevant.

The early debate about *Spheres of Justice* sometimes dealt with people who would finish first or last in all societal spheres, having been blessed with a multitude of talents or by contrast lacking talents of any kind. Usually, Walzer-followers assumed that these discrepancies must have been caused by some sort of transgression of spheres. With regard to those blessed with multiple talents they could point out how rich parents often hire tutors to help their less talented children get good grades (Elffers 2018). They may pressure their children's hockey or football coach to select their son or daughter as first-team players by threatening to withhold donations or sponsorships. They may buy dental treatments or cosmetic surgery to improve their children's appearances. They may even hire psychological expertise to help their children be kind and compassionate. To remedy these types of unfair competition, Walzerians would argue that it was up to the government or institutional authorities to prevent this type of transgression by creating a level playing field, for example by offering tutoring free of charge to students from low income families or by institutionalising the selection of first-team players in such a way that their parents' donations would not be a factor to be taken into consideration.

With regard to people drawing the short end of the stick in each and every societal sphere, Walzer himself argued that in the daily reality of an imperfect, less than just society, this was surely caused by (subtle) forms of exclusion, racism or discrimination by various institutions and offices of the welfare state: "Fully incompetent individuals do not exist; at any rate there is no such thing as a class of fully incompetent individuals." (Walzer 1994, p. 192). Talents are diverse and randomly distributed. Hence in a society based on complex equality, you are bound to succeed in some societal sphere. If that does not happen, this means the scales are tilted and need to be adjusted, presumably by state intervention. It is important to realize that these adjustments should consist of improved border control between the spheres at issue; they should not consist of within-sphere adjustments. A good illustration of this is the Danish Netflix drama series *Rita*. Rita teaches an unruly class with very little academic talent. At some point a football tournament is organized and Rita's class contains several talented players. In a traditional spheres-of-justice vein Rita hopes that her class will finally be able to excel and finish first. But then management explains that there is a maximum number of goals that teams can score in one game. Once the maximum has been reached a team is advised to slow down to give their opponents (less sporty, nerdy students) a fair chance of winning. In the series this is especially hard on Rita's students because no comparable levelling down approach is used with regard to academic performance. But if the school were to adopt an equalizing operation across the board, one might still argue that this would constitute a distortion of our shared understandings. Nerdy students are often bad at sports and sporty students may be bad in mathematics and grammar. Adjusting the criteria to spare students' feelings is no solution; we ought to make sure that the spheres (or in this example the evaluating criteria) remain distinct. A student should not receive a diploma because he helped the school team win a trophy and neither should academic excellence be rewarded with a higher mark in physical education. Adjusting within-spheres criteria cannot be a solution to an acute issue of justice. Within-spheres criteria can change, but they do not change quickly. Walzer's examples of within-spheres changes tellingly contrast the meaning of medical care in medieval times with its present-day equivalent and the importance of romantic love in marriage under a traditional regime compared to modern times.

The picture of multidimensional man helps us accept our own and others' shortcomings. It also protects us against distributive or evaluating actors abusing their powers; this is the second idea underpinning the master principle that spheres should be kept separate. Medical care can mean the difference between life and death; it is reassuring that doctors will not consider your merits in other parts of life when distributing it. It would give them too much power if they would weigh up your flaws and good qualities to determine whether you would qualify for medical treatment. Likewise, it is reassuring that a lecturer at university is precise and sphere-specific when grading essays: an essay needs to be evaluated for its academic merits and the fact that the student who wrote it is very kind and enthusiastic or extremely annoying and arrogant should have no bearing on their mark. Again an integral assessment of students' merits as full human beings would give the lecturer too much power over their lives. Sphere-specificity served as a safeguard against a cumulation of power. In Dutch law and jurisprudence sphere-specificity has become codified as an underlying guiding principle, aptly called the specificity principle or the principle of *détournement de pouvoir*. Governmental institutions are supposed to use their authority for the purpose mentioned in the law that granted them this authority. They are not allowed to use their law-based instruments as a general toolbox for creative policy making (cf. Bovens 1994).

Identity Activism and Integral Policy Making

Walzer's second master principle—spheres of justice should be kept apart—rests on two underpinning ideas: the picture of moral man as multi-dimensional and the idea that it prevents the abuse of power in society by limiting the use of different kinds of power to their allotted spheres. However, the two-pronged underpinning of the second master principle is currently being threatened from two sides. On the one hand the recent rise of what is referred to as "wokism" or "identity politics" questions the attraction of the picture of multidimensional man. On the other hand, the rise of what is called "tailor-made policies" or "integral policy making" questions the idea that power should be limited by tying distributive agencies and actors to their respective societal spheres. I will discuss these developments in turn.

Mounk's *The Identity Trap* (2023) starts with recent social justice issues in America. He describes how racial equity plays a role in the division of medical care where the criterion of distribution according to medical need is sometimes replaced by a "race sensitive protocol for medical triage", giving preferential treatment to certain patients because of their race (Mounk 2023, pp. 4–8). Mounk argues that this phenomenon is part of the advancement of the "identity thesis", an ideology with various intellectual roots (postmodernism, postcolonialism and critical race theory), which argues (among other things, I will only regard what is relevant to the philosophy of *Spheres of Justice* here) that injustices in society are interconnected and should be discussed and fought as such. Thus, Mounk gives examples of special interest groups that used to fight against one particular form of injustice but now adopt various other causes simultaneously, which, to the Walzerian-inspired spectator might feel as a form of mission creep (Mounk 2023, p. 102). Mounk describes an environmentalist group which now issues statements on "a bewildering range of topics, from demanding that the Biden administration 'tear down the wall' on America's southern border to joining calls to 'defund the police'" (Mounk 2023, p. 105). A recent telling example would be renowned environmental activist Greta Thunberg simultaneously taking on the cause of justice for Palestinians in Gaza (Thunberg et al. 2023). Present-day activists seem to demand that their fellow activists have their heart in all the right places at once. Mounk argues that this will make human beings even more groupish than they already are.

The identity thesis as portrayed by Mounk represents a whole-human-being kind of thinking that requires people to consider one another as right or wrong across the board, instead of assessing and evaluating bits and pieces depending on the issue at stake, like the Walzer approach suggests. Mounk's argument provides another reason why the separate spheres principle is so appealing. It presents a sympathetic picture of moral man that is not overly demanding, and it prevents the accumulation of power in the hands of distributive actors and agencies, as argued above. But it also provides an antidote to polarization. It might be appealing to cooperate with soulmates who share your opinion on every single issue that comes up, but in politics it seems safer and better to consider fellow citizens as people with whom one agrees on certain issues but not on others, for certain moments in time.

In the world of leftist woke activists that Mounk describes the separate spheres-principle is threatened by the idea that injustices overlap and should be fought in coherence. In the world of policy making a different development also strives to transcend or overcome the separate spheres approach. Dutch political theorist Frissen recently published a book entitled *The integral state*, in which he argues that present-day policy making is mostly presented as "having to accommodate necessary societal transitions". For example: there is an environmental catastrophe hanging over us and in order to prevent this from happening the country needs to "transition" toward sustainable energy. This is a huge challenge that transcends all traditional policy boundaries. Hence policy makers, organizations and citizens from different backgrounds have to cooperate to rise to this challenge. Similar arguments can be made with regard to the crisis of migration in times of globalization or the demographic crisis caused by an ageing population. Integral policy making has become the cure-all for every major transition that is perceived as absolutely necessary. Frissen observes: "Only very rarely can you hear that the world is fragmented and that therefore compartmentalization is in order. To the contrary, fragmentation and compartmentalization must be fought and overcome." (Frissen 2023, p. 51). Policy makers who take the challenges ahead seriously are assumed to put societal problems first; those who cannot do that are presumably more interested in the interests and parochial moral standards of their own organization or policy sector (Frissen 2023, pp. 51–52 and 84).

The trend toward integral policy making is visible in policy documents about necessary transformations toward sustainability, but it can also be observed at the micro level when it comes to social policy (Frissen 2023, p. 56). A brief look at the history of social assistance in the Netherlands can illustrate what this entails.

Before 1965, social assistance to poor people was delivered by various societal organizations, first and foremost churches and local authorities.

Getting help usually involved an assessment of the claimant's situation: their finances, living conditions, but also marital problems, addictions, problems with raising children and so on. Social assistance was tailor-made and based on what might be termed an integral needs assessment. Financial help could be conditional on seeking treatment for addiction, getting marital counseling and engaging social services for advice on the children, along with the customary demand that clients had to do their best to find paid employment. In 1965 the system was changed. Under the new law people were entitled to social assistance on the basis of financial need alone, without an additional assessment. Social workers taught each other that they had to refrain from paternalistic interference in the families of the poor. They were no longer supposed to look at their clients' problems in coherence and come up with integral solutions. If clients needed psychotherapy, rehabilitation or marital counseling they should find counseling services but in and through a separate trajectory. The social assistance office would only address their financial situation (Trappenburg 2020).

Recently, in 2015, the system was changed again, this time to reintroduce tailor-made help and an integral assessment of poor people's needs (Bredewold et al. 2018). Municipalities installed neighborhood teams consisting of social workers, counsellors, and sometimes policemen or psychologists and the teams were to evaluate the whole situation of needy families. Before 2015 so-called multi-problem families were often assisted by a multitude of support workers one of whom would try to keep the family's son on the straight and narrow after a period of juvenile delinquency, another would be counseling the mother for her depression, a third would be dealing with the father's drinking problems and a fourth one would look into the family's accumulated debts (Kruiter and Pels 2012). This type of specialized help from different organizations by different professionals was widely considered time-consuming and inefficient; hence the call for new forms of integral assistance, often advocated with the rallying cry: "One family, one plan, one support worker" (slighted by Frissen [2023, p. 56] as a somewhat North Korean sounding slogan).

The Netherlands was not the only country to reintroduce tailor-made integral help. Watkins-Hayes (2009) studied American frontline workers who had to implement the Personal Responsibility and Work Opportunity Reconciliation Act of 1996. The PRWORA created ample space for frontline workers to help needy citizens in all sorts of ways, unhindered by legal obstacles, sphere-specificity or professional boundaries, in what Watkins-Hayes calls a "catch-all bureaucracy."

Integral help seems to fit many American front-line workers and support workers in Dutch neighborhood teams (Trappenburg et al. 2022). Clients do not oppose the interference in their private lives. Indeed, there is historic evidence that they did not appreciate the formal, bureaucratic approach of the 1965 social assistance law to begin with, even though it was less interfering and less paternalistic (Trappenburg 2020). Still, Frissen's analysis that the new sphere-transcending approach to policy making increases governmental power is quite convincing. If the government (or its helpers on behalf of the government) may approach you as a whole human being and subsequently offer to help you with all cards on the table, there is no place left to hide.

Like identity activism, the advancement of integral policy making seems a fundamental attack on Walzer's spheres of justice framework, because both ideas start from assumptions that are intuitively plausible, respectively: that injustices are connected and that societal problems require concerted efforts beyond organizational boundaries. With regard to both attacks reminding ourselves of the lessons from *Spheres of Justice* might cool our enthusiasm to proceed in a direction that we might regret later on. With regard to identity politics, it seems important to remind ourselves of the modest and therefore realistic idea of Walzer's multi-dimensional moral man and to agree with Mounk that addressing one issue at the time with one group of fellow citizens might help us fight polarization.

With regard to the attractions of integral policy making, we might start by acknowledging that the objections against across-the-board assessments and integral policy making are still part of our shared understandings. While many people generally respond positively if they are confronted with sphere-transcending plans to fight climate change or demographic change, and while they respond equally positive to integral help to multi-problem families, they tend to respond much less enthusiastically if told that the government sits on a huge amount of digital data, acquired by separate governmental authorities and public organizations. Combining all sorts of datasets (much like computer experts tend to do in American police series on tv) would really allow government to forge ahead in the direction of integral policy making. Yet, this, according to experts in digital data-sharing would take the integral policy ideal way too far. Data-sharing is associated with Big Brother and is frowned upon in the European Union. It is important to realize that large-scale data sharing is considered possibly harmful, not just because it would give big tech companies even more of a hold on all of us, but also because the idea of a government trusted with all kinds of information about us, turning us into near transparent citizens, is frightening because it gives government too much power.

Acknowledging this might make us more cautious with regard to other forms of integral policy making, such as the sphere-transcending battle against large-scale problems like climate change or help to multi-problem families discussed above. With regard to the latter, the spheres-of-justice approach may also remind us to look beyond the problems at hand: why did a family turn into a multi-problem family, or why did an individual become a multi-problem citizen? Instead of immediately launching an all-encompassing assistance trajectory, we might also reconsider the Walzerian assumption that manifold misfortune may have been caused by a transgression of spheres in an earlier stage. If multi-problem individuals and multi-problem families are very exceptional, integral help might be the right approach. But if the multi-problem phenomenon is more widespread, if there appears to be a class of individuals failing across the board we might take a closer look at the specific causes of the cumulative misfortune befalling certain families and wonder whether they were not caused by some sort of unjustified exclusion in one or another societal sphere rather than just accepting the multi-problem situation as is and get to work remedying it.

Still Useful After All These Years

Reassessing *Spheres of Justice* after forty years we can say that it proved exceptionally valuable in the long era of marketization and neoliberalism, helping us to uphold shared understandings regarding the distribution of social, non-market goods. In addition, it would be good to realize that there is more to spheres of justice than distribution alone, and that it is necessary to cherish other shared understandings (for example professional norms) as well.

After the heydays of neoliberalism and marketization new dangers threaten our shared understandings. The Walzerian picture of moral man—multifaceted or multidimensional, failing in certain ways but doing well in other parts of life—might be replaced by the whole-person approach advanced in parts of the leftist woke movement where people are expected to be fighting all forms of social injustice simultaneously. It is good to remember the modest moral demands of *Spheres of Justice*, that allow us to form partial and temporary bonds thus preventing polarization. A political community does not fare well when persisting cleavages resurface with each new issue that pops up. It is better to have many cross-cutting cleavages that will lead to different winners and losers with every new issue.

The second danger threatening Walzer's master principle that spheres of justice should be kept apart is the advent of integral policy making. Integral policy making sounds forceful and effective: do not just stick to your assigned duty, government officials, join forces, merge organizations and fight major policy problems together. However, the lesson we learned from *Spheres of Justice* is that governmental organizations were kept separate for good reasons. Having separate organizations in separate spheres prevents the accumulation of power. It is important to at least take this lesson into account when looking at policy problems that seem to warrant a coordinated effort: is it really wise to assemble power rather than divide it? And do we want organizations to have all-encompassing data on citizens so as to enable them to rule more effectively? With regard to integral policy making in social policy—providing across the board assistance instead of separate bits of help for different problems—it seems important to first study the phenomenon of citizens needing across the board assistance. While it might be good to offer integral help if this group forms a tiny minority, it is less appealing if the group is much bigger than that. In the latter case a Walzerian investigation might show how and where boundaries between spheres were ignored or transgressed, which caused the cumulative misfortune to come into being.

Spheres of Justice still offers guidance and inspiration. It is still eminently usable after all these years.

Competing Interests The author has no conflicts of interest to declare that are relevant to the content of this chapter.

References

Ackerman, B.A. (1981). *Social Justice in the Liberal State*. Yale UP.

Berlant, J.L. (1975). *Profession and Monopoly: a Study of Medicine in the United States and Great Britain*. University of California Press.

Bovens, M. (1994). Detournement de pouvoir: een Walzeriaans perspectief op juridisering. In Berg, Paul van den and Margo Trappenburg (eds.), *Lokale rechtvaardigheid. De politieke theorie van Michael Walzer*, Tjeenk Willink, pp. 97–106.

Bredewold, F. et al. (2018). *De verhuizing van de verzorgingsstaat. Hoe de overheid nabijkomt*. Van Gennep.

Dean, M. (1999). *Governmentality. Power and Rule in Modern Society*. Sage.

De Rijk, M. (2024). *Gekaapt door het kapitaal. Zorg, onderwijs, wonen en kinderopvang*. Pluim.

Diefenbach, T. (2009), New Public Management in Public Sector Organizations: the Dark Sides of Managerialistic 'Englightenment'. *Public Administration*, 87, pp. 892–909.

Dwarswaard, J. (2011). *De dokter en de tijdgeest. Een halve eeuw veranderingen in de beroepsethiek van huisartsen en chirurgen*. Boom Lemma.

Dworkin, R. (1981a). What is Equality? Part 1: Equality of Welfare. *Philosophy & Public Affairs* 10(3), pp. 185–246.

Dworkin, R. (1981b). What is Equality? Part 2: Equality of Resources. *Philosophy & Public Affairs* 10(4), pp. 283–345.

Elffers, L. (2018), *De bijlesgeneratie. Opkomst van de onderwijscompetitie*. Amsterdam University Press.

Freidson, E. (1970). *Professional Dominance: The Social Structure of Medical Care*. Atherton Press.

Freidson, E. (2001). *Professionalism: The Third Logic*. University of Chicago Press.

Frissen, P. (2023). *De integrale staat. Kritiek van de samenleving*, Boom.

Hirschman, A.O. (1970). *Exit, Voice and Loyalty. Responses to Decline in Firms, Organizations and States*. Harvard UP.

Hood, C. (1991). A public management for all seasons? *Public Administration*, 69(1), pp. 3–19.

Illich, I. (1975). *Medical Nemesis. The Expropriation of Health*. Marion Boyars.

Jacobs, J. (1992). *Systems of Survival. A Dialogue on the Moral Foundations of Commerce and Politics*. Hodder & Stouhgton.

Kruiter, A. and K. Pels (2012). *De dag dat Peter de deur dichttimmerde. Waarom mensen die onze hulp het hardst nodig hebben niet geholpen worden*. Prometheus.

Larson, M.S. (1977). *The Rise of Professionalism*. University of California Press.

Mol, A. (2008). *The Logic of Care. Health and the Problem of Patient Choice*. Routledge.

Mounk, Y. (2023). *The Identity Trap. A Story of Ideas and Power in Our Time.* Allen Lane.

Nozick, R. (1974). *Anarchy, State, and Utopia.* Basic Books.

Rawls, J. (1971). *A Theory of Justice.* Harvard UP.

Sandel, M.J. (2012) *What Money Can't Buy: The Moral Limits of Markets.* Allen Lane.

Schram, S.S. (2018). Neoliberalizing the Welfare State: Marketizing Social Policy/Disciplining Clients. In Damien Cahill et al. (eds), *The Sage Handbook of Neoliberalism*, pp. 308–322.

Singer, P. (2009). *The Life You Can Save: Acting Now to End World Poverty.* Random House.

Singer, P. (2015). *The Most Good You Can Do: How Effective Altruism Is Changing Ideas About Living Ethically.* Yale University Press.

Thunberg, G. and Fridays for Future Sweden (2023). We won't Stop Speaking about Gaza's Suffering – There is No Climate Justice without Human Rights. *The Guardian.* https://www.theguardian.com/commentisfree/2023/dec/05/gaza-climate-justice-human-rights-greta-thunberg

Tonkens, E. (2008). *Mondige burgers, getemde professionals.* Van Gennep.

Trappenburg, M.J. (2000). In Defence of Pure Pluralism. *Journal of Political Philosophy*, 8(2), pp. 343–362.

Trappenburg, M.J. (1997). Defining the Medical Sphere. *Cambridge Quarterly of Health Care Ethics*, 6(4), pp. 416–434.

Trappenburg, M. (2005). *Gezondheidszorg en Democratie.* Inaugural address, Rotterdam.

Trappenburg, M. (2020). Wie hulp nodig heeft, wil maatwerk. De historische zoektocht naar een rechtvaardige bijstand, in: T. Kampen et al. (eds.) *Streng maar onrechtvaardig. De bijstand gewogen.* Van Gennep, pp. 23–44

Trappenburg, M., T. Kampen & E. Tonkens (2022). Street-Level Bureaucrats in a Catch-All Bureaucracy. *Administration & Society*, 54(10), pp. 2021–2047.

Walzer, M. (1983). *Spheres of Justice. A Defence of Pluralism and Equality.* Basil Blackwell.

Walzer, M. (1987). *Interpretation and Social Criticism.* Harvard UP.

Walzer, M. (1994). Uitsluiting, onrecht en de democratische staat. In Berg, Paul van den and M.J. Trappenburg (eds.), *Lokale rechtvaardigheid. De politieke theorie van Michael Walzer.* Tjeenk Willink, pp. 181–196.

Watkins-Hayes, C. (2009). *The New Welfare bureaucrats. Entanglements of Race, class, and policy reform.* Chicago University Press.

CHAPTER 10

Response

Michael Walzer

I am grateful to all the contributors to this volume; they have engaged the arguments of my book in ways other authors will envy. Justice does not require, as I wrote somewhere, that all authors get the same appreciation or the same criticism. But I do wish for all of them the same careful attention that I have gotten here. I owe special thanks to J. Toby Reiner (in his introduction) and Astrid von Busekist (in her essay) for their summary presentation of my key arguments; they have done this better than I could do. Astrid's emphasis on comradeship (she is one of my comrades) rightly identifies a driving force in my life and work—and an ideal that I have not always honored as I should. Working together with others is a necessary feature of political life; recognizing others as equals is a necessary feature of a particular kind of politics.

Both Toby and Astrid recognize that I am a political theorist for whom politics is often more important than theory. One purpose of political theory is to explain how politics works, how political power is pursued, how institutions are developed to restrain the pursuit, how ambition and conviction interact, and much more. Spheres has nothing to say about

M. Walzer (✉)
Institute for Advanced Study, Princeton, NJ, USA
e-mail: walzer@ias.edu

J. T. Reiner (ed.), *Walzer and Justice: Spheres of Justice in the 2020s*,
https://doi.org/10.1007/978-3-031-87809-1_10

these questions. For me, the purpose of political theory is to advance a political position. Astrid here and Toby here and in other places, provide generous accounts of my political engagements. It is no accident, as Astrid notes, that the earliest version of the argument for complex equality appeared in *Dissent*, a magazine strenuously committed to a cause, where I was an engaged writer and editor for many years. My theories come out of my engagements.

* * *

Spheres of Justice was published in 1983, conceived and written in the decade before that. Looking around now, watching the news, reading the papers, it seems as if we live in another world. Several of the contributors to this volume invoke the differences and speculate about their meaning. I will try to address their speculations. My book is indeed the product of its time, the glory years of social democracy in Western Europe and, though with less glory, in the US, too. Those years were already drawing to a close in the '70s, but news always reaches the academy a little late.

Spheres is an optimistic book: I thought that I was joining a conversation about equality (begun by John Rawls in 1971) that was of central importance not only in the academy but also in the world of politics. All of us who participated in that conversation wrote with a sense of possibility: that ideas might become policies. (There were law professors, I remember, who thought that the Supreme Court might soon begin enforcing Rawls's difference principle.) Today academic discussions about equality seem, no, they are narrowly academic. There is indeed a politics of opposition to inequality, but it is immediate and practical (and at the moment not very effective) with little publicly resonant theoretical discussion.

Pretty much everyone recognizes the extreme polarization of political life today, and several commentators here argue that this makes "spherical" arguments difficult or impossible. Polarization, it is said, disrupts shared understandings. I would rather say that it forces us to engage in arguments that are not interestingly philosophical; it makes it hard to get back to the discussions about justice of forty or fifty years ago.

Consider the far right's embrace of (a crude) libertarianism, its opposition to all the welfare-regarding uses of state power. A good example is its opposition to the mandated vaccinations and the requirement to wear masks during the Covid years. Certainly, the country was polarized, but it was not divided about the meaning of health or longevity as social goods. Liberty versus life was not the issue, for the right-wing politicians who claimed to champion liberty insisted at the same time that masks and vaccines did not, in fact, defend us against Covid. They did not deny the common understanding of the value of longevity. The people shouting, "Don't tread on me!" did not believe that their health was in any way less important than the rest of us believed our own health to be. The disagreement was about the scientific account of Covid, about statist conspiracies, and about the facts of the case. I think this is the point of Steven Lukes's detailed description of contemporary polarization: that it is most crucially a radical break in our understanding of the factual world, but not necessarily a break in our understanding of social goods.

The test of my argument in *Spheres* might come if there were a citizens' assembly considering (an immediate and urgent issue as I write) America's immigration policy. The first thing that is required in these assemblies as they have been described by advocates and practitioners is that all the participants be informed of the facts of the case by some authoritative figure. The assembly might hear from "experts," as Steven writes, who disagree about the economic effects of immigration, but they would simply be told, for example, that the crime rate among immigrants is lower than that among native-born Americans. The discussion begins only after basic information is accepted. What would it focus on? I suspect that the citizens would agree about the value of membership, the meaning of asylum, the rights and obligations of new and old members—and then argue about the policies required by these understandings. These would be spherical arguments, qualified, perhaps, by memories of the participants' own membership history—and by universal moral principles like those that David Miller invokes (I will come back to them). Steven believes, as I do, that the assembly could and often would reach consensus.

But the disagreement about facts and "alternative facts" points us toward another issue, which has been raised with me by friends. Perhaps we should consider "information" a social good and worry about how it might rightly be distributed. The good might better be described as "accurate information" and surely it should be universally available. How to make it so? We try to prevent fraud in medical care by licensing physicians and regulating the sale of medicines; this is possible because there is broad agreement about good and bad medical practice. But there is no similar agreement about the provision of information. I can imagine psychological arguments about the appeal of conspiracy theories and "fake news" but the only spherical argument that seems possible is an appeal to those who provide information to defend the principle of truth-telling. And that defense turns out, in practice, to be political, not philosophical. The value of truth is a matter for philosophy, the identity of truth-tellers, the content of statements about the world, is a matter for public debate and political struggle.

Is that the whole story? Let's turn from the provision of information in the adult world to the education of children. Education is a social good and, again, distributive justice requires that it be available to all the country's children and that it prepare them for citizenship. We have to argue about its content (how, for example, do we present the history of our country?), and these arguments will result in curricula whose teaching we enforce in different ways—in public schools controlled by elected school boards, in legally required courses in private and parochial schools, in the regulation of home schooling. We accept coercion in the education of children even though we don't always agree on what should be taught; we agree about enough. If that agreement was lost, an inclusive public education system would be impossible. We would have to have church schools, liberal secular schools, socialist schools, nationalist schools, and so on. And that's more or less what we have with regard to information today. Our different understandings of the world reflect the different newspapers and magazines we read and the media we tune into. I can imagine, with Orwell, a Ministry of Truth. I can't recommend it as a means of distribution.

The arguments about education are spherical: we interpret the meaning of a social good. What exactly gets enforced is decided politically, but then there are a host of other arguments about factual matters: are school nurses helping or enforcing sexual transitions? Are children being indoctrinated in alien ideologies? Are they being "groomed" for sexual promiscuity? These claims, versions of which seem to be widely accepted, require both counter-information and, again, political struggle. But they have nothing to do with justice—except insofar as they get in the way of the justice arguments that we need to have.

* * *

Polarization is less of a threat to complex equality than the fact that egalitarians are losing the political wars—losing to political forces that advocate what is best called simple inequality. As Michael Rustin argues, a long series of political defeats has left us with an increasingly steep hierarchy, where wealth is the dominant, indeed overwhelmingly dominant, good. What is needed now is a radical redistribution—what Michael describes as "a substantial advance in the direction of equality simply conceived." I agree with this, with the caveat that the advance stops somewhere short of a "simply conceived" equality of income and wealth, and then we begin to argue about what is and isn't a commodity and what can and can't be traded on the market.

Michael, together with Toby, rightly characterize *Spheres* as an argument for social democracy. That it certainly is, and I continue to believe that this argument can be sustained through the interpretation of recognized social goods. The internal resources for social democratic advocacy exist in our (American, Western) everyday world. I am heartened, therefore, by Margo Trappenburg's account of the usefulness of Spheres in the fight against neo-liberalism—this from someone who seems to have been intellectually (actively?) engaged in the fight. Her discussion of professionalism is a useful rebuke; I should have recognized the value of professional standards in spherical arguments. Margo also suggests that the principles articulated in *Spheres* might help in the fight against the "woke" left; I am not there yet, but I hope she is right.

Nothing I have written should be taken to mean that other justice arguments are not also available and useful—arguments about human rights, about the requirements for human flourishing, even, as Kurtz suggests, about creation in the image of God. The more, the better. In fact, the different arguments are interconnected. Consider "blocked exchanges": the reason for blocking the sale of human beings, for denying that men and women can ever be commodities, is, as Michael writes, our regard for the intrinsic value of human life, for the rights of those men and women. All the blocked exchanges in the market and the state rely on arguments like that. Flammable pajamas are blocked because they are dangerous to human life. Commodities are supposed to be commodious, but it is other values that will determine what we consider commodious and what not. I suspect that these other values will also lead us to something like social democracy—though that may seem a stretch to some readers in the case of creation in the image.

I agree with Michael and Toby that the version of social democracy that emerges in *Spheres* is pluralist and activist in a way that social democratic regimes and parties have not always been. Worker participation in corporate decision-making, worker owned companies, as Toby writes, is my clearest example of democratic activism. Strong unions and worker and consumer representation on company boards might also serve the cause of complex equality. But I think it is important to recognize that the overall stability of complex equality depends on active citizens in all the spheres—teachers defending the integrity of public education; judges and lawyers resisting the pressure of wealthy or powerful individuals; doctors opposing insurance company profiteering; ordinary citizens demanding the provision of essential services.

I also imagine a lively political sphere, which may, as Toby suggests, be crucial to everything else, since the regulation of the boundaries of all the spheres takes place here. It is in the sphere of the state that citizens debate the uses of political power, join parties and movements, choose representatives, participate in local and national elections. This isn't the same thing as decision-making, which at the state level will most often be delegated. What is crucial is that the active agency of citizens precedes governance.

I like Toby's response to the argument that private property and corporate ownership do not belong exclusively to the market sphere; they involve the exercise of power over others and so must be subject to democratic control or regulation. Consider (for fun) one of those weird examples that I usually avoid: a hotel owner advertises room and board for a price and then tells his customers, who have paid the price, that they are not allowed to read Marx in their rooms and must listen to rightwing political talks at breakfast. That is an exercise of power that his customers would oppose—and the democratic state would uphold their opposition. Regulations relevant to the maintenance of the hotel would fall within the owner's purview, but not the intellectual or political life of the residents. Now suppose the owner claims that reading Marx is a challenge to his ownership of the hotel and that the breakfast talks are essential to sustain the economic project of renting rooms—just as banning the distribution of union literature in a factory is a defense of efficient factory production. These claims are rightly opposed, again, by hotel residents and factory workers, and the democratic state should uphold the opposition. Power exercised to sustain a particular economic arrangement is political power.

I don't mean that the residents should run the hotel, but if we turn the hotel into a town, it seems obvious today that the people who live there (though not the visitors) should govern the town. But I like the idea of a hotel run cooperatively by its workers, and certainly a large corporation owning many hotels should be run by a board that includes representatives of the men and women who manage and maintain the buildings and serve the residents. So, we respect the privacy of the rooms and the agency of the workers.

* * *

I think that Georgia Warnke's suggestion that the interpretive arguments in *Spheres* are like interpretations of literary texts is apt; it helps us understand the character of the arguments and their endlessness. So, it invites, as she says, a kind of mutual respect, or at least tolerance, among the participants. But there are also critical differences: the stakes are much higher when we argue about the distribution of hard work or leisure time than when we argue about the meaning of Moby Dick. Interpretive victories may still be temporary, but they nonetheless have immediate material consequences—which may make the disagreements fiercer than those of literary critics.

All the contributors to this volume agree, I believe, with the most important claim that Warnke makes: that there are better and worse interpretations but no final definitive interpretation. Sometimes the arguments seem to end and then, suddenly, some ambitious young man or woman produces a very smart defense of an idea we all thought was disposed of long ago. (I read somewhere of a MAGA disciple describing, not smartly, the mutual benefits of the Southern slave system.) What applies to the interpretive arguments that I hope for applies also to all other interpretive arguments. It is not the case that we can resolve spherical disagreements by moving (upwards?) and appealing to human rights, for there again we will find ourselves disagreeing.

Democratic politics produce endings: laws enacted; policies forcefully pursued. But these are only temporary endings, for the arguments are immediately resumed. Indeed, the temporary character of all political decisions is a necessary feature of democracy. Shouldn't we also say that it is a necessary feature of philosophy—that no theory can be more than momentarily triumphant? And then the arguments resume. Ideologies are different; their authors look for an authoritarian state to make the ideology pervasive in intellectual life and permanently established in law. But that doesn't work either.

* * *

David Miller has thought longer and more deeply about immigration than I have, and I am inclined simply to accept his revisions of my argument. Certainly, the distribution of membership is sometimes constrained by principles of justice (anti-racism, for example, as Miller argues). And sometimes distributions are required by justice—as in the case of refugees coming to the US from countries in which we have been malignly involved. But I don't know what to say about a possible future in which millions of climate refugees fleeing rising waters and spreading deserts are pounding at the gates of countries that are at the same time dealing with their own internal refugees fleeing similar dangers and disasters. Then, perhaps, compassion and its limits will figure more importantly in our discussions than justice and its requirements.

I also agree with David that there could be just arrangements for temporary guest workers that barred exploitation and provided for the enforcement of rights (short of citizenship). Perhaps we should think of those workers as citizens of their home countries, protected by the governments they and their relatives elected. Men and women not protected but persecuted by their governments might be given work permits that guarantee their rights, but if it is clear that they are here, wherever here is, not temporarily but for the long term, I would want them set on the road to citizenship.

* * *

I have left Geoffrey Kurtz's plea for a founding argument or, at least, an "orientation" that gives readers some sense of where my arguments come from or how they might be grounded—I have left this for last because I am reluctant even to attempt a response. Perhaps I should just let Geoffrey speak for me—he is both eloquent and wise. Do I have anything to say for myself?

The phrase "complex equality" describes a social arrangement that bars the domination of some people by others—an arrangement where the arrogant few don't rule the fearful or deferential many. *Spheres* is an argument against hierarchy, but it isn't, as many critics have pointed out, an argument against inequality, which rightly prevails in many, perhaps in all, the spheres that I write about. But there is a moral requirement that we attend to the qualities, the needs, the talents, the agency of each person in each sphere in the same way. My argument depends on equality of attention or, perhaps better, equality of respect. This is obvious, I suppose, in the case of health care or welfare, but it applies everywhere, even in the market where we respect the entrepreneurial green thumb, and certainly in the state, where we respect political skillfulness and ideological persuasiveness. Hence the commitment to the equality of citizens, which simply means equal attention by all the citizens to all the citizens—to everyone's skill and persuasiveness—and which doesn't preclude the radical inequality between elected officials and the men and women they govern. But what explains or justifies this very basic equality? That is Geoffrey's challenge, which I have avoided these many years, because I don't have, or I haven't found, the right words.

The ordinary language of politics is perfectly adequate for the struggle for power, adequate, too, for the uses of power and even for the restraint of power, the making and re-making of constitutions. But it doesn't seem adequate for the ideas and values that make politics important. For me, the basic equality of all human beings is the key assumption of all political activity, the key to how everyone should "do" politics. Geoffrey thinks that the words that describe basic equality can't be said or, at least, can't be said by secular writers like me—hence we can only allude to the religious language in which those words are more readily spoken. Tawney, a Christian socialist, both alludes to them and then speaks them openly. Is God necessary, as he says, to human equality? I want to say no, but I don't know what to say after that. There are good secular arguments against the hierarchical arrangements that I want to oppose, and there are good secular arguments against any defense of those arrangements. We know the cruelty that inequalities of that kind license. We want, I think, to join political struggles against that cruelty. Solidarity with the oppressed may be the way we express or act out the meaning of equality.

Beyond that, maybe, religious language does best, even for unbelievers: the arrogance of the rich and powerful is blasphemous; the equality of humankind is a mystery.

Competing Interests The author has no conflicts of interest to declare that are relevant to the content of this chapter.

Index

J. T. Reiner (ed.), *Walzer and Justice: Spheres of Justice in the 2020s*,
https://doi.org/10.1007/978-3-031-87809-1

The manufacturer's authorised representative in the EU is Springer Nature Customer Service Centre GmbH, Europaplatz 3, 69115 Heidelberg, Germany. If you have any concerns regarding our products, please contact ProductSafety@springernature.com

Printed and bound by CPI Group (UK) Ltd, Croydon, CR0 4YY
01/10/2026
02225967-0006